A Philosophy of Morals

To the memory of my father,
Pal Heller (born Vienna, 1888; died Auschwitz, 1944)

A Philosophy of Morals

AGNES HELLER

Basil Blackwell

Copyright © Agnes Heller, represented by EULAMA, Rome, 1990

First published 1990

Basil Blackwell Ltd
108 Cowley Road, Oxford, OX4 IJF, UK

Basil Blackwell, Inc.
3 Cambridge Center
Cambridge, Massachusetts 02142, USA

British Library Cataloguing in Publication Data

A CIP catalogue record for this book is
available from this British Library.

Library of Congress Cataloging in Publication Data

Heller, Agnes.
    A philosophy of morals / Agnes Heller.
    p.   cm.
    Includes bibliographical references.
    ISBN 0–631–17083–9
    1. Ethics. I. Title.
BJ1012.H46 1990
170—dc20   89–37500
                                            CIP

786 91045

Typeset in 10½ on 12 pt Sabon
by Vera Reyes, Inc.
Printed in Great Britain by
T.J. Press Ltd, Padstow, Cornwall

Contents

Preface

Tradition holds that Aristotle addressed his main discussion of ethics to his son, Nikomachos. Nowadays, even books of a very limited range of academic interest are dedicated to the authors' children. This kind of dedication, however, is not 'addressing someone', for the authors' children may never even become interested in the subject matter of the book or, for that matter, care to read the book. It is not even implied in the dedication that they should. For the thankful gesture is not aimed at prospective adults; it is indeed addressed to authors' children who created a pleasant atmosphere for the writer under stress. Children only properly become *addressees* of one's book when one writes what should be passed on to them. Theoretical knowledge can be passed on to one's children, but it would be ridiculous to state that it should be. For the children might simply become interested in something totally different. It is practical knowledge, ethics, moral wisdom alone that *should* be passed on.

One need not answer the question of why ethics should be passed on, since the very injunction is a constitutive element of morality itself. Morals *should* be passed on by everyone and to everyone. In this respect, the philosopher or the theorist is no exception. Such persons pass on practical knowledge to their offspring irrespective of whether they write books on moral philosophy. Yet, if the philosopher decides to pass on practical knowledge through the medium of philosophy, she or he does what others do and, in addition, something else. The medium of writing and the institution of publishing carry the message far beyond the limits of direct, oral communication. The children who are addressed thus stand for all members of their generation.

Passing on moral experience through the medium of philosophy carries with it both advantages and disadvantages when compared to the everyday mode of passing on moral experience and knowledge. Generalization is certainly an asset, especially if everyday moral perceptions are not being distorted while being reshaped by philosophical categories as well as redefined in a broader context. However, the traditional medium can carry away the writer to such a degree that the asset turns into a handicap. A book, after all, is only a book, and someone can write a moral philosophy which is quite alien to his or her own moral practice. Of course, philosophers are not the only ones liable to the discrepancies which arise between acts and deeds, principles and practices; such failings are all-too-human. If, however, the morals that a self-righteous person preaches are completely different from his or her practice, that person will very soon be found out, because all his/her contacts with others are personal, immediate, oral and practical in character. This is not the case with philosophy. Our utter ignorance about the author's character may even lead us to assume – falsely – that the relevance of the book has nothing to do with whether the author has lived up to his or her moral principles. In the case of a complete discrepancy between the views professed and the ethics practised, the philosopher's moral philosophy would lose its relevance, attraction, indeed even its meaning. In morals, only that for which we are ready to accept personal responsibility can be accepted as true.

At this point, the gesture of addressing our moral philosophy to our children appears in a new light. The gesture now means 'I turn to you, I talk to you, I pass my moral life experience on to you as the representatives of a generation to which I am bound to pass them on.' At the same time, the gesture also means that you (my children) are the only ones among all members of the new generation who know me as a person, who see me day after day in my deeds and acts. You are therefore the only ones who can check up on me, who can ascertain whether my acts and way of life are in harmony with my written words. The author's dedication is therefore an injunction to his or her children: 'Be my witnesses to the fact that I have at least tried to live up to my words; vouch for the authenticity of the message conveyed by this book on moral philosophy.'

It is easy for us to fathom the continuous process of 'passing on moral experience and wisdom' in Aristotle's times. Yet it appears as if the continuity has been disrupted in modern times to such a degree that addressing a new generation has become rather illusory. The gap between fathers and mothers on the one hand, and sons and daughters on the other, is so deep that it seems to be unbridgeable. Mutual alienation of generations is strongest, almost beyond remedy, when and where modern and pre-modern attitudes clash. This happens frequently and repeatedly; moreover, one cannot even draw a line of demarcation beyond which it is likely to vanish. We may hope, however, that, between generations both of whom are intrinsically modern, the continuity of the process of passing-on moral experiences will be assured as it used to be.

Since the field of morals is not a sphere and since we do have a moral relation to certain norms, rules, ideas and values, what we can call our 'moral life' is always dense. We develop attitudes towards, and make decisions within, concrete situations. Passing on all of our positive commitments as mandatory is the pre-modern way of passing on moral experience and wisdom. This was the rule in traditional societies. And whenever it was followed in good faith, sincerely and authentically, it worked. These days, however, it no longer works, not even under the conditions of good faith and authenticity. This is precisely the kernel of the story of fathers and sons in Turgenev's famous novel of the same name.

In the modern world, men and women continue to develop their attitudes, and make their morally relevant decisions, in fairly dense ethical milieux (situations), if not to the same extent or in a uniformly all-encompassing fashion. And yet this density no longer authorizes one to pass on one's *concrete* ethical commitments as mandatory ones, for such commitments are different for different people even within the selfsame generation. The modern person still can, even should, pass on his or her concrete commitments, because the field of morals is practice, and one practises morals in concrete situations. However, these concrete commitments and ethical choices are now passed on as the exemplifications or applications of certain general attitudes and commandments. The modern person attempting to act in an exemplary fashion does not transmit his or her action as the one to be actually performed by others (by all others). She or he rather presents it as the one act which exemplifies the kinds of action to be performed, or the kinds of attitudes to be developed in a similar situation. Kinds of action which exemplify the same general type of action or attitude can be completely different, not only in intensity but in quality as well. Therefore, this is the language of the modern person when passing on his or her moral experiences: 'I did that then and there; I do this here and now. In doing that then and there, and in doing this here and now, I have tried to live up to the general norms and ideas A, B and C. For your part, try to live up, as best as you can, to the general norms and ideas A, B and C in your own actions and choices.' The modern person would not say, 'Do as I did, practise the same virtues as I practised, believe in the same ideas, etc., as I believe in, and be the same kind of moral person as I am.'

Pre-modern and modern patterns of life are closely interwoven in the everyday life of most women and men. One has to learn how to pass on moral experience and wisdom to one's children in a modern way. Many people learn this 'modern way' not for moral reasons, but rather only in order to avoid the threat of generational conflicts and to preserve the affection of their children. Above and beyond our longing to keep our children as our friends, there are other urgent factors, some of which are political, which speak to the need to accelerate this transformation. In passing on morals in a traditional fashion, transmission can only work in so far as the socio-political milieu remains the same. Yet children brought up in a liberal democracy should acquire the moral stamina to be able, eventually, to live up to the best possible moral standards in a totalitarian state, while children brought up in a totalitarian regime should learn how to act and behave democratically, as well as how to develop liberal attitudes. Children born at the bottom of the social hierarchy should acquire the capacity to be decent at the top; they should also learn what *not* to do in order to get to the top. Alternatively, those born at the top should learn how to act and behave decently if they happen to land at the bottom; they should also learn what they should not do in order to avoid arriving there. Since men and women of the modern age are contingent persons, they must learn moral attitudes which will serve them well in all possible situations. This is the most urgent reason for acquiring the modern way of passing on moral experiences and ideas.

This modern way of passing on moral experiences has changed the status of the *moral ideal*. There is no lack of exemplary moral personalities in modern life, but they have no plasticity, at least not in the traditional sense of the term, because they do not *embody* the unity of the general, the particular and the individual (which is at least one of the main reasons for the decline of one representative and traditional type of sculpture). Every exemplary modern moral individual has, so to speak, his or her own style, an unmistakably personal touch. This is why, despite the existence of exemplary modern moral personalities, there are no longer *public moral ideals* on display for general imitation and emulation. As a result of this situation, which has prevailed since the end of the nineteenth century, media cynicism of a kind has been gathering momentum, under the tutelage of its own self-appointed sages, and backed up by its pseudo-Socratic logic which asserts, 'Every human is a scoundrel. We are human, and aware that we are scoundrels. That is why we are more knowledgeable than other scoundrels.' Exemplary modern moral individuals are not in the limelight; they rather stand in the shadow, unseen, unmarked, unnoticed. Only the members of their families, only those few who are in touch with them, have met the exceptional, the exemplary, the moral ideal in a personal style. The cynic who states that every human is a scoundrel is, indeed, a scoundrel. But he does not know that he is also ignorant: he was never capable of recognizing the good person because he has eyes only for things which are on public display.

Moral ideals on public display, saints and heroes, are indeed gone. Yet, however strange it may seem, the greatest moral philosophers were the least likely to illustrate moral goodness by invoking exemplary figures. Still, they simply had to have a model in mind in order to draw the portrait of the good person; otherwise their images of goodness would not strike others as so sharply 'true-to-life' as they certainly do. There are strong autobiographical elements in every original philosophy – 'original', that is, in the sense of comprising new attempts and innovations, regardless of the level of achievement. The autobiographical element is normally transformed, abstracted, transubstantiated, even hidden. Yet for perceptive eyes it is always discernible and thus recognizable. What is difficult to believe is that any moral philosopher of consequence could have designed the image of the good (honest) person as self-portrait, however transformed and transubstantiated. There are too many factors in a philosopher's life that make him or her singularly unfit for the role of model good person. On whatever level one does philosophy, there is always 'blessing' on this activity. The very circumstance that allows one to write about morals is already a special 'gift of fortune' which the philosopher by definition does not share with others. Over-reflectivity and the speculative mind of the philosopher diminish the element of spontaneity in his or her life as compared to others'. All in all, the model of the good person is purer the less the particular traits of excellence and the special gifts of good fortune, all autobiographical elements, enter the picture.

Obviously, the 'wise man' can serve as the moral ideal. In selecting him, no autobiographical features are mixed into the portrait drawn by the philosopher, for the 'sage', like the 'saint' or the 'hero', is a public model figure. Yet, even when the philosopher invokes the traditional ideal of the 'wise man' and provides it with a few new attributes, he normally presents us with the companion figure of his or her philosophy, the upright person pure and simple, lacking in outstanding marks other than those of common honesty.

It might appear to be a far-fetched idea, and one which cannot be corroborated by evidence, yet I have strong suspicion that moral philosophers have always painted their image of the good person after a particular model. They had a certain model in mind, alive or dead; they were keeping the figure, the voice, the smile, the deeds of this person clear in their minds whenever they were writing about the honest, upright person. We may find it ridiculous that the *megalopsuche*, Aristotle's truly upright man, walks slowly and speaks with a deep voice. But the much too particular description would lose its almost comic side if it were true that Aristotle modelled his image of moral excellence on one of his best friends, the most upright person he had ever known, and that this person, furthermore, had walked slowly and had a deep voice. We know somewhat more about Kant than we do about Aristotle and we are therefore aware that his men of good will, who, as we know, shine as jewels, must have been modelled after his parents. One truly cannot write about the good person without having a particular good person in mind.

This book is a humble attempt at moral philosophy written with modest objectives in mind. Modesty is not the philosopher's virtue; pride befits him or her far better. Yet in this venture modesty is the attitude of realism. My intellectual powers do not reach as far as they should to overcome the immense difficulties towering before a new beginning in moral philosophy. But my shortcomings have nothing to do with my model. The hidden hero of this book, the one whose image I have never lost from my mind, was not inferior to any of the upright, honest persons who had ever been models for the portraits of moral philosophy. He was my father. My father was blessed with many talents, without ever being endowed with the opportunity to develop them. To support his widowed mother, he practised a profession which he disliked and had no talent for. He was poor, suffering under the daily pressure of constant misery. He was a Jew exposed to harassment and discrimination living in the first officially racist country of the world. He had all the 'reasons', if 'reasons' are necessary, to lament his misfortune, to take it out on others, to care only for his own business, to be one of the many loveless, bitter egoists. And yet he was the exact opposite. I still see him visiting internment camps in order to do all that he could to help, and more. And I also see him cherishing a flower or a tree, or gazing at the starry sky with wonder; I recall him loving, wise and merry. In the concentration camps, we were told, he cheered up his fellow inmates, not as if he bore any false hopes. He, who had never believed in God, still held that our life is a prayer, a thanksgiving for the blessings of hearing, seeing, tasting, loving, and of being here.

My father had a wonderful ability to pass on moral experience and wisdom in a modern fashion. Among the many stories I could recount about him, one in particular stands out vividly in my mind. There were times when the unhappy Jews of Hungary believed that, if they converted to Christianity, they could save their own lives as well as those of their children. Some old friends of my father, all confessing Jews, had therefore decided with sinking hearts, to take this step. They were absolutely sure that my father, who had nothing to do with Judaism, would follow suit. I was present at the conversation. My father said an unequivocal 'no'. His friends tried to point out that for him it was an easy step to make, for he had never believed in God. To which he simply answered, 'But I do not believe in the Christian God either.' Further attempts at persuasion followed, with plenty of references to me – the innocent child who should be saved by such a step. My father only answered, 'One does not leave a sinking ship' – and that was the end of the story. In listening to the conversation, I learned something which has stayed with me my entire life. Had my father consented for my sake, nothing would have been the same. He did the most for his child by rejecting this argument. What my father passed on to me from his own moral experience was not the concrete norm of remaining faithful to the religion of my forefathers. It was rather the general attitude: one should not leave a sinking ship or a lost cause merely for the sake of survival.

My father was not a philosopher. He therefore had the courage to commit to paper ideas that 'professional' thinkers would shy away from addressing in *oratio recta*, thoughts we would only hint at in a manner that Kierkegaard called 'indirect communication'. My father had the courage to write this in his last will and testament:

> My dear daughter Agi, if you think of me, you should remember that if you choose the path of love, your life will be outbalanced and harmonious; you only need a little greater share of luck than had been allotted to your father, and all will be right with you. . . . In spite of everything that had happened in the last years, I have not lost my faith. . . . Evil can carry a victory for the time being – but it is goodness that, finally, will be victorious. Every good person contributes a grain of dust to its final victory. . . . Please keep me in your friendly and merry remembrance.

In this book I have invented nothing. I have only written variations on the theme that had been passed on to me by my father. These variations do not alter the main message. They reflect new life experiences and they are drawn from the philosophical tradition. I have taken my father's legacy, I have been working on it, and I pass it on to my children: *Zsuzsa* and *Yuri*.

A Philosophy of Morals is the second part of my trilogy on ethics, *A Theory of Morals*. The first volume, *General Ethics*, addresses the problem of what 'moral' is; this volume seeks answers to the question of what we, modern men and women, ought to do; the third part, yet unwritten, will explore the possibilities of good life. The working title of the completing volume is *A Theory of Proper Conduct*, but I would rather term it a theory of moral wisdom, for this is exactly what the book is meant to be.

This volume, *A Philosophy of Morals*, speaks for itself. One can fully understand it without having read *General Ethics* first. Though I frequently refer to ideas explored and elaborated in the first volume, I explain them again, albeit only briefly, in the notes to this book whenever such explanation is needed to avoid misunderstandings. But I hope that this book will whet the appetite of the readers for *General Ethics*, and also for *Beyond Justice*, a book in which I deal with similar problems as they appear at the conjuncture of ethics, political philosophy and social philosophy.

I express my thanks to the research assistants of the Philosophy Department at the New School for Social Research – Peggy Heide, Wayne Klein and April Flaken – and especially to Graham Eyre for his conscientious editorial work.

Throughout this project my best friend and husband, Ferenc Feher, offered generous and constant assistance in a way that has become habitual with him during the twenty-five years we have spent together. Feelings do not need to be made public; acknowledgements should. These lines express my acknowledgement of the part he paid in the conception and making of this book.

1

The Contingent Person and the Existential Choice

I

Moral philosophy offers an answer to the question 'What should I do?' People normally do not pose this question in general terms, nor do they expect to receive a complete moral philosophy as an answer. It is in concrete situations, particularly in situations of choice, that men and women turn to one another with a plea like this: 'Please, advise me, what should I do, what is the right thing for me to do?'[1] Most often, they are given the following advice: 'You should do X rather than Y'; or the same advice put in a different form: 'If you want to do the right thing, do X rather than Y.' *Moral philosophies should be formulated in order to provide guidelines for all possible moral advice given to any actor who asks, 'What is the right thing for me to do?' in any given situation.*

Persons who turn to others with a plea for good advice intend to make a moral choice. If the answer contains a moral advice, the adviser and the one advised are on common ground. Moral philosophies should be formulated in such a way as to provide guidelines for actors who intend to decide, as well as act, on moral grounds. Persons are in need of moral advice if they do not know by themselves what is the right thing to do or if they seek confirmation of their choice. This occurs when it must be decided (a) whether the choice (or the action) is morally relevant or rather adiaphoric (indifferent, open to mere pragmatic considerations); (b) if the alternatives open to choice are all *equally* valuable; and (c) if the alternatives are all equally binding. Moral philosophy can only provide general guidelines for cases belonging to (a) and (b), not for cases belonging to (c).[2]

Moral philosophies are not religions: their authority rests on themselves. They do not issue commandments; rather, they offer a body of earthly wisdom which is to be consulted. They provide moral service (or disservice). Kant's grand attempt at providing actors with a lay philosophy endowed with the authority to formulate the categorical imperative is no exception to this rule: we consult the Kantian philosophy in the same way as we might consult others. And, in the same way as we can change doctors if the one we have been visiting has cured others but not ourselves, we can choose another moral philosopher if the consultation with Kant's moral philosophy turns out to be a disappointment.

We are not often faced with decisive moral choices. And yet we do make moral choices all the time, without even noticing it, in the continual flow of doing, acting, behaving, reacting, speaking, listening, interfering and non-interfering which is the business of our daily life. Although moral philosophy is of special significance if decisive choices are to be made, its aim is also to provide guidelines for a decent way of life in general, a disposition for all the good choices. Just as any randomly selected person whom one addresses with the plea 'Please, tell me, what is the right thing to do?' must have previously fathomed what a decent way of life is in order to be able to give advice, so moral philosophy has to devise a general guideline for a decent way of life to be able to answer this question. In offering a general answer to the question 'What should I do?' philosophies also have to offer a general answer to the question 'How should I live?'

Just as a doctor must have authority in order to heal, and preventive medicine must have authority in order to devise a healthy way of life, so moral philosophy too must yield an authority on the basis of which we can seek its advice in cases where we are faced with moral choices and in all matters of moral relevance. Because moral philosophies are not religions, the body of the philsophy itself must be vested with an authoritative appeal. In pre-modern societies, this kind of authority presents itself in a simple and natural way. The philosopher is a member of a community that he (or she) addresses. He is a participant observer. He is a participant in so far as his fundamental values, images of virtue, moral precepts, and so on, are shared with other members of his community in general, and with the most virtuous members of this community in particular. He is an observer in so far as he registers, dissects and exemplifies ethical behaviour, deliberation and choice, or in so far as he interprets and explains them. The authority of a philosophy is established if the philosopher's case for the good life is a strong one, and within the grasp of his addressees. Authority is, so to speak, derived from the addressees. The religious moral message, if it falls on deaf ears, can be imposed on the addressee, sometimes even by force. This is not the case with the message of moral philosophy. Since its authority is derived from the addressee, the latter can accept or reject it. Viewed from a broader perspective, rejection of a moral philosophy is also a kind of reception. Those who reject the message understand what it is all about, and are aware of being addressed. No sharp conflict between the philosopher and the addressee, not even the death sentence meted out to Socrates, severs the lifeline between the authority and the addressee. It is in the modern world where the real problem starts.

Moral philosophy cannot resign the task of providing guidelines for all kinds of possible moral advice to any actor who formulates the question 'What is the right thing for me to do?' Nor can it resign the simultaneous task of offering a general answer to the question 'How should I live?' Philosophers who in a pre-modern fashion continue to address the members of one particular community deriving authority from their membership will perforce fail to offer this kind of general guideline. Their blueprint will be out of touch with the concerns of the members of another community or group whose moral customs, ideas and values are of equal relevance. In addition, modern philosophers address men and women who simultaneously dwell amidst a great diversity of concrete norms. For example, they share professions and their professional ethics but they do not share each other's family, religious and civic ethics – or *vice versa*. As a result, the old-fashioned philosophical message only has one of two options. In the first place, it can make a case for granting unconditional priority to one community as against all others in all our commitments and choices. The fruit of such an approach in modern times is moral fundamentalism. Fundamentalist ethical theories behave as a religious morality, even if the substance of their moral precepts and goals is non-religious. Alternatively, philosophy can be departmentalized into branches such as business ethics, family ethics and sexual ethics. It can even go further by affixing adjectives to the branches and terming them 'liberal'/'conservative' business ethics, 'lay'/ 'religious' family ethics, 'gay'/'straight' sexual ethics, and the like. To summarize: moral thinking which derives its authority from the speaker's membership of a particular group may turn fundamentalist and thereby pose a threat to members of other communities. Or, in a best-case scenario, it can present moral options, rules and recommendations which have direct relevance to the lives of some people in certain walks of life, but not for others.

In universalistic ethics, the relation of authority to addressee is structurally quite similar. In fact, here too philosophers derive their authority from their membership of a community; and this is how they address its members. However, to put the matter bluntly, the community whom they both address and derive their authority from, namely humankind, does not exist as an integrated entity. As a result, humankind has not developed an ethos, not even in the form of a few common norms that would be binding for every member of the human race. In so far as they live up to the inherent norm of moral philosophy which has remained unfulfilled by particularistic quasi-moral philosophies, fundamentalist or departmentalized, moral philosophies such as the Kantian (in all its versions, including communicative ethics) do in fact, by virtue of their authentic universalism, provide guidelines for all possible types of moral advice to be given to any actor who might ask in any given situation 'What is the right thing for me to do?' However, since the addressee of the universalistic philosophy (humankind) has not developed even the semblance of a common ethos, and its members do not have a single moral norm in common, the guideline provided by moral universalism must remain merely formal (lacking in any substance whatsoever). One cannot really address humankind, for it does not listen. One can, however, address 'humankind' as manifested in every human person, in every human relation, in every human speech act. This kind of approach does not have to end up in mere formalism, although in fact it has so far. For 'humankind' has always been identified with 'Reason' or with some versions of 'Reason'. As a result, universalistic philosophy has failed to take into account the unique embodied in each individual. In the end, mere formalism leaves the initial task unaccomplished. The guideline provided by formalistic moral philosophies is not *the* guideline for all possible types of moral advice in all possible situations, as they must leave certain situations unrecognized. (This was the case with Kant in relation to the conflict of duties, and with Habermas in instances where the fundamental principle of universalization does not apply.)

I have only briefly mentioned the two extreme solutions to the predicament of modern moral philosophy. One can also choose to address the members of a particular movement or of a particular class (as attempted in 'socialist ethics' or in 'proletarian ethics'); or one can choose one's own nation or ethnic group or race as the 'special addressee'. Such attempts may flourish for a while only to disappear later; or they may develop towards a powerful fundamentalist ideology. In either case, the basic pattern remains the same. The philosopher (the moralist, the moral adviser or manipulator) claims authority on the grounds of membership of a (particular or universal) community. She or he then goes on to address the members of the selected community with an authority based on the claim of shared membership.

Instead of choosing between the above solutions, I would recommend leaving the whole configuration behind. The model has been taken over from pre-modern philosophies and made perfect sense in the pre-modern world, where, in the main, moral norms, virtues and ideas were divided along the lines of social stratification. That is why it worked there and then, and no longer works here and now. The shift of the model towards universalization has brought the message home even more forcefully.

In seeking for new solutions one cannot renounce the claim of moral philosophy to provide a guideline for all possible types of moral advice in all possible situations; nor can one rescind its specificity (as compared with religion) in drawing its authority from its addressee. Philosopher and addressee *must share something* which is morally relevant as well as something that may provide the foundation for mutual understanding. Yet this 'something' need not be membership of an integrated entity, whether it be a religious community, family, state, class, caste, nation, or even humankind. This 'something' could perhaps also be non-membership in all of them.

II

The philosophical metaphor that man is 'thrown into the world' expresses the fundamental life experience of modern men and women. *The modern person is a contingent person.* In a broader sense, contingency is one of the main constituents of the human condition, for nothing in our genetic equipment predetermines us to be born in precisely such and such an age, in such and such a social condition, caste, class, and the like. Yet pre-modern men and women were rarely aware of this contingency. Blood ties on the one hand, and domicile (the home) on the other were normally perceived as determinants of a person's existence.

The modern person is 'thrown into the world' because his or her condition is that of *dual* contingency. In addition to the initial, mostly unconscious, contingency of the person, a secondary one *qua* 'form of existence' in the modern world has been gaining momentum in the last 200 years. The modern person does not receive the destination, the telos, of his or her life at the moment of birth as happened in pre-modern times, when people were born to do this and not that, to become this rather than that, to die as this and not as that, for better or for worse. The modern person is born as a cluster of possibilities without telos. This newborn bundle of possibilities, furthermore, without socially patterned telos cannot make its choices within the framework of a socially determined destination: it must choose the framework for itself. The existentialist formula of 'choosing oneself' can also be read as a descriptive comment on the form of existence in modernity. The modern person must choose the framework, the telos, of his or her life – that is, choose himself or herself. One can say with Kierkegaard that, if you do not choose yourself, others will choose for you. Those 'others' do not convey the socially patterned telos as did the 'others' in pre-modern times, for they are as contingent as the one instead of whom and for whom they choose, whose life they determine. If you do not choose your own life, but let others choose for you, no telos will appear on the horizon of your life. You will remain completely contingent throughout life. Born as a cluster of possibilities, you will not realize any of them in full. You will die without having lived. By contrast, to choose your own telos, destiny, pattern of life, and so on is to choose yourself, which is more than a figure of speech.

The modern condition of being born as a bundle of possibilities with no socially patterned telos to rely upon, as well as to be limited by, can also be experienced as being 'thrown into freedom'. This freedom, however, is empty, or, in existentialist jargon, it is Nothing (Nothingness). It is 'Nothing' in a triple sense. First, it indicates the mere absence of a socially patterned telos. There is no handrail to be grasped; one walks the tightrope over the abyss. Second, if one fails to choose oneself, but instead lets others choose for one, life becomes a kind of lingering towards death. One lives only in order to die, to become Nothing. Finally, this freedom is Nothing in the Hegelian sense. Out of the dialectic of Being and Nothing, Becoming emerges as the mediator. One is born, one *Is Nothing* in order to *Become*. The choice of oneself is to become what one is. Here 'Nothing' is freedom in a positive sense.[3] The statement 'One can become everything', whether true or false, is irrelevant. Yet the statement 'One can become oneself' is both true and relevant. We need only to look around to see people who have indeed become themselves: there are plenty of them.

To be contingent in the dual sense of the word is both a blessing and a curse. Whatever one's choices, one never chooses to be born, and, in particular, one does not choose to be born as a dually contingent person. Freedom as Nothingness becomes freedom as blessing if, and only if, the choice of self is successful. In becoming yourself while choosing yourself, you become as free as a person, *qua* contingent person, can be. You become free as a person if you transform your contingency into your destiny. You transform your contingency into destiny if you freely choose what you did not choose in the first place: to be born precisely in this world, in this time, as a dually contingent person, if you understand your self-created path as your destiny and dearest property.

The contingent person is not the abstract Man or Woman; no one is thrown into the world as such. Concrete human beings are born, each of them singular, all of them with different clusters of talents, unique childhood experiences. They can be possessed of a merry constitution or a melancholic disposition. Yet all of them are contingent persons, and equally so, irrespective of whether they were born poor or rich, children of loving or of uncaring parents, in war or peace, in democracy or under dictatorship, predisposed to merriment or to sadness. The situation into which one is thrown at birth conditions the 'likelihood' of, or the 'objective chances' for, one or another course of life. Yet it does not provide the newborn with a socially pre-patterned telos for such a course of life.

Modern men and women have something in common: they are all contingent; they share a fundamental life experience and they are all in the same predicament – either they choose themselves or they let others choose for them. There are many things in others' lives that they do not understand. One cannot expect them to agree with one another on issues that spring from their concrete life conditions, experiences, ideas or goals. Yet, because contingency is shared, modern men and women can understand each other on this *universal ground*. It is on this shared life experience and predicament that modern moral philosophy can be founded. A contingent person can communicate with all other contingent persons in addressing what they all share: contingency. Every contingent person has the authority to discuss the predicaments of contingency, because she or he is contingent, as are all those with whom she or he communicates. The relationship between the speaker and the addressee is one of *symmetric reciprocity*.

In what follows, I shall not address 'humankind as such', nor shall I address humankind as it dwells in Reason or in the reasoned speech of everyone. I shall rather address concrete persons who feel, enjoy, suffer, choose, reason and speak. I shall not turn to any specific human group, class, party, profession, race or nationality. I shall not address any cluster in particular with the authority of being a member of the same cluster. I shall address the contingent person regardless of the concrete institution, profession, party, country, group or class to which he or she belongs. I shall address contingent persons of both sexes, although I myself belong to the female gender and I do not claim honorary membership of the male gender. Perhaps I do therefore address humankind. Yet, if this is so, it will not be humankind *in us*, but humankind that *is us*, that will be addressed; each of us, all of us. Not the general will but the will of all.

III

To be contingent does not amount to being rootless. Among modern individuals there are 'hotel-dwellers',[4] but there are also men and women who feel at home in a particular habitat. Moreover, finding a home, achieving the feeling of 'being at home', may result from having transformed one's contingency into one's destiny. Persons who choose themselves, and thus their life's telos, their destiny, 'settle in' on the earth in general, in our time and world in particular, and perhaps also in their environment, relationships and attachments as well as the institutions to which they are affiliated. Modern moral philosophy appeals to all contingent persons, to those who 'feel at home', as well as to those who 'settle in the world'. But pre-modern, non-contingent persons are not addressed directly by a moral philosophy of this kind. And yet we inhabit the world along with human groups and cultures which are still characterized by the division of moral customs along lines of social stratification, in which people, at the moment of their birth, are slotted into their social telos and destiny. Moral philosophy does not have a prophetic power; one cannot foretell whether in the future all cultures will become modern. Therefore one cannot foretell whether the addressee of modern philosophy will ever be coextensive with 'every human being'.

The decision to address the contingent person in his or her 'personhood' at the initial stage of a moral philosophy, instead of beginning by arguing for the validity of certain rules and norms, has neither an ontological nor an epistemological status. One can make this decision and go through with it irrespective of whether or not one subscribes to the paradigm of language, communication, action, consciousness, collective consciousness, work, or whatever, and from the standpoint of any metaphysics or anti-metaphysics. One can provide different answers to questions concerning the formation of the human person, the source of the person's knowledge and self-knowledge, the (subjective or intersubjective) constitution of the world, and yet still agree with others that persons *qua* persons simply exist, that one can communicate with them (as they can communicate with us), that one can address them (as they can address us) *qua* persons.[5] Yet to address the contingent person in his or her 'personhood' at the initial stage of a moral philosophy is certainly a matter of *decision*, precisely because this kind of gesture 'does not follow' from the metaphysical, ontological, sociological, epistemological or historical system or creed of any particular philosophy.

At this point, the suspicion might arise that 'choosing oneself' is simply a fancy term for 'making oneself', and that the gesture of addressing the contingent person in his or her personhood at the initial stage of this moral philosophy has therefore, in fact, been derived from the paradigm of work, and follows from that paradigm. But in reality 'choosing oneself' is the modern equivalent of 'knowing oneself' and not of 'making oneself'. The metaphor of 'making oneself' carries with it associations with self-creation. One perceives the self as indeterminate, as raw material. At the same time, one also perceives the same self (or a particular aspect of it) as the creator, the worker, the artist moulding the raw material into a predesigned shape according to a goal set by the actor himself. Once the creative–artistic dimensions of the metaphor are dismissed, one easily arrives at the positivist image of a mere goal-oriented general actor who has a life strategy and who chooses every step she or he takes rationally, fitting it into a preconceived 'goal'. The other metaphor, 'choosing oneself', generates altogether different associations.

One cannot know oneself by mere introspection. If 'choosing oneself' is the modern version of 'knowing oneself', the interplay between the selves (at least between two 'selves') is presupposed.[6] Yet a modern knowledge of the self is not derived from the others' perception, from their regard, alone. We cannot know ourselves, nor can others know what we 'really' are, *before we become what we are.* (If we fail to become what we are, we behave like characters in Goffman's puppet theatre.[7])

The pre-modern interplay between action and character was accurately depicted by Aristotle, and has since then been depicted by many others. The person's character is formed by action, and the more it becomes formed, the more the character determines every further action. Yet the kinds of action the pre-modern person was supposed to perform were, so to speak, 'on display' for the person at a very early stage. There was the father; the youngster was introduced into a circle of citizens; he knew exactly what he could become if he acted in such and such a way. Specific actions were affiliated with typical ideals (the ideals of the accomplished gentleman–citizen). The circumstances in which modern men and women are unaware of what they are unless they become what they are do not modify the interplay between character and action; rather they change the framework within which it takes place. The dictum of Browning's hero, 'I go to prove my soul', summarizes the story with poetic brevity. Since the actions which form your character are not predesigned for you at the time of birth, because your course of life is not set by social expectations, ideals and determinations, you have to 'reach out' in order to find the kind of actions which are fitting to your character. Yet, since it is actions which form the character, how can you know in advance what kind of actions you should seek? You could try to prove your soul and engage in all kinds of action in the wrong way – by which I mean, in a way whereby you do not become what you are. The soul that has never proved itself is the lost soul who will never know what 'it' is. Yet, if 'choosing yourself' is the modern equivalent of 'knowing yourself', but you know yourself only when you become what you are, how can you choose yourself at all? It is assumed on the one hand that, once you choose oneself, you become what you are, while on the other it is also assumed that you do not really know what you are prior to the choice. Yet we only appear to be moving in circles. Choice of yourself is the choice of destiny; more precisely, choosing yourself is tantamount to knowing yourself as a person of a particular destiny. You do not 'have' a self whose knowledge predates choice. Existence and the consciousness of existence are indivisible. The choice of self is an *existential choice*, for it is the choice of existence. Existential choice is by definition irreversible and irrevocable. You cannot choose your destiny in a reversible way, for a reversible choice is not the choice of destiny, by definition not the existential choice.

Since the existential choice is irrevocable, it generates the telos of the person's life (it 'restores' what was absent at birth from the modern person's life). Life now has a destination because the person has a destiny. The interplay between character and action is restored in so far as the existential choice pre-empts the possibility of acting in any way other than the one predestined by the choice itself. As Kierkegaard once remarked, after having made the existential choice you continue to choose all the time. Yet these consecutive choices occur within a framework that was already predestined by your choice of yourself.

The inherent telos of a self-chosen life must not be confused with life strategies and goals that are devised in terms of rational-choice theories. Existential choice is our choice of ourselves, and not the choice of a concrete goal, not even *the* goal of life. No means can be applied in order to realize the goals of an existential choice. The end inherent in the existential choice is truly an 'end-in-itself'. To quote Aristotle, it is 'the activity of the soul throughout the whole of our lives'. Whatever one chooses existentially in choosing oneself is *energeia*. It is the activity, and not the end result, which men and women choose existentially, the 'activity toward something', the 'activity that we are', the 'activity that we become since we are'. Whatever you choose, this will invariably be the case. You can (existentially) choose yourself as an activist of a movement (a party), as a member of a religious community, as a scientist, and so much else. Lukács did not choose the victory of communism (*the* goal); rather, he chose himself as a communist. Weber, as he so movingly confesses in his 'Science as a Vocation', did not choose 'the progress of sciences' but rather chose himself as a social scientist, as a person of this particular calling and no other. Whatever you choose existentially is irrevocable (as a choice). Once you revoke it, you lose yourself, your own personality, your own destiny, to relapse into contingency.

It is only in the existential choice, in choosing themselves, that modern men and women can transform their contingency into destiny. If they fail to do so, others will choose for them. All of their choices will then become revocable and, in due course, they will reverse all of them. They will then endlessly ponder what would have happened had they chosen otherwise, what they could have become had they done this and not something else, had they married another man or woman, had they emigrated instead of staying where they were born, had they taken this particular course and not another one, and so on *ad infinitum*. They will be busy with making a living, with choosing means for the realization of goals, and, once having realized them, they will feel weariness instead of satisfaction. They will always be dissatisfied with 'life', with themselves, with the people around them. They will regret whatever they have done, and equally regret whatever they failed to do. They will run to the analyst, who will not ease their neuroses. For, ultimately, an analyst is a person who creates the conditions for another person to choose him- or herself. And, if the person does not choose, the analyst has reached the limits of his or her power and can do no more.

If you choose yourself as the 'person of this particular cause' or, in Weber's terms, the 'person of this particular calling', you choose yourself as *difference*. The choice is irrevocable, and this is why it is existential. It is through the choice that you become what you are. You will never regret it, for, if you do, you will lose yourself. The choice is unambiguous, because it is yourself that you have chosen. However, for others the same choice may appear ambiguous, for what you have chosen is the difference. It might even occur to you that, in other people's eyes, to revoke your choice and thus lose yourself would be a morally better decision than to stick to your destiny – especially if this destiny is vested in a cause. This kind of existential choice ultimately separates individuals from others, rather than uniting them with them.

Persons who choose themselves existentially under the category of difference thus expose themselves to external powers, the bearers of blessing or curse, of good luck or bad luck. Such powers are external to the individual's existence, to his or her existential choice. They do not threaten one's well-being, position or happiness alone; they can even poison one's choice of oneself. Or, alternatively, they can make the choice seem so much better than the one who made it could possibly have dreamt. Thomas Mann, who without a doubt chose himself as the 'writer of his nation', as the 'Goethe of the twentieth century', and whose subsequent actions, for better or worse, were determined by this existential choice, once stated emphatically, 'Everything depends on blessing' ('Alles hängt vom Segen ab'). Blessing was upon him; he was luck's favourite child – but what about the others who were not, and who are not? An existential choice that does not come off, because the gods were in a bad mood, makes the one who has chosen bitter, misanthropic and rancorous. One's choice of one's own self cannot be blamed in this case and, as a result, someone else must be blamed. All modern Timons of Athens made an existential choice at some point in the past that did not come off. If a cause, and not a calling, is existentially chosen, it is the caprice of external powers that can play the dirty trick. To be more precise, a cause is by definition an external power which has been existentially chosen. Thus, blessing or curse, good or bad luck, depends fully on the course which the cause itself will take. Should the cause take a bad turn, one which is at odds with the initial choice, then, because this existential choice is irrevocable, the degeneration of the cause cannot be recognized by the person who made the initial choice, even less confessed privately or publicly.

Whether you have chosen oneself as a person of a particular calling or cause, as the friend (or lover) of a particular person, or anything else in particular, you stand under the category of difference, and everything in your life will depend on blessing or curse.[8] If the choice does not come off, there will be a discrepancy between your self-perception and the way you are perceived by others. Other people will regard you as irrational, while you will continue to regard yourself as rational.

However, irrespective of the outcome of the choice made under the category of difference, in choosing yourself you transform your contingency into your destiny. At this point, however, we might come to the conclusion that there is very little a moral philosophy could possibly do with the gesture of the existential choice. Modern moral philosophy turns to the contingent person – so far so good. The choice of the self as a person of a particular calling, or a person of a particular cause, is of little moral relevance unless the virtue of constancy is made an absolute, or unless it is proved that people who have transformed their contingency into their destiny are morally better than the rest of us. But there is nothing to indicate that this is the case. On the other hand, moral philosophy can do very little with people who have never even attempted to make an existential choice, those who never choose themselves but let others choose for them, who therefore can hardly be approached as responsible moral agents. Only people of character can be people of good character.

Yet there is a way out of the impasse. Instead of further considering the kinds of existential choices that all can be made under the category of difference, we may instead pose the following question: is there an existential choice that can be made under the category of the *universal*, an existential choice of a kind that does not separate the person who chooses from the rest of us, but rather unites that person with us? Kierkegaard was not the first thinker to present such an existential choice, yet he was certainly the one who made the strongest case for it. Weber made a new, and to my mind theoretically problematic, attempt at the issue in his swansong lecture on politics as a vocation. Since twentieth-century existentialism, in particular Sartre, offers a strongly subjectivist version of the original idea, I would rather fall back on Kierkegaard in order to introduce a less subjectivistic interpretation of the choice.

IV

Choosing ourselves under the category of the universal is tantamount to choosing ourselves as *good persons*. This is *the* moral choice because this is the choice of morals. In Kierkegaard's formulation, to choose ourselves ethically means to choose ourselves as persons who make the choice between good and evil. But, he adds, if one chooses oneself as a person who makes the choice between good and evil, one has by definition chosen the good. This does not mean that in the future one cannot choose an evil course of action. Rather, it means that one will not choose an action because it is evil. The person who has chosen himself or herself ethically will do good for good's sake, but never evil for evil's sake. As a consequence, making the choice between good and evil by definition means choosing the good.

I recommend a slight modification of the Kierkegaardian rendering of the ethical choice of our selves. The modification deradicalizes the idea to a point where it becomes acceptable for thinkers of a different philosophical background, as well as more empirical, and thus more palatable for everyone. 'Choosing ourselves' means to *destine* ourselves to become *what we are. Choosing ourselves ethically means to destine ourselves to become the good persons that we are.* Let me briefly elaborate on this. We are children of particular parents, we had a particular childhood, we suffer from particular neuroses, we were born into a particular milieu, rich or poor, educated or uneducated – this is what we are. In choosing ourselves, we choose all these determinations, circumstances, talents, assets, infirmities: we choose our ill fate and our good fate – in short, everything that we are. Therefore, we also choose ourselves as the good persons *that we are* and choose ourselves precisely *as we are.* We choose all our determinations and thus we make ourselves free. With the same gesture, or, as Kierkegaard put it, in the same instant, we choose ourselves as persons who choose between good and evil and who thus choose the good, as well as choose ourselves as persons to be destined to be good. I shall be a decent person as I am, for I, as I am, destine myself to be a decent person. This is a very simple idea. Whoever chooses to become what she or he is – that is, a decent, good person – chooses all his or her determinations with the same gesture. For, only if one does precisely this can one destine oneself to be good. Suppose that I do not choose myself completely, but make a selection. I choose my talents but not my infirmities, I choose my tribe but not my parents; I do not rechoose the sufferings of my childhood or my disappointments. If I selectively choose in this manner, I cannot destine myself, because I am not free: that which I have left unchosen will, at least partially, *determine* my life and my fortune. People who have chosen themselves completely cannot make excuses like 'I did it because I had such an unhappy childhood' or 'I could not help doing it for I had to make up for the disappointments of my tender age' – rather, they have chosen all this. In choosing themselves existentially–ethically, they have no 'alien' power, no compulsion, built into their singular character. They have no excuses because they don't need any.[9]

The existential choice of the ethical was said above to be the choice of the self under the category of the universal. This sounds strange, because in this kind of choice people choose precisely what they are, as they are – all their singular determinations. Yet since we can all choose ourselves ethically to the same extent, the choice of our singularity, as the gesture of freedom, falls under the category of the universal: 'every human being'. This statement may appear unconvincing at first glance. All individuals as individuals have their own determinations. However, not all of them can equally serve as a trampoline for an existential choice; for some, the choice may be easy, while for others it may be difficult. But this counter-argument is irrelevant. Whether it is easier or more difficult, the existential choice of goodness is the same, and equally possible for all human beings. In this respect, the existential choice shares the propensities of all universals – moreover, of all norms. 'Do not murder' is an equally valid norm for those who cannot harm a fly and for those who have strong inclinations to physical violence. It is possible for both of them, and to the same extent, not to murder their fellow creatures.

The existential choice of the ethical falls under the category of universality. It is possible for all of us freely to choose all our determinations and to decide whether to become the decent and good persons that we are, as we are. However, the concept of the existential choice under the category of difference implies that not everyone can make the same choice. Everyone could choose a particular calling, but not the same one; still less can everyone pursue this calling on the same level of quality. Everyone can choose a cause, but not everyone the same cause (even less pursue the same cause with the same attachment) – yet everyone can destine himself or herself to be a good, decent person.

The existential choice made under the category of difference can play a dirty trick on the person who has chosen, while the existential choice under the category of the universal cannot. This is not to say that the decent person is happier than the one who has chosen himself or herself as a person of calling. A successful outcome of our choice of ourselves as difference may sometimes fill us with the triumphant feeling of infinite happiness. Yet, although an existential choice cannot, on pain of losing one's 'personhood', be revoked, once the source of choice becomes polluted one often wishes the choice had not been made at all. Since the source of a choice made under the category of the universal cannot get polluted by any subsequent event, whether it be good luck or bad fate, no one could wish that such a choice had never been made. Put another way, in choosing yourself under the category of the universal you destine yourself to authenticity. Becoming what you are (a good person) is bound up with the authenticity of your actions, attitudes and gestures. An authentic person cannot desire to become an inauthentic one, although she or he can certainly complain about the ill fate of goodness in the world, past or present.

The existential choice under the category of universality is the fundamental moral choice: it is the choice of morals. Undoubtedly, either a discourse held in moral terms, or the distinguishing (in certain situations) of good from evil does not presuppose a moral choice. Furthermore, one need not speak the moral language in order to understand it. Hutcheson found the simplest and most convincing argument to support his thesis of *minima moralia*. He remarked that even those who mock morals cry out 'injustice' if they are the ones who are wronged. One could add that cynics who hold the view that moral terms are empty, mere fancies void of meaning and relevance, would take serious offence were they called 'dishonest', 'cowards' or even 'illiberal'. Taking offence makes sense if the categories make sense and under no other circumstances. Interestingly enough, the same people as take offence if termed dishonest would not take offence if someone remarked that they had not acted efficiently enough in protecting their interests, or had not sought their pleasures fully.

'Distinguishing' and 'choosing' between good and evil are not conterminous. It need not be demonstrated, however, that choices between good and evil can be, and are actually, made by everyone, irrespective of whether they have chosen themselves existentially as moral agents. People in general choose between good and evil if it so happens that they must choose, if they cannot avoid or sidestep it and if they care to know the moral implications of their choice. All those who have chosen themselves existentially as good persons will to choose between good and evil, for they will to choose the good (to become what they are: good persons). They cannot and will not wait until told that a choice implies the choice between good and evil. Whenever they embark upon an action, or during the course of an action, they will raise the question (to themselves) of whether the action implies the choice between good and evil. They will scrutinize all possible actions under the guidance of the categories 'right' and 'wrong'. One does not have to be morally rigorous to behave like this. Placing all one's actions under scrutiny from the perspective of 'right' and 'wrong' by no means implies that all choices are between good and evil. Scrutiny may lead to the conclusion that the choice is adiaphoric, even if one is told that it is not. Yet, once certain alternative courses of action present the choice between good and evil, the choice of the good takes absolute preference over all other kinds of possible choices, as well as over all reasons for making other choices, such as goals, interests, passions, (private or public) benefits and any values whatsoever (excepting moral values where a conflict like this does not arise). Needless to say, if one chooses oneself existentially under the category of difference, one gives priority to those actions which are inherent in one's particular destiny; these actions will by no means be the morally best possible ones.

There is nothing paradoxical in the Kierkegaardian assumption that the person who has chosen himself or herself existentially as a good person also chooses the evil, for there would be no choice at all if one could only choose the good. However, the issue at stake is not merely whether the choice between good and evil includes the possible choice of evil as a category (which determines the character of an action); rather the issue is whether a choice may include the *actual* choice of evil. The commonplace wisdom that good persons sometimes do wrong things is in this context less trivial than it seems. Since, in modern times, morals are more reflexive,[10] and theoretical reasoning must, more than ever, lend support to practical reason if it is to find the right decision (though theoretical reason can itself be in error), the person who makes the choice can be mistaken about the moral character of his or her choice, choosing evil without knowing that it is evil. Furthermore, since one is sometimes presented with a choice where each course of action is equally good and each includes moral transgression of a kind, one sometimes 'cannot help' but choose evil knowingly. Having chosen oneself existentially, one chooses freely. Therefore, one cannot plead innocent on the grounds that one 'could not help' but choose. To this question I shall return in chapter 3. To sum up, if one chooses oneself under the category of the universal, one chooses oneself ethically. One chooses oneself ethically if one chooses to become what one is and as one is. In choosing all one's determinations one makes oneself free to be a good person, a person who is self-destined to be good. In choosing to become a good (honest) person, one chooses the choice between good and evil.

One need not subscribe to Kierkegaard's assumption that men and women never choose evil for evil's sake in order to regard this problem as irrelevant for our present discussion. I trust Shakespeare more than Kierkegaard when it comes to knowledge of human nature. There can be (there have always been) people who choose evil for evil's sake. Radical evil may exist, yet it is certainly untypical and uncharacteristic of our human race in general.[11] Thus, even if there are people who choose evil for evil's sake, they are the exception rather than the rule, while choosing good for good's sake is, if not the rule, at least the ideal norm. It is the ideal norm not because people generally do good for good's sake, but rather because, in general, people highly esteem those who do so.

V

Existential choice is inherent in the modern form of existence. Pre-modern societies neither provided conditions for such a choice nor did they necessitate them. So long as, and to the degree that, a particular pre-set way of life was *socially* allotted to persons at the moment of their birth, these persons could not choose themselves. For what has been allotted may be peacefully, gaily, dutifully, modestly, humbly or even proudly accepted or enthusiastically embraced; but it cannot be *chosen*. One can choose something only if one can also *not* choose the same thing.

This is one of several reasons why life's telos in pre-modern societies was not, and in fact could not be, dissected under the aspects of the unique, the difference and the universal. The socially allotted telos was a *typical* end in this world. The social position and the activity ascribed to the person occupying a given position carried with them the moral norms and virtues which the person in turn had to live up to. It should be mentioned that, the more the aspect of morality develops, the more the possibility of making an existential choice of goodness arises.[12] Since, however, my goal here is not to produce a historical inquiry, I shall discuss only the pure model cases. Given this, I shall repeat the point I made earlier: it is only in the modern form of existence that the choice of self under the category of difference and the choice of self under the category of universality can be completely separated. And yet the two kinds of choice can also be mediated and in this sense combined, albeit never fully united.

In principle as well as in practice, a person can make an existential choice under the category of the universal without (earlier, later or simultaneously) making an existential choice under the category of difference and *vice versa*. To avoid misunderstanding, it should be noted that choosing ourselves as good persons without choosing ourselves as being destined toward a particular cause is *not tantamount* to remaining without a calling, cause, concrete goal, value commitment, or the like. Having chosen oneself ethically, one becomes (or is likely to become) involved with causes, people, institutions, family, friends, neighbours, developing talents, collecting and enjoying things of beauty. Yet this is not the same as choosing oneself as a person who becomes what she or he is through one particular kind of calling, or cause, or something similar. Choices of a cause or calling that are not existential ones can be revoked whenever one wants. Moreover, such choices can be switched as often as desired without exposing oneself to the danger of losing oneself: the continuity of one's character has been established by the (existential) moral choice. However, having made this choice, one would lose oneself and fall apart if one failed to make a choice between good and evil, if one began choosing activities or causes irrespective of their moral qualities.

The ethical choice of self brings us into the vicinity of the ancient (Aristotelian) vision of virtuous life. Aristotle's 'man' was not contingent, while the modern person is. It is precisely because of their contingency that modern men and women have to choose themselves existentially as good persons. Yet, after choosing oneself existentially, one need not put one's own contingent uniqueness under the constant pressure of a universal moral law; nor does one need to suffer under the onerous weight of rigorous universal imperatives. Living up to one's own destiny can be satisfying, good and pleasant – even if it entails suffering injustice and pain. For, having once chosen ourselves existentially as good persons, nothing is more threatening to us than losing our destiny and thus ourselves.

Plato's famous dictum that it is better to suffer wrong than to cause wrong to someone else is neither true nor untrue. Moral philosophies can employ this dictum as an axiom if they support it through metaphysical absolutes. Once, however, the latter are either rejected or sidestepped, as should duly happen when the contingent person becomes the addressee of moral philosophy, one must admit that the statement cannot be proved and thus must not serve as an axiom either. Irrespective of whether they are believers or a disbelievers, committed to a rationalist world-view or not, involved in a particular cause or not, all contingent persons have one feature in common: in so far as they choose themselves as good (decent) persons, Plato's dictum will be true for them. Those who have chosen themselves ethically are committed to, and partake of, *the common truth that it is better to suffer wrong rather than to cause wrong to others*. The ethical choice of the self brings the vague dreams of humanist classicism to fruition. Persons who have chosen themselves as good love doing the right thing and do the right things with gentleness, predilection, gusto and joy. They are like Aristotle's man of 'good character' (*heksis*): he cannot do the wrong thing, for doing the right thing already follows from his character.[13]

As mentioned earlier, a person can make an existential choice under the category of the universal without (earlier, later or simultaneously) making an existential choice under the category of difference. Yet it is entirely possible to choose oneself as a good person (under the category of the universal) *and* choose oneself existentially (earlier, later or simultaneously) as a person of a particular calling or cause – that is, under the category of difference. A radical conception

of existential choice that rules out such a possibility thereby reintroduces moral absolutism – if not exactly of the Kantian brand, then of
a type which represents a more recent version of the old theory and is
equally unfit for mediation. To my mind, philosophy has to pay its
due to our incompleteness, and it can do so by forgoing the claim to
absolutes and by becoming incomplete itself. There are thus decent
persons who have only made the existential choice of the ethical,
while there are others who make two existential choices. Even if
moral philosophy models itself on the image of the good (decent)
person, it is not authorized to exclude one kind of decent person from
that image because she or he does not fit into the system.

Absolute choice and fundamental choice are distinguishable in
precisely this context. If a person chooses himself or herself both
under the category of the universal and under the category of difference, there must be a hierarchy of choices, even if both are irrevocable. Since conflicts between goodness and calling, and thus
decisions about their relative priority, cannot be eliminated, 'irrevocability' cannot mean the same in the case both of the superordinated
choice and of the subordinated one, where there is conflict between
them and a need to place them in order of priority. The first is our
absolute and the second is our *fundamental* choice.

If the ethical choice is the absolute, and the choice under the
category of difference is the fundamental choice, one will give the
absolute and incontestable priority to moral considerations in action,
judgement and so much else if a conflict arises between the two
existential choices. However, even in this case, the original choice
under the category of difference never needs to be revoked. Precisely
because one's absolute choice is superior to one's fundamental choice,
one will never come to regret (and in this sense revoke) one's fundamental choice. 'Irrevocability' of the fundamental choice then simply
has the following meaning: one does not 'take back' the fundamental
choice, for this is what has made one what one is (what one has
become), and this has been built into one's character. However, all
this does not mean that one would choose again the *object* of one's
choice.

The existential choice of the ethical may or may not permit *free
perseverance* in the object (objective) of fundamental choice in the
case of collisions. It does not permit it if, and only if, one would lose
oneself in persevering in the object (objective) of the fundamental
choice. It is painful, indeed tragic, to disavow the object (objective) of
a fundamental choice in such a way, but it is not tantamount to the
full reversal of that choice. It cannot be emphasized enough that the
fundamental choice is a kind (in this case, a subordinate kind) of the

existential choice and, as such, irrevocable. If I give myself a law and later, led by moral integrity, I change this law, this gesture has no retroactive effect. But it must be stressed that the *ethical* choice of self has *no object or objective* other than the subject itself. There are no dual aspects of this choice. This makes us wonder whether the relationship between the absolute and the fundamental choice can possibly be reversed. Can the existential choice under the category of difference be the absolute one, while the existential choice under the category of the universal simply plays second fiddle to the fundamental choice? Can the universal be subjected to the difference as a result of the gesture of self-determination (of choosing our destiny)?

Forceful external powers hold sway over the person who has chosen himself or herself under the category of difference. The choice can either come off or not. However, the existential choice of goodness is sheltered: it can never be contaminated by the interference of external forces. If, on the one hand, the universal is my absolute and the difference my fundamental choice, the ethical choice cannot protect me from being exposed to the whims of external powers to whom I have exposed myself in the act of choosing myself under the category of difference. Yet it can prevent the source of fundamental choice from becoming contaminated. This happens every time someone in a moral conflict disavows the objective of his or her fundamental choice (without revoking the choice itself). It is exactly the disavowal of the objective (object) which prevents the source from being contaminated. I have mentioned a 'tragic' conflict, which is to be understood in the most traditional meaning of the term: cathartic, purifying, as well as simultaneously annihilating and elevating.

If, on the other hand, the difference is my absolute and the universal my fundamental choice, I shall give an absolute, incontestable authority to those actions which will guide me towards my self-given destiny (a cause, a calling, a relationship and much else), as against moral considerations, in the case of conflicting loyalties, duties, passions, wishes, and the like. However, because I have also chosen myself as a good person, I should risk my own integrity, the unity of my personality, my own autonomy if I did something in which my choice of good would indeed be revoked. I should be walking a tightrope above an abyss, and therefore in need of a good sense of balance, good reflexes, tremendous luck and, most of all, a network of friends able to hold my hand. 'Tightrope dancing' here means giving priority to 'what one has destined oneself to become', without losing one's identity under the category of the ethical. Choosing oneself under the category of difference absolutely, while choosing oneself also under the category of the universal, is the *absolute risk*, for obvious reasons. If you have chosen yourself under the category of difference alone, you may not even notice if your choice does not come off. While cutting a comic figure in the eyes of others, you will not even be unhappy, but will instead live and die in the conviction that you have been good at the thing you have chosen (a cause, a calling or a particular person) while the others are just fools. But if you also choose yourself under the category of the universal, you cannot seek and then find consolation in self-deception. You may even resign your absolute choice and thus cease to be 'the person destined to become this and this', and thereby become infinitely unhappy. To be good (decent) will be no consolation for you. People in this kind of predicament are the likely candidates for suicide.

Everyone who has chosen himself or herself under the category of the universal as a good person, intends by definition to make a moral choice every time a situation, an alternative, an issue so requires. Viewed from this perspective, it is of no (or very little) relevance whether the person has made an existential choice under the category of the universal alone, or a dual choice under the category of the universal *and* that of difference, and, in the latter case, whether the ethical choice was the absolute or the fundamental one. Such a person will invariably ask the question 'What is the right thing for me to do?', thereby expressing the intention – indeed, the *resolution* – to do the right thing or, at least, never to do the wrong thing. This kind of person is the natural addressee of a moral philosophy which provides guidelines for all possible moral advice to be given to actors who ask in any given situation, 'What is the right thing for me to do?'

Modern moral philosophy turns primarily to its 'natural addressee'. In this instance, 'natural' does not stand for 'according to nature', but (roughly) for 'self-evident' (*selbstverständlich*). The relationship between moral philosophy and an addressee is natural in so far as philosophy answers *only* questions which have been raised. Answering (hypothetical) questions which no one has actually asked is a different exercise from the one called 'answering a question'. And, if one replies that moral philosophies only answer questions which have been asked by moral philosophers, my rejoinder will be (as in section I) that the questions raised in a moral philosophy are themselves derived from the answers which are embodied in the very existence of good persons. 'Good persons exist – how are they possible?': this is the fundamental question of moral philosophy. All other questions that this kind of philosophy tries to answer derive from this fundamental one. No wonder then that good persons, those who have chosen themselves under the category of the universal, ask questions the same as, or similar to, those that a good, relevant moral philosophy asks. In this sense, moral philosophy is indeed always *dialogical*. Philosophies are in a continual dialogue with good persons, for they could not otherwise provide guidelines for actors who intend to decide and act on moral grounds. The norm of a modern moral philosophy is to provide such general guidelines as would have been provided by all decent persons, had they destined themselves to be philosophers.

The dialogical relationship does not include everyone. A phone call is made in vain if the other party does not answer the phone. A moral philosophy cannot be blamed if it makes no attempt to establish contact, and dialogue, with people who shun this contact, or even ridicule the attempt at making such contact. As will be discussed in detail in chapter 4, *moral philosophers are not moralists* who let loose their gall and witticism on human foibles, vanities and follies. Moralism can be wholesome, while moralists make it their *point d'honneur* to make us laugh (at others, not at ourselves). But this is simply not what moral philosophy does. Moral philosophy is not interested in human vanities, foibles and follies – not because they are uninteresting, but because moral philosophy is not interested in the 'interesting'. Moral philosophy is interested in the good, which is not necessarily the boring but might not always be what we tend to describe as 'interesting'.

On the other hand, those who have no questions to put to a moral philosophy will not receive any answers either. There will simply be no contact between these people and moral philosophy. Simply put: moral philosophy will not be at their service. One cannot conceive of a moral philosophy which caters to everyone. Ancient moral philosophy could pinpoint certain eternal moral laws and commandments, as well as unconditionally valid values and virtues. It was also authorized to threaten evil with worldly and other-worldly punishment. As mentioned earlier, modern moral philosophy lacks such an authority. In it, one contingent person turns to another contingent person. What we have in common is our contingency, and the possibility of transforming our contingency into our destiny. This is why a moral philosophy cannot volunteer an answer when the contingent person fails to ask the question 'What is the right thing for me to do?' A moral philosophy which attempts to address everyone in the same way, irrespective of whether the addressees have chosen themselves as good persons or not, is not a moral philosophy of the modern kind. For it tries to impose on men and women something which can no longer be imposed on anyone: a good, decent, honest way of life. To say this is simply to reaffirm, from our new perspective, our initial statement that modern men and women are contingent.[14]

Modern moral philosophies do not issue commandments; rather, they offer an earthly body of wisdom to be consulted. It is understood that men and women who have chosen themselves under the category of the universal must consult moral philosophies in order to find one which provides them with general guidelines for a decent way of life. Furthermore, they find what they need, for they are the addressees of modern moral philosophies. But there is only one answer which a moral philosophy can give to men and women who have not chosen themselves under the category of the universal. It goes as follows. *Choose yourself as a human being who is destined to be good. Destine yourself to become what you are: a decent, good person. Choose yourself under the category of the universal. Be the addressee of a moral philosophy so that it can speak to you.* All these formulas are variations of one and the same address. And all of them boil down to the simplest answer of all: *be a person who asks the question 'What is the right thing for me to do?' whenever such a question should be asked.* If you do it, you will become a model for a moral philosophy. The portrait of the good person that such a philosophy paints will also bear your features.

VI

An existential choice is neither rational nor irrational. More precisely, between the state prior to the choice and the one after the choice, there is a *leap*. One does not choose to become what one is *because* one has previously listened to all arguments for and against this choice, and then one arrives at the conclusion that the arguments supporting the 'choice of self' are better or weightier. Anyone who has ever made an existential choice (of a calling, a cause, a person, and of honesty and goodness respectively) knows that the choice does not happen like this. Sometimes one remembers having once made a decision, without even being able to locate it in time and space. We often refer to salutary accidents, sudden illumination, of being 'carried away' by a stronger power, and much else. Yet, whether a particular instance of deliberation and decision can be recalled or not, no one who has ever made an existential choice would doubt that it was indeed a choice, that once upon a time there did exist the possibility not to become what one really is, and that only one's resolution excluded this possibility for good.

Since an existential choice yields destiny, it appears as if it were destiny; if one becomes what one is, one cannot imagine becoming other than what one is. Viewed from another perspective, the same existential choice appears as if it were completely accidental, for it could have never taken place. Anxiety grips the soul of persons who have chosen themselves existentially, and who fix their eyes on the abyss of the past, on the mere possibility of never having made this kind of choice. The momentous character of an existential choice cannot be forgotten. People choose several times in their lives, irrespective of whether or not they have chosen themselves existentially. In all instances of choice, it is very easy to imagine that one could have chosen otherwise, as well as ponder the various modalities of the fictitious choice. An existential choice, however, imposes limits on the imagination. One knows that, theoretically, one could have made another existential choice, or could have stayed put without making any choice at all. But one cannot conceive how it would have been possible, for one simply cannot imagine oneself back in the situation of being able to choose something else or nothing at all. This is the case for the simple reason that the subject of the imaginary–hypothetical situation is not identical with 'myself'; it is another self who happens to be 'me' before the existential choice or after another choice. If 'I' have chosen someone existentially, I cannot imagine myself (my life) with any other person, for then this 'I' would not be 'me'. If one has chosen oneself as a good person, one cannot imagine 'oneself' living a life (what kind of life, indeed?) where one would not prefer moral values to values of other kinds.

When, in the spirit of Kierkegaard, I referred to the existential choice as a 'leap', I registered a well-known life experience. Of course, to a greater or lesser degree every, or (more modestly put) almost every, choice is a leap. One listens to reasons, and finally one makes the decision. More often than not one has to decide quickly and the time for deliberation is limited. Thus one takes the risks and dives in, choosing one course of action rather than another. The leap can be very small and it can also be long. The choice called 'existentialist' is the longest possible leap in a person's life, for, in the case of the *holistic* choice, the *whole* of life is put at risk.

The existential choice under the category of the universal is normally made earlier than existential choices of other kinds; even children frequently make such choices. This in itself indicates that the existential choice is not irrational in so far as it is condition-dependent. I shall return to this question shortly. Yet the same circumstance underscores again that the choice is not rational either. It cannot be repeated frequently enough that the statement 'It is better to suffer wrong than to cause wrong to someone else' cannot be proved. For those who have chosen themselves as good persons, the statement is true, even self-evident; for those who have not made this choice, it is false, even meaningless. One could argue along with Kant, departing from a 'dialectic of pure practical reason', that both thesis and antithesis can be proved equally, for there are equally good reasons to support both of them. Obviously, people do not make a choice of goodness because they are convinced that the thesis is true (right) and the antithesis false (wrong). And even those who dare to make the leap because they are convinced that the thesis is true and the antithesis false do in fact dare a *leap* in the same way as others do, for they accept the truth of the thesis by faith. Had they pitted reasons against reasons, they could have never made the choice (the leap) at all.

It is utterly unlikely that children would rationally consider the truth content of thesis and antithesis. But, if one listens to the recollections of good people, one will frequently hear the story of a decisive childhood experience which was focused on suffering or committing the wrong thing. Interestingly enough, it is more often than not a negative experience, the experience of suffering and of pain which, in the retrospective view of the adult, seems to have been the decisive condition for the choice of goodness. Feeling pain because one did something which one believed was all wrong, or watching the suffering of others, can induce such torments that the person decides to act in such a way that she or he *never feels these torments of conscience again* (for it is better to suffer the wrong than commit it). But where then is the leap? For, if we lend credence to the 'existential story', which we normally do, then it stands to reason that the person had already been good when she or he chose to be good. This in itself corroborates, rather than refutes, the presence of an existential choice. In choosing existentially we choose what we are (in this case, we choose to become what we are: good human beings). Yet the choice is still there. For the child can equally decide (and a decision it is) to kill his or her conscience in the cradle.

Naturally, children can have this kind of tormenting experience without being aware of the existence of moral categories. Children are often similar in some degree to Parsifal, who was able to feel the sufferings of someone else before being clear about the concepts 'right' and 'wrong'.[15] However, in order to choose oneself as a good person, two conditions must be met. First, moral categories and concepts must somehow be around 'in the air'. And, secondly, the child's fate must not be predestined by dense ethical regulations as in pre-modern times. If the first condition is absent, there is no possibility of choosing *goodness* existentially. If the second condition is absent, it is neither possible nor urgent to choose *existentially*.

'Leap' is a metaphor, as is the expression 'existential choice', but they are meaningful metaphors for they stand for the experience, the perception and self-perception of the contingent (modern) man and woman. And they are powerful metaphors for the same reason. One can of course put these metaphors under empirical scrutiny, or create puppets of ideal types out of their infinite variations and possibilities. 'Leap' can be discussed, for example, from a quantitative aspect and be divided into completely irrational, halfway irrational and almost completely rational types. One can also create a typology of the existential choice by applying the category of temporality. Without doubt, there are existential choices which are made in an *instant*, while others drag on for months and years, yet both have the same result. One can toy with the notion of 'fundamental' (not absolute) choice and invent the model of an existential choice which can be replaced by other existential choices. One can perhaps empirically enumerate 'in-between' types, pinpointing people who have 'almost but not quite' chosen themselves existentially, or who let others choose for themselves and yet still preserve a kernel of an autonomous personality such that they are 'not quite' determined by others. Moral philosophy allows for such and similar empirical specifications, but it does not perform them. It is on purpose that I employ the terms 'leap' and 'existential choice' as powerful metaphors without additional empirical or quasi-empirical qualifications.

We already know that the existential choice of goodness is neither rational nor irrational. The circumstance that one has equally compelling reasons to choose A and B (or A and non-A) does not make one's choice (either of A or of B or of non-A) irrational. One's choice is irrational if either one has no reasons (at least no strong reasons) to make the choice, or one has far more and stronger reasons to do something else. However, choosing something which one has good reasons to choose, when one simultaneously has good reasons to choose something else, is far from being irrational. There can be good things in both courses, but life requires a choice. In addition, there may be certain preconditions which make a particular choice in one direction more likely than a choice in another direction (for example, an extremely ethically self-aware and influential milieu may precondition a child for the existential choice of goodness, and thus this choice would be as close to rational as possible). An existential choice is always a *bet* in the Pascalian sense, but it is very rarely a bet with equal odds. There is neither certainty nor calculable probability in it. Yet there is attraction, desire, intuition, even impulse. The Kantian blueprint may render the character of many a concrete choice correctly, but it is certainly at odds with the pattern of the existential choice of the ethical. Since reason alone cannot determine an existential choice, forceful desire, illumination and exposure to a kind of spiritual attraction are all concentrated in such an act of faith.

The existential choice of goodness is frequently made in childhood, but it can be made in any period of life. As time goes by, this kind of choice becomes an ever more dramatic event. When, in his late *Aesthetics*, Lukács remodelled the Aristotelian category of 'catharsis', he interpreted the experience of purification through the intensive feelings of fear and pity as the existential choice. He discussed the 'tragic' as an event and experience of life in the sense of a crucial collision from which one emerges as an entirely different person from what one has hitherto been. One becomes different in so far as one is elevated to the level of 'species essence', that of the very essence of the human race, the universal. The formulation is very close to the Kierkegaardian: in an existential choice, one 're-pents' oneself back into the human race. In addition, Lukács made a distinction between authentic catharsis and what he termed, with allusion to Dostoevsky, disorderly repentance. Disorderly repentance is inauthentic catharsis in which no genuine attempt at the existential choice is made, or an attempt is made but miscarries. The person of disorderly repentance is longing for the existential choice, but is afraid to make the jump. Such a person finally remains on the shore waiting for others to choose for him or her. In a way, Lukács suggests, in the wake of Dostoevsky, it is better not to make an attempt at the existential choice than to miscarry the choice. So far as I am concerned, I plead ignorance in this matter.

2

Everyday Virtues, Institutional Rules, Universal Maxims

I

When a person chooses himself or herself ethically, the category under which she or he chooses is universal. Goodness is universal in so far as we can all choose ourselves as good persons. Yet what one chooses is not the universal, rather the unique – as one's own personality is unique. What Kierkegaard termed 're-penting oneself back into the race' is not meant to denote becoming a universal man or woman, a bloodless abstraction, or what amounts to the same thing: the mere embodiment, the 'becoming-corporeal' of pure reason or reasoned speech. There is no 'good person as such'; there is only this or that good person. All good persons are different; each of them is unique: every good person is good in his or her own way. Or, to formulate the issue in a more Kierkegaardian way, every good person is an exception. It should be remembered that choosing oneself as a good person is choosing *oneself*. To repeat once again everything which is involved here: the chooser chooses his or her sex, family, childhood, race, former experiences, wealth or poverty, neuroses, anxieties, talents and follies, health or sickness – absolutely everything that she or he is. And in so doing the person decides to become what she or he is: a decent, good, honest person. It is in this gesture that determinations are transformed into autonomy.

Once you have achieved autonomy, your soul no longer has a prehistory. Nothing that you do is causally determined any more. And this is so not because of the absence of objective conditions and constraints or because you cannot explain many of your propensities in terms of causality; rather, it is because you have chosen all these causalities. In whatever paradigm you decide to explain your own genesis, the same genesis, once chosen, resides in your freedom.

Once you have chosen yourself as good you are the unity of the individual and the universal in a non-Kantian sense. You are not the composite of the universal (reason) and the particular–singular (nature). Your 'natural' self is not subjected to your 'rational' self. You are a *unified self*. You cannot be cut into the pieces of 'soul and body', 'soul and mind', 'reason and senses', or 'essence and appearance'. You are essential as you appear. You are essential as such and such a person.

Let us suppose that you (the unity of the individual and the universal) are confronted with a situation of choice, and want to find out what is the right thing for you to do. Let us also assume the obvious – namely, that you will turn to others (another) for advice. You will of course seek the advice of decent persons, though you cannot be completely sure whether the persons whom you address have indeed chosen themselves as good persons, or whether they are decent only for the time being, or whether they are only pretending to be good for gain or convenience. A similar problem arises in Kant's moral philosophy, for one cannot be sure whether others act out of duty or merely 'dutifully'. Yet this circumstance does not lead to difficulties in Kant's moral philosophy, for in it it is not the other person, but rather the moral law itself, that should be consulted. For the moment, the same circumstance is far more embarrassing in our model. In turning to another person for advice you are exposed to the danger that the advice is not going to be good advice. Of course, the existential choice of goodness is by no means shaken by the circumstance that in following the bad advice you do the wrong thing instead of the right thing. Yet the circumstance that you rely on another's advice reveals the vulnerability of the model under discussion, for there is no higher (or other) moral instance but the other singular person who, like you, has chosen himself or herself as good, and has thus united the universal with the particular. The alternative to relying upon the advice of others would be self-advice. Yet when you turn to others you do so precisely because you are ignorant of the answer to the question 'What should I do?', because you are unsure what would be the right thing for you to do.

The model of existential choice is *dialogical* in nature, and it is based on the assumption that several persons, not just one, have chosen themselves as decent persons and that they all are good in their own ways. This is quite a reasonable assumption. The dialogical character of the model pre-empts the accusation of 'abstract morality', an age-old objection of Hegelian provenance. True enough, the model of existential choice places a strong emphasis on subjectivity *qua* moral subjectivity, even if it does not profess epistemological subjectivism. Moreover, the birthmark of romanticism is not completely erased from it as long as the existence (and the character) of *Sittlichkeit* (shared values, norms and rules) remains unmentioned in the story. However, the model does not exclude *Sittlichkeit*. On the contrary, the moral dialogue is in itself the manifestation of *Sittlichkeit*. I turn to someone else and I ask her, 'What is the right thing for me to do?' She turns to me and asks me, 'What is the right thing for me to do?' – and so on at any time when she and I are in need of such advice, when we are in need of listening to our fellow creatures' judgement.

What then is the cause of embarrassment? Is there any reason for being embarrassed? For once, we can combine the most attractive features of the Kantian and the Hegelian models. From Kant we preserve the idea of moral autonomy, from Hegel the idea of *Sittlichkeit*. And we can even add the most attractive aspect of discourse ethics to the list. We have morally autonomous subjects who are, in addition, not abstract but concrete, who unify the individual and the universal, who participate in the *sittlich* (ethical) life by entering into constant discussion with one another. Finally, this discussion will be a real moral discussion, and not a theoretical discourse conducted about moral problems, for people seek advice for their actions, and it never occurs to them to substitute moral discourse for moral decision and action. And yet there is reason to be embarrassed. For the model works, and works well, primarily under the condition that there exist communities, or networks of friends, who are not subject to the division of labour, who already share a *Sittlichkeit*. Moreover, they share not just any kind of *Sittlichkeit* but one which has respect for the uniqueness, the 'thusness' of each and every human person. In other words, the model works well under certain *utopian* conditions.

However, people who turn towards moral philosophies as well as to each other with the question 'What should I do?' do not normally live under utopian conditions.[1] Rather, they live amidst conflicting *Sittlichkeiten*, in a world of diverse cultural spheres, in a society consisting of many subsystems, each with rules of its own; in a world where the contingent person can successfully reproduce himself or herself without ever making a conscious moral choice, in a culture where psychology, examination and therapy have been substituted for morals, moral consideration and judgement.[2] *Those living here and now choose themselves as persons who live here and now, and not as persons who live in a utopian reality*. Persons who choose themselves here and now existentially choose the conflicting *Sittlichkeiten*, the diversity of cultural spheres, the subsystems, each of which has an intrinsic rule of its own. They also choose the world where the contingent person reproduces himself or herself smoothly, without ever making a moral decision. They choose a culture where psychology, examination and therapy have been substituted for moral consideration and judgement. They also choose the world which gave birth to the idea of humankind, an idea which, so far at least, has been unable to cross the threshold of reality. They choose the world of global wars, inequality, crime, starvation and tyranny, as well as the world of democracy and liberalism, of human and, in particular, women's emancipation. They choose all of this, not because they like all of it, not because they do not despair or revolt, but rather because they choose to be good, decent persons exactly here and now, under such stars. They do not choose themselves as persons dwelling in a utopian reality, even if they choose such a reality.

If someone chooses himself or herself in the modern condition and transforms his or her contingency into destiny by destining himself or herself to become what she or he is, namely a good person, that person has to choose the 'how' together with the 'what'. For one cannot choose to be a good person without also choosing the way of becoming one.

There is a dialectical relationship between the 'what' and the 'how'. We choose the 'what' (ourselves, our becoming what we are: good persons). However, this 'what' is never devoid of content. Nor is it filled with content. One has to have an idea about being 'good, decent, honest' before choosing oneself existentially under the category of the universal. One such idea is that a good person is someone who would suffer wrong rather than cause it or, what amounts to the same thing in another formulation, one who chooses to do the right thing (to observe moral norms) irrespective of the ensuing consequences. Yet, in order to make this kind of existential choice, the chooser must know that certain actions are good while others are wrong. She or he must even know about certain actions which are good and others which are wrong. When a person becomes what she or he is (as a result of the gesture of the existential choice), namely good, the 'what' of choice is filled with content, it is *concretized*. A decent person's whole life is a process of such 'filling up', such a concretization. Every good person is not just *a* good person in general terms, but such and such a good person in whom the process of concretization ends only in the hour of death. The contingent person who devises his or her own destiny is in this respect dissimilar to Aristotle's virtuous Greek. The latter stabilized his *heksis* (good character) in manhood. From this period onwards he acted spontaneously, for all his actions already derived from his character. The modern person never reaches the point of a completely fixed *heksis*. She or he is a character which, though not malleable, is not 'rounded off': it is still open to further concretization. In our world, values are colliding, as are virtues, and different forms of life impose upon us different obligations; the world can become unfathomable, the connection between action and results hidden from human eyes, transparency gone. How can we be prevented from committing serious moral mistakes amidst such circumstances? How can we avoid committing fatal mistakes?

If a person who has chosen himself or herself as good were to do something *evil*, the moral mistake would prove fatal. Doing evil while believing it to be good is in Hegel's view the moral trap of modern subjectivity. In a transparent world, in a freely chosen community, even in the realm of *Sittlichkeit* as devised by Hegel, the existential choice of goodness precludes fatal mistakes. Yet in the model designed by us not even the constant readiness for moral dialogue seems to prevent anyone from doing many a wrong thing, or even from doing evil things. For the person whose advice one seeks might turn out to suffer from a moral self-delusion. To commit crimes out of ignorance is an old pattern of action, but the modern version is more complex and devious. Ignorance concerning the moral status of norms, values and obligations is now added to the list of the kinds of ignorance which might result in grave, sometimes fatal, moral mistakes. In a simple face-to-face situation of giving moral advice, one fatal blunder leads to several more. Clever and dull alike can fall into this kind of trap, if not for the same reason. The clever person would make an argument for or against everything offered as advice, while the dull one would accept everything at face value.

The choice of oneself as a good person is no guarantee against committing wrong, including fatal mistakes. But it certainly includes the firm determination not to commit such mistakes; hence the attempts to figure out how best they can be avoided. And, indeed, only if we know *how* to become *what* we are (good persons) can we become *what* we are (good persons). There is a difference between the 'what' and the 'how'. If there were none, people could not possibly commit moral mistakes once they had chosen themselves ethically. In the choice, one chooses both the 'what' and the 'how' – in their difference as well as in their final unity (the personality itself).

Let us now return to the situation of a face-to-face moral dialogue. The plea 'Tell me *what* is the right thing for me to do' makes sense if both the addresser and the addressee (the one who seeks advice and the one whose advice is sought) hold certain values in common, especially those values, norms or images of virtue which are relevant for the case or action under deliberation. Unless two persons (or more) have certain values (norms, virtues) in common, they have no basis for advising each other on matters pertaining to good and evil, right and wrong. If in the course of mutual counselling it turns out that what is right for one is wrong for the other, then the participants must share certain notions of 'right' and 'wrong' in order to understand and clarify why this is so, in order to approve or disapprove each other's actions by giving reasons which each of them regards as moral.

It frequently happens that I want to tell someone what is the right thing for him or her to do and that the person wants to tell me what is the right thing for me to do – and this for one very simple reason: we are engaged in action together, we share the course of action, the process of deliberation, and we both want to do the right thing. Let us assume for argument's sake that there are many norms that we do not share. Yet, however different our normative engagements may otherwise be, we both know that it would be the right thing to act. However, we cannot act but together. In order to do what we believe is right, we must obviously find a value, a norm, a virtue which we share, as well as agree on the interpretation of this value, norm or virtue, for only under this condition can we act together in a way which we both consider to be good and right. *We are bound to find out whether any given norm or value can be shared by us without offending either person's concrete idea concerning the good and the right.*

The stronger the relationship is between people, the more norms they have in common and the simpler it is for them to give and receive advice. The weaker the relationship is, the more they find themselves in a situation where they miss the 'natural' common ground for mutual understanding. Yet we know that we cannot be decent persons if we shun participations on a broader scale. *Therefore we are bound to figure out what kinds of norms we can rely upon if involved in action on such a broad scale.*

It can also happen, as it frequently does, that one is a member of different institutions, integrations, forms of life, and that therefore one's loyalties are split. If I find myself in this situation, then I am compelled to choose among alternative courses of action that conflict with different loyalties. The advice I get from others in such a situation will be dependent upon the shared loyalty of the adviser. I thus remain split in mind, and yet I have to act and I want to do the right thing. Obviously I have to figure out whether there is a *hierarchy* among my loyalties. I thus have to ponder whether there is a higher norm, value, virtue, something I can rely upon in ordering my conflicting loyalties in a hierarchical manner. (The case in which the different loyalties are equally weighty will be discussed in chapter 4).

Thus we are back to Kant, though on the grounds of a completely different ontology. The categorical imperative (and all its later variations) is the formula which qualifies for an *absolute* yardstick. Any maxim for action, any duty, can be checked and tested by this formula. It is simple and easily applicable. Kant claimed that a ten-year-old already completely understands the categorical imperative, and he was right. The categorical imperative, or some other but similarly universal maxim, is the crutch which modern persons need to rely upon if they have chosen themselves existentially under the category of the universal 'here' and 'now'. Unless they reach out for such a crutch, they will be exposed to the threat of external powers. And, in the case of tough luck, they would commit a fatal mistake. Today, contingent persons who choose themselves existentially also choose themselves as persons who are exposed to certain moral conflicts and collisions; but they cannot find the good and the right way out of these unless they use a universal crutch as a yardstick.

For Kant (and in all similar philosophical conceptions) the categorical imperative or its equivalent is the Moral Law writ large. It is the object of awe for it stands higher than all individuals, sensual, passion-ridden, interest-steered as they certainly are. And law it is in a dual sense. It is obligatory and unconditionally binding as judicial laws are, and it determines us as the Law of Nature. Yet it is not necessary for an individual to know anything about Kant, still less accept his philosophy, in order to understand what a universal maxim is all about and how such a maxim can be used as a crutch. One need not hold a formula in awe and term it 'Moral Law', one need not recognize 'the universal' as a Platonic idea which dwells above us, or as a Kantian idea of reason which dwells within us and at the same time above us sensual beings, in order to use it as a crutch. Nothing and nobody stands higher than the good person (and to this Kant would not have raised any objection). The good person is good just as she or he is, in his or her ipseity, as such and such a person, as a unique being, as a whole, for this person has chosen himself or herself as such. (Against this Kant would have raised several objections.) The Kantian formulas were devised for the modern contingent person. In formulating the categorical imperative, Kant did a service to contingent persons who have chosen themselves as good, because he devised the model of a crutch which such persons need. And, since they need it, they will use it in so far as they need it. They will use it in a context where they need it. The Kantian Moral Law writ large is a good model for a crutch, but there can be other, less solid, crutches which may do instead.

We need a crutch only when we cannot walk without it. We need the yardstick of a universal maxim or norm whenever everyday norms and rules, tribal norms and rules, virtue norms, and so on, do not provide us with an answer to the question 'What is the right thing for me to do?' It is decidedly odd that in elucidating the categorical imperative Kant mainly cites cases in which no person would need a universal formula to find out which action was right. A person who has chosen himself or herself as a decent human being does not need a universal formula in order to figure out whether murder is right or wrong, whether telling an untruth can be accepted as a valid maxim, or whether it is all right to embezzle. An obvious objection to this is that Kant formulated his philosophy not for persons who have chosen themselves as decent human beings but for everyone. However, this does not change the situation. For bad persons or persons who systematically let others choose for them will not consult the categorical imperative or a similar formula anyway. Only people who have chosen themselves as decent human beings will be ready to consult the Kantian formulas. Yet they will need to consult them in far more complex situations than the ones that Kant analyses.

The individual is the universal. Individuals who want to remain decent seek an answer to the 'how' ('how to be decent?') in the modern world, in the world they have chosen for themselves. They use the crutch of moral universals for their own sake. Otherwise they cannot fence themselves off from external powers which might play a dirty trick on them. The Kantian ontology (and the Jewish–Christian tradition from which this ontology sprang) have left such deep traces on our moral understanding and self-understanding that one cannot emphasize this frequently enough: one is good for one's own sake. Good persons are the ones to whom the Platonic dictum that it is better to suffer wrong than to cause wrong to others applies. Aristotle once said that justice is the sum total of our virtues in relation to other persons, by which he implied that all virtues are good in relation to ourselves. *It is good for us to be virtuous.* Goodness, decency, honesty is not the strenuous way, the way of self-denial, the way of sacrifice, the way to Calvary, unless this is the only alternative to violating and crucifying others.

That decent people are good for their own sake is only another formulation of the idea that virtuous activity is an end-in-itself, as Aristotle put it. Reaching out for universals is by definition an end-in-itself, for it helps the person to continue to live a life that she or he prefers to any other kind of life. To avoid misunderstanding, I do not say that the good person is necessarily happy, nor do I say that goodness is its own reward. I merely mean that one is decent for one's own sake[3] and that, as a result, one turns to the crutch of universals also for one's own sake. Admittedly, a good person often acts for others' sake. However, acting for others' sake and being decent and good for others' sake are entirely different propositions. To distinguish between 'being good for one's own sake' and 'doing the right thing for one's own sake' is of primary importance. The failure to realize that we are confronted here with two completely different, even unrelated, issues has often resulted in the hackneyed discussion of the 'egoism' of the decent person.

Being decent for one's own sake does not make a person an 'egoist', for decent persons by definition act on behalf of others as well, even sometimes make sacrifices on behalf of them. However, people who are decent for their own sake are not altruists either, for every time they act on behalf of others they also remain decent for their own sake. The discussion on this issue is still revolving around the image of the self-righteous person. The image of the self-righteous person is a carry-over from pre-modern *Sittlichkeit*, and we can still come across such persons where traditional ways of life survive or where dense norms are legitimized or underpinned by ideologies, traditional or modern. Self-righteous persons obey meticulously and fully all moral prescriptions, or at least pretend to do so in order to collect credits, external signs of recognition, in their urge for self-aggrandizement. It is easy to spot self-righteous persons. They will always compare themselves, covertly and overtly, to others, and they will invariably be the ones who come out of this comparison with flying colours. As a rule, self-righteous persons reap what they sow: others hold them in awe unless they are unmasked as Tartuffes. It must be added that not all self-righteous persons, not even the majority of them, are in fact consciously hypocritical. Yet on an unconscious plane that is exactly what they are.

However, all this happens in a traditional setting where people receive their destiny prepackaged from the day of their birth, where people know exactly what kind of behaviour is expected of them. As a result, their behaviour does not testify to a great deal of reflection or resolution, let alone the existential choice. True enough, a new type of self-righteous person emerged early in the modern age. To the self-righteousness of *Sittlichkeit* (the traditional element) the self-righteousness of morality (subjectivity) has been now added. In this compound, self-aggrandizement surpasses all proportions and it can result in madness as in Shakespeare's Timon. I cannot provide here any typology of self-righteousness. I would rather return to my starting point: one needs to make the distinction between being good for one's own sake and acting (in a good sense) on behalf of others. Self-righteous persons do indeed do the right things for their own sake; (their acts are done in order to gain recognition, to fulfil their urge for self-aggrandizement); but they are not good for their own sake. Their self-esteem is dependent on the recognition of others, or at least on the comparison with others.[4] Needless to say, persons who have chosen themselves existentially, under the category of the universal, do not compare themselves to anyone, because what they have become, their personality, is unique and in principle incommensurable.

Self-righteous persons (other than the types just mentioned) are disappearing fast from the modern West, which could give the impression, not entirely unfounded, that no virtue, goodness or decency is left there. When people cannot expect to reap high recognition for observing all moral norms more fully and meticulously than others, when the idea that one is morally superior to others will no longer suffice for the purposes of self-aggrandizement, when it is no longer a common everyday phenomenon for people to boast of the purity of their heart and body, *moral life itself must gain a fairly problematic status*. In such an atmosphere people are indeed no longer, or not very frequently or continuously, compared and ranked by the standards of concrete norms. And this is exactly why men and women can make the existential choice to become good, each in his or her own unique and inimitable fashion. And this is also exactly why in addition they can become what they are: good for their own sake.

Good persons now exist by virtue of their existential choice under the category of the universal. They become what they are through that choice. They preserve themselves as good persons in a world which has been chosen by them as their own habitat, while designing, discovering and using as many 'crutches' as they need in order to avoid committing a fatal mistake (a moral crime). These crutches are *their* crutches as well as ours in so far as we accept them. General norms, universal maxims, abstract values, virtues and the like are exactly these kinds of crutches. Philosophers render a service to decent persons by devising the crutches and by giving them a theoretically presentable form.

And this is what I too am going to do while paying the respect due to Kant, who devised the most solid crutch of them all when he gave a fraction of content to his universal formula. For the most solid crutch is the universal moral recommendation that a person should not use another just as a means but also as a goal-in-itself. The phrase 'universal moral recommendation' is deliberate, for in my view all universals (all crutches) are in fact recommendations for the decent person. They read as follows: if you accept this, you can avoid making fatal mistakes.

In what follows, then, I make my own recommendations. I do not begin the discussion with universal maxims; rather, I choose to follow the life way of a decent person. Decent persons, like the rest of us, start their life on an everyday plane. More likely than not, they will first distinguish right from wrong in elementary everyday decisions. I suppose that they have already made up their mind about certain tribal norms when they confront the momentous decisions amidst which they need a crutch, among them a universal crutch.

To follow a decent person on his or her life's way is a reconstruction of a kind. Persons who embark on becoming what they are do not yet know anything about universals, nor do they know that they will need them. The philosopher, who is aware of this in advance, also knows that persons who start treading the way of an honest life will in all probability need these crutches, and knows which one she or he is going to recommend. In so doing, *the philosopher starts to imitate the regard of a decent person who had already become what she or he is*, and who passes on his or her experience and wisdom to other decent persons who have just begun to walk this way.

Moral philosophies should be formulated in a such a way that they can provide guidelines for all possible kinds of moral advice given to any actor who asks in any given situation, 'What is the right thing for me to do?' The person who turns to another person seeking such advice wants to know what the *right* thing is, for she or he wants to choose the right thing as against the wrong one. But such persons also want to know what is the right thing *for them* to do. For a particular kind of action may be right for some but wrong for others. They want to receive custom-made advice, advice which fits them (their situation, biography, conflicts, alternatives, strength and weaknesses) completely. Yet moral philosophies are not custom-made. When they narrate the stories of good persons who seek advice and give advice in a concrete and dense life situation, they are hopelessly clumsy, unpoetical and short of breath. It is left to poets, not to moral philosophers, to narrate *a* story which is *the* story. Only the reader can infuse real lifeblood into moral philosophy; only the good person can make it real.

II

Kant was baffled by man's *unsociable sociability*. In the main, all the wrongs people do to others are done in order to secure the recognition of their fellow creatures. They humiliate others in order to be elevated in the eyes of others. They seek power, wealth and fame in order to get a strong emotional response from others, be it fear or love. They fight for positions while trampling their rivals underfoot in order to become 'somebody' in the eyes of others. And, by and large, people also do all the right things in order to achieve recognition, to avoid shame. Only other persons can elevate us. Only other persons can humiliate us. A good word from another person makes it a happy day, an offence an unhappy one.

The need of human beings for one another (for recognition, love, affirmation, appraisal, approbation on the one hand; for fear, humiliation, craving on the other) cannot be quantified. And it is not some attempt at quantifying the unquantifiable that leads me to believe that this need, and the 'amount' of this need, is a constant. A cursory glance at the contemporary human condition would clearly support such a guess. The modern world is characterized by a functional division of labour. Within our institutions of work (in the broadest sense of the world) we perform a function, and we communicate or co-operate with other people as the manifestation or 'embodiment' of another, similar or identical, function. We do not encounter others as whole persons; skin does not touch skin, flesh does not touch flesh. The interior life of one person is of no concern to another, and *vice versa*. We walk on streets where we know nobody; we are surrounded by millions of strangers. If we choose not to have a family, we can live alone, be alone, stay alone: no one cares. We can have as many 'casual affairs' as we want without establishing any bonds. Yet, if we believe that all of this has somehow decreased human vulnerability, we are certainly mistaken. Rather, it is the case that, the less intense people's contacts with each other are, the less they share each other's life skin to skin, flesh to flesh, every day, hour and minute, the less constant their human ties are, the *more* sensitive they become. People who do not tolerate the smell, let alone the constant presence, of another human being remain as sensitive as small children: they never become adults emotionally. Where people are squeezed together in a metaphorical sense, they certainly learn that they are different, that not every offence was meant as such, and, even if it was meant, that this does not always matter and one can forget about it. The circumstance that the need of human beings for each other is rather constant (as needs for human beings and not for the manifestation of functions) makes the claim of certain contemporary philosophies that in the modern world only justice has remained of morals patently absurd.

That modern morals work in a different way from pre-modern ones is one proposition, and that there are no morals any more is another. The latter, moreover, is a patently false proposition. Modern moral norms are patchy, and even when and where they are not, the quasi-organic ties between norms, values and virtues have been severed. This is why people will be, and already are, less inclined to do the right thing *in order to achieve recognition* except in a normative environment which is still dense. It is under such conditions that goodness as well as persistent and continuous honesty and decency results from the existential choice. Morality as self-destination is not pitted against *Sittlichkeit* here as in Hegel's model. It is amidst the dried-out and patchy fibres of *Sittlichkeit* that it stands its ground. It asserts itself as the carrier of a new kind of *Sittlichkeit*. Good persons create *Sittlichkeit* in everyday life, within institutions, in the political theatre, on a world scale. They do not create *Sittlichkeit* out of nothing; rather they create it, custom-made for themselves and for others, out of the patchy norms, values and virtues which are floating around them. Decent persons need other men and women. As repeatedly stressed, they need the others' good advice, but they also need *them*; rather they need them first of all. And, in a similar fashion, decent persons are needed by others; others need their advice, but, above all, they need *them*. Nothing is more needed than a good, decent, honest person – not because such persons have a good heart (sometimes they do not have an exceptionally good heart at all), but because they turn towards others, because they are the embodiment of 'social sociability' (*gesellige Geselligkeit*).

III

A decent person cares for others.

Heidegger invented the beautiful metaphor of the 'shepherd of Being'. I read this metaphor in the following way: everyone who has been born into this world has the task of taking care of this world. The world is left in the care of human beings. The decent person takes care of the world (of all beings) but does not literally 'take care' of human beings. Rather, she or he cares for them. The honest person is the shepherd of all beings, and a good shepherd at that, in so far as she or he cares for them. Caring for other humans is taking care of all beings, of Being. The person who chooses himself or herself existentially has to learn how to care for human beings.

Care for other human beings: this is the universal orientative principle of morals.

It is a universal principle because in all spheres, all forms of life, all kinds of activity people can care for each other as well as not care. As a result, the principle orients and steers people in everyday life, within institutions, in the public realm. Actually, very different kinds of action are oriented by this principle. The principle is orientative (and not constitutive) not because its content is meagre (a substantively thick principle is not a proper principle anyway), but because it cannot serve as a moral crutch which one can rely upon in all cases when one needs a crutch. Indeed, a great many interpretations of the principle need to be checked by universal maxims. Using a spatial metaphor, it could be said that the universal orientative principle (care for other human beings) is the lowest universal, while universal maxims (the 'universal crutches') are the highest, because one checks the content of the former with the latter. Yet spatial metaphors are misleading. If we began the discussion with human goodness, and not with establishing a 'moral law', and if one insisted, as I do, that the universal yardstick should be understood from the concerns of decent persons and not *vice versa*, we could then even conclude that the universal orientative principle is actually the highest principle of them all – since, in the final analysis, it is caring for other people and taking care of all beings that ethics is all about.

The good person first learns how to care for others. By definition, that person learns how to avoid harming another person.

Orientative principles as a rule encompass commandments and prohibitions. In modern times, most specifications of the universal orientative principle are also orientative in character. There are still prohibitions left (although no more positive commandments). If prohibitions are infringed, judicial or social sanctions follow (albeit not in all cases). Although the negative formula 'Do not harm another human being on purpose' is orientative to the same extent as the positive one 'Care for other human beings', there are certain acts of doing harm which carry sanctions, while failure to care for others does not unleash sanctions unless harm is done.

The decent (good) person is one who does the right thing irrespective of social (judicial) sanctions. In addressing men and women who have chosen themselves existentially under the category of the universal, moral philosophy *cannot* start the specification of the orientative principle ('Do not harm another human being on purpose') with the prohibition 'Do not murder.' Murder is certainly the most heinous of all crimes, yet precisely this is why no decent person needs to be confronted with such a prohibition. She or he has built-in inhibitions about committing murder anyhow. And since (to look at the matter the other way round) the most serious judicial sanctions apply to murder anyhow, not to murder is no merit, at least not in modern society. Abstaining from murder adds nothing to the portrait of the honest person or, for that matter, to that of any person. Nor does modern society leave much room for killing on moral grounds in private life. The kind of killing which can be regarded both as a sacrificial offering and as a heinous crime, the kind of murder to which no sanction applies, the type of murder committed under the guidance of evil maxims and the like, will be discussed in conjunction with far more complex situations than the ones emerging from a normal everyday setting.

I have already mentioned that the specifications of the universal orientative principle are also orientative in nature in the manner in which Aristotle discussed virtues. One cannot tell other people *exactly* what they should do in the event that they want to follow orientative principles in full. One can only make a tentative formulation, on the following lines: it is better to do something in this direction rather than in that one; it is better to do more of this and less of that; not even the best things should be done to excess, for, if they are, they can cause more harm than good. One should add, still in keeping with Aristotle's spirit, that orientative principles are 'situation-sensitive'. In following such a principle, one cannot do the same thing in every situation and to everyone. Principles are applied by dynamic adjustment. Orientative principles are not to be applied to the single case by a determining judgement. One can certainly subsume a case under one or another principle, yet proper subsumption alone will not prescribe the handling of this particular case. If it does, the application of the principle may suffer some harm as a result of rigidity. Reflective judgement and determining judgement must constantly oscillate in order for the 'proper measure' to be determined. All this is subject to the fact that the case is already regarded as one to which the universal orientative principle applies.

Orientative principles are not only adjustable to situations and to persons for whom one cares; *they are also adjusted (and adjustable) to the (good) person who cares.* One cannot emphasize frequently enough that everyone is good in his or her own way. One also cares for others in one's own way. 'Mutual dynamic adjustability' is the proper term to employ here. In caring for another, a person cares in his or her own way. Yet one has to consider how 'caring for someone else' is interpreted by the persons for whom one cares. And anyone who feels the care of another person, or is in need of such care, must make allowances for the other person's need to care, for his or her interpretation of 'caring for', for his or her need for 'being cared for by someone'. Orientative principles do not always offer a smooth ride. Phronesis, or practical wisdom, is more important when people have to make allowances for each other in the process of mutual caring.

Finally, the observance of each and every orientative principle can be waived by universal moral maxims, norms, or laws. In addition, the observance of certain orientative principles can also be waived by institutional rules (to which I shall turn shortly). Yet waiving the application of this or that orientative principle does not result in waiving the validity of the *universal* orientative principle. It is universal and thus it cannot be waived.

In what follows, I shall enumerate a few orientative principles. All of them are interpretations and concretizations of the universal orientative principle 'Care for other human beings', and of its negative formulation 'Do not harm another human being on purpose.' I do not pretend to offer a catalogue of all principles. Every decent person can correct me as well as add his or her own principle to the list.

1   *Have a proper regard for other persons' vulnerability.*

   (a)   Do not offend another human being in his/her person and in anything she/he holds dear.

      (i)   Do not show contempt for another person (unless morally justified).

     (ii)   Do not ridicule another person or put another person to shame (unless morally justified).

   (iii)   Do not express contempt for or indifference to persons and causes which another person holds dear (unless morally justified).

   (b)   Learn to express your feelings of love, sympathy and respect towards other persons.

      (i)   Do not be afraid of self-exposure in the expression of your feelings.

     (ii)   Learn to express your feelings in such a way that the other will not misread them.

   (iii)   Never feign a feeling for personal gain.

   (iv)   Do not conceal your feelings even out of the best motivations – for example, pity (unless there are strong indications to the contrary).

     (v)   Emotional expressions should not be accompanied by self-humiliation.

   (c)   Respond to another person's need for your person sincerely.

(i) If a person says 'I need you' and you need him or her, you should not cause suffering or insecurity in the other by withholding the satisfaction of that need (unless there are moral reasons not to satisfy it).

(ii) If a person says 'I need you' and you do not need him or her, it is better to refuse the satisfaction of that need. But you should not refer to the other person's shortcomings in rejecting him or her (unless the shortcomings are moral ones).

(d) Help the other person to 'save face'.

(i) Try to find the gesture or the word which may help the other to escape from an embarrassing situation.

(ii) Do not let people enter into situations which will be embarrassing for them, if you are in a position to warn them. Learn how to tread the line between meddling in other people's affairs and outright indifference.

2 *Have a proper regard for other persons' autonomy.*

(a) Do not violate another person's body.

(i) Do not murder (non-orientative).
(ii) Do not rape (non-orientative).
(iii) Do not deliberately inflict bodily harm on another person.

(b) Do not violate another person's soul.

(i) Do not humiliate others.
(ii) Do not deliberately make others emotionally dependent on you.
(iii) Never attempt to break another person's will.

(c) Do not manipulate others.

(i) Do not withhold information (do not lie) in order to make others do something which is for your own pleasure or benefit, even if the act is good.

(ii) Do not influence others to do what is pleasant or

beneficial for you but not for them, even if the act is good.

(iii) Do not use your charisma (if you have charisma) to recruit a following with the purpose of prescribing or dictating to them what to do, even if they will benefit by it and the intention is good.

(d) Do not keep others in tutelage.

(i) Do not use others' financial dependence to keep them in tutelage.

(ii) Do not use others' institutional dependence to keep them in tutelage (see section VII: institutional rules).

(iii) Do not use your superiority (intellectual, artistic, etc.) to keep others in tutelage.

There is a *non-orientative* principle which *encompasses a, b, c and d*:

Do not violate another person's body or soul; do not manipulate others or keep them in tutelage because of their race, sex or membership of other human groups.

(e) Help others achieve greater autonomy.

(i) Let go a person who wants to go, even if you could hold him or her back, and even if parting causes pain (see Goethe, *Iphigeneia in Aulis*).

(ii) Seek to transform work relationships in the direction of greater autonomy for all parties.

(iii) It is better to base an exclusive relationship on a greater autonomy than on a lesser one. Only a freely chosen exclusivity is autonomous.

(iv) Do not sacrifice your autonomy for another person's autonomy. In so doing you either make the other guilty or infringe the other principles listed under point (e).

3 *Have a proper regard for other persons' morality.*

(a) If your opinion holds weight in the deliberations of others, you must warn them every time they embark on a wrong, bad, criminal or evil course of action.

(i)   It is better to seem troublesome and be exposed to rebukes than to omit the duty of forewarning.

(ii) It is better to cause pain to a person than to let him or her do something that you know to be wrong.

(iii) It is better to be accused of impertinence or interference for insisting on warning people than to veer to the opposite extreme of moral indifference.

(iv) Do not push your own self into the foreground when warning others. Self-righteousness has nothing to do with caring for others.

(b) Pay attention to moral merit.

(i)   Good persons stand in the shadow. Bring them into the light so that they can be seen.

(ii) Recognition is due to all persons.

(iii) Praise is due to excellence and merit. Never miss the opportunity to praise meritorious actions, irrespective of the actor's goodness or otherwise.

(c) Learn how and when to pass moral judgements.

(i)   Learn to distinguish adiaphoric actions from actions of ethical relevance. It is a moral debit to pass moral judgement on adiaphoric actions.

(ii) In the case of small offences, only phronesis can decide whether moral judgement should be passed. In the case of major offences, one should always pass moral judgement.

(iii) Moral judgement should have a proper regard for the autonomy of the offender. The aim in passing a moral judgement should not be to 'reform' the offender but to offer that person insight into the character of the offence. (The offender may rely upon this insight if she/he chooses to reform himself/herself.)

(iv) Moral judgement should be passed (in the above way, under the above conditions) irrespective of others' lack of concern or outright hostility, and irrespective of the consequences.

(v)   To withhold moral judgement is legitimate or advisable if you have committed the same offence as the person to be judged, or have committed an offence of equal or greater gravity.

    (vi)   It is better to express approval or disapproval face to face than behind the other person's back.

    (vii) In the case of disapproval, the judgement should not cast aspersions on the character of the person to be judged (unless there are strong moral reasons to the contrary). In the case of approval, it is better to extend the judgement to the character as a whole.

(d)   Learn when to forget and when to remember.

    (i)   If you realize you have wronged someone, say 'I am sorry'. Apologize under no other circumstances.

    (ii)   If someone says 'I am sorry' to you, forget the offence if you were the one who has been offended (unless you have strong moral reasons for remembering).

    (iii) Irrespective of whether you are more inclined to remember or to forget, apply the same standard to yourself as to others.

    (iv) Avoid keeping a catalogue of small offences in your memory.

    (v)   You can be decent and good without forgetting serious offences committed against you. (You need not be a saint to be good.) But you cannot be decent and good if you forget the serious offences you have committed against others.

4 *Have a proper regard for other persons' suffering.*

(a)   A decent person notices the suffering of others.

    (i)   Learn to perceive suffering in all its forms, even if you have never contributed to it.

    (ii)   Never be indifferent to another persons' sufferings. Find out whether their sufferings have causes that can be remedied.

    (iii) Learn to express regard for other persons' sufferings.

(b)   A decent person does his or her best to alleviate another persons' sufferings.

    (i)   Do your best to alleviate the sufferings of those who rely upon you.

(ii)   Offer a proper part of your time, money and energy for the alleviation of remediable suffering.

All these orientative principles sound simple and quite traditional. Some of them are indeed traditional and this is precisely why they sound simple. However, the few non-traditional (modern) principles among them modify each and every principle in the catalogue, even if their inclusion does not change the wording of the traditional ones. Or, more precisely, they confer new meaning upon the traditional principles by widening the field of their application on the one hand and narrowing it down on the other.

The group of principles which modifies the meaning and the scope of validity of them all is the second group ('Have a proper regard for other persons' autonomy'). Although principles may collide in their practical applications, they cannot contradict one another as principles. No principle can be formulated in such a way as to contradict the principles of cluster 2. From this, several important steps follow. One of the most important is that none of the principles listed above involves a command–obedience relationship. Moreover, none of them refers to any authority but the moral one. If the principles listed as 2 (c), (d), (e) have to orient our actions, obedience is either adiaphoric or wrong, and so is command.[5] The implications of this circumstance are far-reaching. Let us take a quick look at the sub-cluster 3 (d). Point (i) states that you should never say 'I am sorry' unless you realize that you have done something wrong. 'I am sorry', however, does not suggest that you *ask for forgiveness*. From point (ii) onwards, the principles concern *forgetting* but *not forgiving*. One could argue that this makes no difference, that 'forgetting' equals 'forgiving'. But this is not quite true. If people are equally autonomous, if their relationship is one of symmetric reciprocity, if they reciprocally recognize each other's personhood, then, and only then, will 'forgetting' equal 'forgiving'. Anyway, what else can we do in an everyday situation but say, 'Forget it'? What has been done is done. It cannot be undone except in our memory, in so far as we blot out the traces of the event. We do our human best if we behave towards the other person as if nothing had happened. And the one whose deed has been forgotten cannot turn to the one aggrieved and say, 'This is not enough! In addition, forgive me.' This is a pointless injunction, for nothing can be done 'in addition'. It has an unpleasant taste if people of equal standing and dignity turn to one another with the plea 'Forgive me!', because the plea is associated with humble genuflection, lying prostrate, folding one's hands in prayer – all gestures of pre-modern times. It is also irrelevant. However, within self-consciously hierarchical social arrangements 'forgiving' and 'forgetting' do not coalesce. 'Forgiving' then means, precisely, that in response to the humble apology of the one standing lower in the hierarchy the one standing higher restores the offender to the position that she or he held prior to the offence. The case is similar where the offender is a child in an authoritarian family. Moreover, in such cases 'forgiving' does not necessarily mean 'forgetting': a person who has been forgiven can still be daily reminded of his or her offence.

I have spoken at length about this problem because it serves as an example of the modification which traditional principles undergo when they are combined with the orientative principles of autonomy. However, the same principles of autonomy – sub-clusters 2 (c), (d), (e) – do not just modify the wording (and thus the substance) of certain orientative principles. They also reset the stage for the application of all principles (naturally, with the exception of the non-orientative ones).

The principles listed above are orientative in a traditional sense, like Aristotle's virtue norms, in so far as they orient our actions and behavioural patterns in a general direction, letting phronesis (good judgement) decide about the 'what', the 'how', the 'when', the 'towards whom' and the 'to what extent'. In addition, they are orientative in a non-traditional sense, for they are formulated so as to avoid any reference to concrete norms, rules, even virtue norms. The principles frequently mention 'offence' without making any attempt to determine what kind of offence is meant, or what is and what is not to be regarded as an offence. In a pluralistic moral universe, which is the modern moral universe, an act that is an offence in one particular way of life may be adiaphoric in another. Some of the principles include the proviso 'unless there are strong moral reasons to the contrary' or 'unless morally justified', without making any attempt to further concretize such provisoes. For moral reasons can be derived from concrete norms, virtue norms and rules, but the orientative principles abstract from those precisely because they are modern. This explains certain, apparent or real, omissions.

In the first place, there is not one single principle in the catalogue which aims at orienting our feelings, emotions and sentiments. No principle enjoins us to love or feel sympathy, though there is a principle which advises us to learn to express our (positive) feelings so that others should be able to read, and not misread, our feelings. Furthermore, there are principles which advise us *not* to express *certain* negative feelings (contempt in particular). Moreover, when it comes to 'proper regard for those who suffer', *empathy is not en-*

joined either (instead, the principles suggest that we should learn to perceive suffering, never to be indifferent towards it, rather to help alleviate it). Yet these are not emotional matters. Kant said that love cannot be enjoined. I would not subscribe to this as a generalized statement. In a traditional society love can indeed be enjoined, and sometimes it is. In a similar fashion, other feelings, emotions, sentiments can also be enjoined. It is by virtue of *modern subjectivity*, of the kind of self-reflexivity which constitutes a unique personal inwardness for each individual (or which at least offers the possibility of such an inwardness), that it becomes odd, absurd, even ridiculous to *enjoin* men and women to *have* (to develop) certain feelings and emotions. However, no 'ontological' statement follows from this. The circumstance that one does not enjoin men and women to have (to develop) certain feelings, and the further circumstance that abiding by the principles may be motivated by feelings as well as by rational insights, have absolutely nothing to do with one another. The orientative principle simply abstracts from the genesis or the motivation of a certain kind (type) of action. What is true about the existential choice of goodness is also true about all concrete actions. If one admits that children can make an existential choice of goodness because they *feel* that what they have done is wrong, because they suffer under the burden of suffering that they have brought on another, how can one possibly deny that strong impulses towards decency and honesty can come from emotions, feelings and sentiments? None the less, these feelings cannot be enjoined (they are either there or are not there). In addition, such feelings can also motivate one towards actions in a direction contrary to the one indicated by the orientative principles.

The second apparent omission is that of norms related to sexuality. This is a contentious issue, for it would seem that one simply cannot discuss orientative principles in everyday life without discussing at the same time one of the centrepieces of everyday life, without providing a single orientative principle to guide us in matters related to what happens to be one of the main forms of human social intercourse.

There was a time when people, on hearing the term 'moral', almost instinctively thought of the regulations of sexual life. In referring to an 'immoral man' or a 'woman of loose morals', they pointed out people whose sexual habits fell short of 'proper' standards. The so-called 'sexual revolution' did not put an end to all normative regulations in the field of sexual relationships. However, it did pluralize these norms and regulations as well as establish a variety of forms of life along traditional (religious) and non-traditional (personally chosen) lines. As mentioned earlier, orientative principles abstract from concrete norms all the way along, and the same holds for all norms regulating sexual relationships. Orientative principles, all of them, obviously steer and guide people in their sexual relationships to the same degree as in everything else. Since orientative principles are subcases of the general principle, the kinds of concrete norms which contradict principles are not permitted. At this stage, it is easy to comprehend why and how modern principles widen, and at the same time narrow down, the territory of what is permitted. They widen it in so far as one can be fully guided by the principles without accepting a single concrete sexual regulation (in other words, a single norm which regulates sexual behaviour and action alone). Yet it also narrows down the field because no sexual practices and symbioses are permitted which would infringe the orientative principles. Among these orientative principles are those of autonomy, and, in fact, if one is guided by those principles, many a traditional sexual practice would become impermissible. It will suffice to look at the catalogue. One should not violate another person's body. One should not violate another person's soul. One should not manipulate others. One should not keep others in tutelage. This simple list will show how far the narrowing-down can go. Kierkegaard, correctly, suggested that sensuality as a principle had been created by Christianity. Foucault, equally correctly, insisted that sexuality as a principle had been constituted by the modern 'scientific' discourse. The 'sexual revolution' still stood under the spell of this discourse. Feminism is just about to begin to challenge it. Once we no longer believe that moral laws, if recognized, should be written on tablets of stone, we shall also cease to believe that committing norms and rules to paper, as is constantly done with traditional concrete sexual regulations, guarantees their validity independently of the persons who stand up for them. If, further, one does not believe that all traditional norms should be tested, or that every norm must be legitimized and authorized by rational speech, but believes rather that good persons uphold norms in order to make decent life possible as well as viable, one will take it as self-evident that whatever makes decent life possible and viable in human relations in general is also the criterion of decency in all sexual matters.

IV

Practising reciprocity is *giving* and *receiving*. This is so irrespective of whether reciprocity is symmetric or asymmetric. By 'symmetric reciprocity' I mean reciprocity among persons of equal standing, while by 'asymmetric reciprocity' I mean reciprocity among persons of unequal standing. By 'equal standing' I do not want to denote social equality (of means and positions), but rather the equality of persons *qua* persons (mutual recognition of personal equality). There is no society without symmetric reciprocity; however, there have been very few societies of symmetric reciprocity. Societies of symmetric reciprocity do not necessarily outlaw all instances of asymmetric reciprocity. Relations of the latter kind exist in them *de jure* (in an institutionalized form) and *de facto* (in merely private personal relationships).

The first sentence of this section ('Practising reciprocity is *giving* and *receiving*') is, on closer scrutiny, a tautology, for what else can reciprocity be but giving and receiving? Where one party gives and the other does not receive, there is no relationship. Where one party only gives and the other only receives, there is a relationship but no reciprocity. One of the most elementary ethical norms, if not the most elementary one, is that *reciprocal relationships are preferable to non-reciprocal relationships*. If you take something, you should also give something. This is so within the framework of all social arrangements, without exception.

So much, of so many things, is given and received, and one can give and receive in so many different ways and forms, that discussing them all would result in discussing practically everything. You can give and receive a piece of bread, advice, encouragement, a kiss, a promise, a kingdom, a kick, a wound, a bad time or a blow. In terms of the elementary norms of social intercourse, whatever you get you return *in kind* – good for the good things, bad for the bad. There may be merit in failing to return the bad things (though not everywhere and not in all cases). Yet it is always a debit, in the dual meaning of the word, to fail to return a good one. A person who receives and does not give in kind is in debit. If that person is in debit for too long a time, she or he loses face. A person who receives a bad thing and returns a good one is regarded in certain cultures (for example, the Christian) as highly virtuous. A person who receives a good thing and returns a bad one is considered to be a scoundrel in all cultures without exception (in an 'in-group' situation).

It is mere guesswork to say that most of the concrete norms regulate acts of giving and receiving. And yet I would venture this generalization. The different levels, modes and forms of giving–receiving are meticulously specified and refined in every known culture. They are sometimes also surrounded by rites and ceremonies. Strong and concrete normative regulation is inherently tantamount to 'yardstick fixation'. If you are familiar with the norms of giving and receiving down to the minutest details, and if you follow the norms meticulously (returning precisely what is required, in exactly the right way), then you match the yardstick of what is termed *equal*. But how can you equalize such absolutely different things as getting a piece of land and giving loyalty; receiving a piece of bread and saying 'God bless you' (giving a blessing); receiving a sum of money and providing the giver's nephew with a position; getting cattle and giving a bride? Quite obviously, it is not only in commodity exchange that qualitatively different 'things' are quantified in the exchange. All acts of giving and receiving quantify the qualitatively different: things, services, gestures. What you are not supposed to return (even now) is exactly the *same* thing as you have received. Many virtues and vices are crystallized out of the practices of reciprocity. Misers fail to give when they should; the ungrateful receive but do not repay – or, what is worse, repay the good with bad. The generous lavishly give without expecting an equal return; the grateful give more than they receive or at least exactly that much. Honesty and dishonesty are also closely related to acts of giving and receiving. So is justice.

One gives something – one receives something. I give – you receive; you give – I receive. What I give is *mine*; I cannot give you what is not mine. Or, rather, if I give you something which is not mine, I must be authorized by an institution or by a third party to do so. Giving *myself* to you is the limit to reciprocity unless you simultaneously give yourself to me. Yet, since giving ourselves to each other is really a metaphor, standing for love and the acts of love, giving myself to you is in fact the limit to reciprocity. What we give away are some of our properties, or the use of such properties. The property can be a thing, an emotion, a position, a relation, or anything else. A property of which use is granted is a possession – an object, a physical power, a talent or whatever – that one allows another to use or puts to another's service.

Where there is a giver, there is also a receiver. Where there is a receiver, there is also a giver. Yet in this interplay 'giving' is the overarching category. This is so for the simple reason that the property, the very medium of reciprocity, must be there in the first place. However, there is obviously an enormous difference between 'giving away something' and 'giving away the use of something'. In the first case 'mine' becomes 'yours' (it is no longer mine, and never will be, unless you return it). In the second case, what is mine remains mine – be it talent, power, a thing, a position, a relation or something else. Emotions and sentiments are special issues and cannot be adequately discussed within this framework.

Where there are givers, there are also receivers; however, the bonds of reciprocity are not necessarily there. One can give something away to unknown recipients, or the other way round: the giver can keep his or her identity undisclosed. Yet such acts are beyond the bonds of reciprocity if, and only if, they are performed not according to social and political rules but as acts of free choice. Whenever and wherever social and political rules regulate redistribution, and such rules constitute social clusters, the giving and receiving that take place in accordance with such rules are matters of *justice*.[6] Little room is left for free choice in this case. Of course, people can try to act unjustly, to keep more of the good things for themselves and less of the bad. But there is always a risk involved, since they can be punished for the infringing of the rules. Attempts at tax avoidance are a case in point. Reciprocity, even if unintended, is built into the social fabric. Paying taxes is not a morally meritorious act of giving, although not paying them is an offence. By contrast, if a wealthy man decides to give a great sum of money to charity while keeping his identity undisclosed (thereby losing the right to set off the gift against tax), his act of giving is generous but not reciprocal (the act cannot be reciprocated).

The maxim of justice enjoins us that the norms and rules constituting a social cluster should be applied consistently and continuously to each and every member of that cluster. If norms and rules are taken for granted (considered natural, divine or just), every person knows what these norms and rules are, and when and how they apply. Or, as Aristotle first put it, everyone knows what is due to whom. All matters of justice have something to do with acts of giving and receiving, and most of them are actually matters of giving and receiving. Giving and receiving are therefore thoroughly regulated. The party that gives and the party that receives, and returns something in exchange, do not act on their own. Not two, but invariably three, parties are involved in the performance of acts of justice, for the *rules themselves* can be regarded as the third party. Moreover, the gaze of the community, of all 'others' whom the rules represent and stand for, is the dominant party in the interaction. Metaphorically, the giver does not confront the receiver, nor does the receiver confront the giver. They look not at each other, but rather at the rules to which their acts of giving, receiving and reciprocating must conform.

Even if most of the rules of justice circle around the acts of giving, receiving and reciprocating, the obverse is not the case. One need not get entangled in empty speculations about 'every society', but this much can be said about modern societies: that certain acts of reciprocity are always practised above and beyond the pale of justice. People give others something which is not 'due' to them, and the like.

Several virtues and vices related to reciprocity have nothing to do with justice. One can be just, yet not generous; one can be illiberal or stingy, yet not unjust.

The emergence of dynamic justice promotes practices of reciprocity between two parties in so far as the 'third party' to the bargain, the dominating rules of justice, themselves are queried, and sometimes even invalidated. Although there is always a new 'third party' recommended by those challenging the old, so long as the new third party lacks power it cannot impose social sanctions. Hence the actions of reciprocity can be termed 'freely chosen' interactions of two parties. In addition, the less stratified ethical behavioural patterns become, the more people are at liberty to choose the other party, to choose the amount and kind of giving and reciprocating, and the more reciprocity can become symmetrical. To the problem of symmetric reciprocity I shall return shortly.

In modern societies, at least the rules of redistribution and retribution are regulated by laws. In Soviet-type societies, distribution and sometimes even consumption are also regulated by a 'third party' (the central agency). Every time people delegitimize such laws or regulations they do so by arguing against them and, mostly within the framework of law, by reaching beyond them in action (in Western societies), or by reaching beyond them by overruling the decision of the central authority (in Soviet-type societies). In addition to legal regulations, there are also patterns of convention, sometimes even ceremonious conventions, in modern everyday life. Thus there is also a private kind of 'third party' to the interaction. However, everyone knows that giving and reciprocating according to these rules has absolutely nothing to do with justice nowadays. It is obvious why this is so. Contemporary conventions are not the kind of rules which *constitute* social clusters, even if sometimes the rules are accepted and conformed with *within* certain social groups (though this is rare). If you are invited by a family and you do not return the invitation, but invite other families instead, no one will call you unjust – rather, rude and impolite. Invitation is not 'due' to the family in question. If, although you have money to lend, you do not lend it to someone who needs it and who has lent you money when you needed it, you will be considered stingy and ungrateful, but not unjust. To give a loan is not an act which is 'due' to another person. Ceremonial acts of reciprocity are acts of urbanity or civility, whereas acts of reciprocity beyond, above or outside all ceremonies or conventions are *not* acts of civility or urbanity, but acts of generosity, kindness, honesty, gratitude, and so on. Neither type comprises acts of justice.

Thus, when certain philosophers insist that nowadays justice is all that remains of morals, I would respond by affirming a contrary trend. Nowadays most acts of reciprocity are no longer acts of justice (even if they were so in pre-modern times), but acts of civility, generosity, kindness, and so on. Virtues beyond the virtue of justice play, or at least can play, a far greater part in our life than ever before.

The proviso 'at least can play' is a reference to the fact of contingency. Acts of justice cannot be chosen in the same way as acts beyond justice can be. The contrast between acts of justice and acts of civility is not stark, but the contrast between acts of justice and acts of generosity is. The rules of civility are still rules, and those who infringe them are not punished by law but can be discriminated against or can meet certain social sanctions. One need not choose oneself as a decent person in order to perform acts of civility. However, if it comes to acts of generosity and kindness, there are no rules whatsoever (except in communities, either religious or lay in character). Thus there is nothing to follow or abide by, there is no 'third party' at play. The suggestion that no other virtue but justice remains in modern society is based on this observation. Indeed, people can successfully reproduce themselves in the modern world without ever having performed a kind or generous act or an act of gratitude. Yet it is exactly this circumstance that makes acts of kindness, generosity and gratitude so *freely chosen*. Modern society offers enormous scope for such acts, yet not that many people choose to perform them (though, again, not so few either). Decent persons put to use the possibility opened up by modern society: it is they who choose to be generous, grateful and kind.

Let me now briefly return to the structure of reciprocity in giving–receiving–reciprocating. What one 'gives away' are certain properties or the use (the practice) of certain properties – be they talents, objects, powers or positions. Of course, the two parties can be singular or plural, individuals or groups. The relation of reciprocity is interrupted if there is any kind of giving without receiving or any kind of receiving without any kind of giving, or if giving–receiving makes up a *real* chain (which does not return to itself). Reciprocity is interrupted (although there is a relation) in all cases of injustice and ingratitude (whether or not the latter are also unjust acts).

To interrupt the reciprocity of giving–receiving or to interrupt relations of such reciprocity on purpose is an offence, except in cases of retribution and in cases of such kinds and relations of reciprocity as are unjust or morally evil.[7]

Theft interrupts the relation of reciprocity, for the thief takes (receives) without being given anything and without intending to return the thing taken or compensate for it in the future. Rape interrupts the relationship of reciprocity in a dual sense. The rapist uses the properties of the woman raped without being offered the use of those properties, and the woman receives something (the semen of the man) that she has refused to receive. In the case of relations of reciprocity between two nations, groups or states, war interrupts reciprocity in so far as the victor takes something (territory, wealth, service) which has not been freely given by the vanquished. Yet not all interruptions of reciprocity which meet the above provisoes (no retribution is involved and the violated habits or relations are neither unjust nor morally evil) are criminal or violent in character. One can talk to someone who refuses to answer (Bergman's movie *The Persona*); one can love and care for another who refuses to notice one's existence: these are not untypical cases of active giving, passive receiving and no reciprocation. And the list can be extended.

At this point the provisoes must be further specified. It is obvious that, in the case of retribution, things or services can be justly taken without having been given (recompensation for a harm done, confiscation of property, and the like). In the case of the second proviso, one may wonder why the distinction between injustice and moral evil has been made. The two can certainly overlap as well as otherwise. People who live in the symbiosis of mutual hatred will never interrupt the relationship of reciprocal harming and humiliating; and yet it would be odd to call Strindberg's characters unjust. At the same time, one can denounce relationships of reciprocity as 'unjust' even if they are not to be regarded as evil, and one can, although only in certain cases, stop practising them (in a non-institutionalized framework).

As a result, we can formulate the following norm, to which a decent person will certainly be willing to subscribe. *Other than in cases of just retribution, do not initiate the interruption of a relation of reciprocity in giving and receiving unless the kinds and/or relations of reciprocity are either unjust or morally evil.* This is a moral norm, and not an orientative moral principle, for it prescribes what one should do or what one should avoid doing. In some cases it will be obvious whether the provisoes apply, but in others it will be necessary for phronesis (good judgement) to decide whether they do, to what extent and why. This is the general norm of reciprocity in giving and receiving.

In what follows, I shall focus my attention on the process of giving and reciprocating itself. Given that we have been following in the footsteps of the decent person in the modern world and focusing on his or her exploits in order to discover how to become what she or he is, namely decent, we can disregard all non-institutionalized instances of asymmetric reciprocity. Even the best of us enter institutions where the reciprocal relations of giving and receiving are asymmetric, at least in certain aspects. (The army is a good example.) The decent person's attitude to institutionalized rules is an issue we shall address in section VII. Here it should be stressed as a matter of decisive importance that the decent person who stands in the relationship of asymmetric reciprocity to another person within the framework of an institution is supposed to stand in a relation of symmetric reciprocity with the selfsame person outside the institutional framework. In other words, the patterns of asymmetric reciprocity within the framework of the institution have no bearing whatsoever on the patterns of reciprocity outside that institution, particularly when it comes to acts of giving and receiving. The decent person relates to all other persons with the gesture of natural equality, where 'natural' stands for 'of course'. As a result, giving and receiving do not take the form of service and patronage. It goes without saying that natural equality extends to the only institution of everyday life: the family. Decent persons choose their family relationships as ones of symmetric reciprocity (they also choose their relationship to their small children as a decreasingly asymmetrical one, especially when it comes to giving and receiving).

Since we distil moral norms out of the attitude of our contemporaries, those decent persons, we can confidently formulate the following norm at this stage of discussion. *Hold firmly to symmetric reciprocity in all your acts of giving and receiving in everyday life, unless moral maxims dictate otherwise.* This is the specific norm of reciprocity in giving and receiving. Similar to the general norm of reciprocity in giving and receiving, this norm is a moral norm proper, and not an orientative principle. Though keeping this norm always in one's sight, one knows exactly what one should not do, and how one should relate to others, when it comes to matters of giving and receiving in everyday life (including family relations), but with the proviso that small children cannot follow the norm in full (nor can adults while relating to them). The condition 'unless moral maxims dictate otherwise' transfers decision-making and deliberation to the authority of phronesis in borderline cases. But it does not transform the norm into an orientative principle.

The norm of symmetric reciprocity in giving and receiving does not maintain that things given and reciprocated or mutual services rendered should be of equal quantity or of the same kind. The norm excludes merely the relationships of service and patronage – that is, the relationships of personal dependency established or reinforced by the acts of giving, receiving and reciprocating goods and services. There are many relationships of this kind; I shall list only a few of them. It should not be forgotten that, with the exception of intra-family relations, the relations in question are non-institutionalized.

It is wrong

- if someone does something for another (gives a thing, renders a service, does a favour) while having in mind the kind of thing, service or favour that she or he expects in return, or does it in order to receive the thing that she or he desires without disclosing his/her purpose to the receiver;
- if someone asks a favour (a service, a thing) of someone whom she or he despises or vilifies;
- if someone pretends feelings in order to make the other party inclined to do a service, a favour, or willing to transfer things to him or her;
- if the reciprocity offered for things received or services rendered is pretended feelings (genuine gratitude is legitimate reciprocity);
- if one renders services or gives things *in order* to be reciprocated with feelings;
- if, in the absence of rules, one demands (insists on) receiving *particular* kinds of services or favours in exchange for services or goods previously rendered or given.

In all the above-listed paradigmatic cases one person *instrumentalizes* another. Indeed, the relationship can be mutual, with each person instrumentalizing the other. Yet, in such a case, double negation is no affirmation. If one person has been instrumentalized, the relation of reciprocity, however violated, should be suspended (see the general norm). Instrumentalizing the other in turn is the wrong answer to the initial offence unless – and even here there is an 'unless' – *no relation* of mutual instrumentalization is stabilized. In principle, one can teach the offender (the one who instrumentalizes) a lesson, make him or her ashamed or look a fool. But we are here on slippery ground, and it is always better to leave such scenes to authors of comedies.

After having excluded those patterns of giving–receiving–recipro-cating which establish or reinforce relationships of personal depen-dency, service and patronage, mutual instrumentalization, we are still left with such an enormous cornucopia of qualitatively different patterns that dealing with them in even the most superficial manner would be out of question. What helps us in our predicament is the circumstance that we can always rely upon the orientative moral principles in case we need to find out which is the better (or the best) course to take.

Although the orientative moral principles do offer guidance in matters of giving–receiving–reciprocating, they do so in such a vague manner that they can by no means replace the two norms we have discussed so far. Yet, once action patterns infringing those two norms have already been dismissed, the moral orientative principles can be relied upon every time one makes decisions or embarks on actions in matters of giving and receiving. However, a few remaining problems still deserve special attention.

How much a person is to give another in goods or services, to whom a person should do favours, from whom a person may accept goods and services, how one should return services rendered, and so much else, is left to the discretion of giver and receiver in modern societies. In delicate issues where no general guidelines are of assistance, there are sometimes fragments of daily wisdom which may help and are therefore worth consultation. Such fragments of wisdom do not orient us, for we may well decide not to follow them, but more often than not we tend to heed their advice.

On the question of 'how much', daily wisdom normally advises moderation. A token service is no service at all. To offer too little of our property, time and capacities is a sign of stinginess, and stinginess is a base (mean) character trait. It does not seem prudent either to neglect our duties towards ourselves. We should think it over three times before jeopardizing our lives, future, well-being or the well-being of people for whom we have responsibility (for example, our children) by giving away too much in terms of goods and services.[8] Put bluntly, it is prudent not to neglect our own interests – at least, not to do so completely. This seems to be pointless advice, for the one thing that people do not seem to need advice on is considering their own interests: they do it anyway. And yet the advice is not entirely pointless. The act of giving is normally, though not always, preceded by the act of promising. People can be extremely lighthearted about promising on the spur of the moment, following an impulse. People with no decency can do this unpunished. They would promise everything in the firm conviction that they would not be taken seriously anyhow, that the other would refuse what was promised or that the thing would be forgotten. And if the chickens nevertheless came home to roost, they would simply back out of their obligations, talking of misunderstandings or of changes in their situation – whatever came to mind – but invariably failing to deliver their promises. Not so the decent person, who would keep the promise even if the promise was made without due consideration. Everyday wisdom therefore suggests particularly strongly to the decent person not to make promises lightheartedly, on the spur of the moment – especially if the promise is momentous and if keeping it puts severe constraints on the person's self-interest (or the interest of those for whom she or he has responsibility). To do the right thing with bad (painful) feelings is deemed a credit in Kant's system, but not by the decent person who could have avoided this painful experience by being more circumspect.

Everyday wisdom also suggests that, if we are not certain about the other person's good character, then, instead of accepting an offer, it is better to wait and see whether it was seriously meant, or whether there was an ulterior motive of instrumentalization behind it. Everyday wisdom likewise suggests that, if we are certain (or almost certain) about a person's good character, and particularly if an offer (of any kind and magnitude) comes from a close friend, it is better promptly to accept what is offered if we need it than to hesitate. One should learn to accept with dignity and grace.

Everyday wisdom suggests too that, if we are in need of something (goods, services, and the like), we should not wait for others to make an offer but rather ask a favour. We first ask those who are close to us, and we take 'no' (as well as 'yes') for an answer. Only mean characters are incapable of distinguishing between real and fake reasons if the answer is a refusal. It is mean-spirited to bear a grudge against a person because he has refused a favour. But, if a person asks a favour and the wish has been granted, it is not only a moral duty (as with every receiver), but also a moral obligation, to reciprocate it.

Everyday wisdom further suggests that gifts, services and favours need not be reciprocated in kind. Gift reciprocity or service reciprocity cannot be quantified beyond the domain of justice. Even money, as a gift, is non-quantifiable. If X does Y the favour of lending him the sum he needs, repaying the money (the same sum of money) has nothing to do with gift reciprocity; it is a matter of justice. Reciprocity comes into play if on another occasion X needs money and Y lends her the money she needs. The favour is then absolutely reciprocated irrespective of whether Y lends X the same sum as he had borrowed from her earlier. What is to be reciprocated is not the equal but the adequate. What is 'adequate' depends on many factors, such as the needs and means of each party, and the magnitude of the gesture – where 'magnitude' stands for quality rather than for quantity.

Gratitude is something that cannot be demanded. What can be demanded, the act of reciprocation, is not gratitude. Gratitude is not merely an act but also an emotion, and, at least in modern times, this emotion is always 'freely given', 'presented'. It is also a present, and one cannot demand a present; one can only demand what is 'due'. Gratitude is certainly not 'due', but ingratitude is, equally certainly, one of the ugliest character traits.[9]

V

It is to Alasdair MacIntyre's credit that philosophers are no longer forced to shy away, for reasons of 'professional competence', from using moral terms such as 'virtue' and 'vice'. Everyday actors make generous use of virtue terms and vice terms, and now philosophers, themselves also everyday actors, can do likewise. I have already taken the liberty of doing so. I paraphrased Aristotle's dictum that people are virtuous first and foremost for their own sake, in order to make it palatable to modern actors. In addition to the virtue of justice, I have also referred to virtues such as generosity and liberality; to virtuous emotions such as gratitude and tact; to virtuous gestures such as accepting something with grace; and so on. I have referred to a range of vices, including stinginess, irresponsibility (in making promises), rancour and the instrumentalization of others (for which we have yet to invent a 'vice term'). If objections arise as to the use of such terms in a moral philosophy, I shall not argue for them. It is only in the process of reintroducing virtue and vice terms into a modern moral philosophy that their relevance or irrelevance can be tested.

MacIntyre correctly demonstrates that in the ancient (Aristotelian) model there is the raw material of human feelings, intellectual and other dispositions on one side, and the 'telos' of the accomplished gentleman, the 'man of all round virtues' on the other; 'upbringing' (*paideia*) aims at moulding the matter into form. Being contingent, modern men and women cannot be moulded into the ready-made social pattern of a 'telos'; so, for them, 'becoming virtuous' must, in so far as there is still such a process, be completely different from what it used to be.

Our experience and our understanding of the two poles 'matter' and 'form' are modern, and our experience and our understanding are in constant interplay. In addition, our patterns of understanding are different in kind, and as such they differentiate patterns of experience, and *vice versa*. There are certain experiences which require one type of interpretation (understanding) rather than another.[10] We may disagree on what our 'matter' consists of as much as we may disagree on what 'form' this matter should take. But isn't then MacIntyre right when he insists that under the conditions of contingency 'virtue' becomes the empty shell of a substance which long ago evaporated?

Instead of attempting the impossible task of defining 'virtue', I shall instead offer a rough approximation of what I mean by the term. Virtues are character traits which predispose persons to support and maintain certain values (common goods), whereas vices are character traits which predispose persons to destroy and undermine, even threaten, the same values (the same common goods). Thus both virtues and vices are related to values, although neither group is related to all the values of a particular epoch, still less to all the values which appear on the horizon of a single individual. In the absence, in modern times, of a general social telos (the 'form' into which the 'matter' of a man was supposed to be moulded), a great many values are decoupled from virtues. Such values are promoted and maintained by excellence, not by virtues.

The term 'common goods' conveys too general a sense before it can be determined how common our goods are. We live in a world of value pluralism, value conflict and even value relativism. A 'common good' can be ours, yours or theirs; in addition we can be shareholders of many a common good, so that 'ours', 'yours' and 'theirs' are not precise qualifications for making an elementary order in the jungle of such (common) goods. To formulate this in different terms, not only may my value (my share in and commitment to a common good) differ from your value (your share in and commitment to another common good) to the extent that a value conflict results; in addition, one value of mine may collide with another value of mine. This problem amongst others should be considered if a sincere answer is to be given to the 'MacIntyre question', as I shall refer to it.

The other consideration refers to the astonishing fact that *no virtue pluralization follows from value pluralization*. Needless to say, decisive shifts in abstract values accompany decisive shifts in the status of virtues and vices. The birth of modern society witnessed the most spectacular devaluation of a supposedly 'eternal' abstract value – that of social hierarchy, alias the natural, the best, the divine world order. Many a virtue went down with this value, or lost general significance (some of them – for example, humility – even came to be viewed as outright vices). However, all these developments, and related tendencies which cannot be here discussed, did not result in a noticeable pluralization of virtues. Who could enumerate all the values people intend to promote, share or not share in our modern world? By contrast, it would be perfectly simple to enumerate our main virtues. On an abstract level one could not even detect the possibility of a contradiction between them. One can now promote any value with constancy and courage. Thus people who hold opposite (or even contradictory) values can agree that courage and constancy are virtues (and cowardice and inconstancy are vices). To whatever value one may be committed, generosity is invariably a virtue and meanness invariably a vice.

Virtues are, then, character traits which predispose persons to promote and support as well as maintain certain values (common goods). If what has been stated about the pluralization of values and the non-pluralization of virtues is valid, then the disappearance of a 'social telos', the very form into which our 'matter' should be moulded, does not of necessity bring about the disappearance of virtues.

Let us draw the following preliminary picture. People are 'thrown' into the world; they are contingent. No 'social telos' is given them at the moment of their birth. They are free to choose their destiny, and they have the possibility of making an existential choice. Suppose that they choose themselves as decent persons and that they try to figure out how they can become what they are: decent persons. If they look round attentively at the world, as I assume they do, they will find the general principle of (moral) orientation and will discover all other orientative principles as well. They will figure out the two norms of reciprocity in giving–receiving–reciprocating ('mine' and 'yours'). If they follow the principles of orientation, which they will certainly do once they have figured them out, they will also develop certain character traits which will dispose them to act in one way rather than another. Such dispositions are certainly virtues and we can easily name them. Everyone who names them will use the same or closely related (similar) expressions, so that we can all understand each other. In speaking of a virtuous person we should be likely to describe him or her as kind, friendly; as one who shows respect and displays self-esteem; as one who appears attentive and tactful, benevolent although not altruistic; as one who appears to exercise good judgement, without rancour or envy, resentment or vanity; as one who is generous and liberal – and so we could go on endlessly adding other virtue terms to the list. Certainly every individual practises the same virtues in a different fashion; as we know, every person is good in his or her own way, which is a fact writers have always known but philosophers sometimes forget.

Yet, in speaking of the virtues to be practised and vices to be shunned by the subject, *no single concrete goal is yet given* to that person, *no single concrete value is proposed* to be furthered by him or her, *no essential activity is predetermined* for him or her, *no form of life is presented* into which she or he must fit. What is still lacking is precisely the much-disputed form into which the matter of the person should be moulded.

Contingent persons who have chosen themselves as good also choose, in becoming what they are, values, avenues in life, professions, public engagements, private contacts, and the like. They choose their own forms in so far as they choose their own destiny.

The forms into which they mould themselves are the forms created by themselves just for themselves. They choose their values, commitments and everything else *in*, and *not as a consequence of*, becoming what they are (decent persons). For one can be decent, and equally so, in many a way of life, in practising various professions, through and amidst a great variety of commitments, and the like. It should be mentioned in passing that similar statements can be made about persons who choose themselves absolutely under the category of difference and who on top of this make an existential choice of goodness.

A paradox seems to be hidden somewhere in this argument. Decent persons, it has been said, share a few virtues, i.e. character traits which predispose them to do certain things while refraining from doing others. It has also been stated that all decent persons are unique (good in their own ways, although they share certain character traits). Finally, and most importantly, it has been stated that there is no direct connection between, on the one hand, the virtues practised and vices shunned by a person, and, on the other, the forms (of life) that the same person chooses and becomes committed to. I should be more specific in order to eliminate the seeming paradox.

For the sake of simplicity and because I began the discussion by picking up the gauntlet which had been thrown into the arena of moral philosophy by MacIntyre, I have accepted the triad of matter–*paideia*–form. Since I have not yet addressed the problem of the first pole (matter), only that of the second (form), I shall modify the problem for the time being, and depart from the pole of 'form'. In giving Aristotle a modernizing twist, I stated that contingent persons, those who choose themselves and thus their destiny (in order to become what they are), are the creators of their own 'form'. This expression, however, does not seem to be entirely appropriate. This is so, first, because the modern person is never 'completely formed' – she or he is always in the process of 'becoming'. In addition, the 'form of life', whatever it may be, cannot be shaped by any one person. As complex networks of human interactions, sedimented in institutions or at least in the repeated and repetitive patterns of intercourse, such 'forms of life' are always collective endeavours which shape the lives of single persons to the same extent as they are shaped by them.

Yet it is obviously not true that a person who has chosen his or her own destiny can actually choose any particular form of life. In making an existential choice one does not predestine oneself to a *single* form of life but one certainly does predestine oneself to a *particular type* of form of life. Decent persons who consult the principles of moral orientation and the norms of reciprocity in giving, receiving and reciprocating, as they certainly do, invariably choose only such forms of life as are fundamentally based on the patterns of symmetric reciprocity within which persons recognize each other's autonomy and have respect for each other's personality. This stands to reason, for one cannot be modern and decent at the same time unless one excludes from among the objects of one's choice all forms of life which institutionalize relations of asymmetric reciprocity at all levels. Both Kant's and Hegel's philosophies of law make a plea for this precondition. In terms of a positive model, decent (modern) persons choose among forms of life where the network of human interactions is constituted by symmetric reciprocity, where the respect of everyone for everyone's else unique personality has been built into the patterns of intercourse. However, established forms of life sometimes do not meet the minimal criterion, and, more often than not, whole forms of life do not meet the maximum criterion. What does it mean in such conditions to 'choose' one form against another and to mould one's own 'matter' into that 'form'? Obviously there are no 'forms' waiting to be 'filled'. It seems difficult to make proper sense of the Aristotelian triad matter–*paideia*–form in relation to the modern person.

As a result, I propose to change for the time being one pole in the triad matter–*paideia*–form – namely the second one, 'form' – and replace it with 'conduct'. This replacement is of major import, for it is rich in ramifications. Whereas 'form' suggests perfection, fulfilment, completeness (for example, once matter has been moulded into form, the *paideia* has come to an end), 'conduct' has no such connotations. Conduct is open-ended, something which goes on and on; it is the identity of being and becoming. Suppose that a person who has chosen himself or herself existentially under the category of universal destines him- or herself to a particular course of conduct in life. That person thus embarks on that particular course of conduct and develops it, making it ever richer in all concrete decisions, in every experience, attachment and commitment of his or her life. If we think in this way of 'conduct', our misgivings with the notion of 'form' – namely, that it excludes 'becoming' in so far as it suggests complete fulfilment, something so alien to the life experience and needs of a modern individual – will evaporate. Let us therefore address the further objections.

A person indeed cannot create his or her own 'form', for a form of life cannot be established by a single individual. However, individuals can develop their own conduct on their own, as in fact we all do. I prefer to talk of 'developing', rather than 'mastering' or 'designing', a course of conduct, for technological terms are highly inappropriate to what is meant here. This has dawned upon even the most ardent theorist of 'rational choice' – Rawls, who first operated with 'plans of life' but finally had to admit that such 'plans' can also be unconscious. However, an unconscious life plan hardly deserves to be called a 'plan'. It could of course also be said that one does not 'develop' one's conduct but that this somehow 'grows out of' or 'unfolds from' one's life activity. Several other biological similes could be used to describe what the phenomenon is all about. And yet I use the term 'develop' on purpose, for the conduct of life is neither an organic event, which can thus be unconscious, nor a life plan of a kind, and therefore completely conscious and rational, nor, finally, the 'median' between the two, but rather the combination of them. As argued in chapter 1, the existential choice can be rooted in an impulse *and* in a series of conscious reflections. The fact that the choice itself, as a leap, is never completely rational, has in itself no bearing on what happens afterwards. One could even imagine a full and whole life plan being designed after an existential choice has been made.

At any rate, the life-plan scenario can be considered only where the existential choice was made under the category of difference – not where it was made under the category of the universal. And the latter is the choice under discussion. It sounds pretty morbid to refer to the existential choice of goodness as the choice of a life plan to be good, thus transforming all acts of decency into so many means (rational choices) of realizing such a plan. Developing a course of conduct means, rather, learning how to be decent. And it is not only our conscious mind that learns, but our impulses, gestures and emotions as well. In other words, we learn to be decent persons as a whole. Developing a course of conduct means developing a course of conduct of the whole person. And it goes without saying that such a development cannot be merely a quasi-instinctual and unconscious 'growing toward'. In modern times, where under certain conditions it is quite difficult to figure out what is the right step to take, where a far greater amount of reflection is needed even within the framework of daily life in order to avoid grave mistakes, a merely spontaneous development of conduct would certainly lead to disaster. Where there is the existential choice at the virtual beginning, and men and women are contingent, a decent course of conduct cannot be developed without the mobilization of our reflective powers.

The virtues common to all decent persons, along with their lack of certain vices, constitute what can be termed the 'backbone' of a decent conduct of life. The backbone is obviously not the whole but the supporting system of something else. Every person is a being in the world, a member of networks of sedimented intercourse, a participant in institutions, a professional man or woman, a mother or a father, a boy or a girl, a politically committed or non-committed person, and committed to particular projects, goals, institutions, and so on, accordingly. It is amid all these determinations and self-determinations that people who have chosen themselves under the category of the universal commit themselves to a decent course of conduct. The different courses of conduct of different persons become richer (as well as more differentiated) as they go on. However, the backbone (the virtuous character) remains the supporting centre around which all experiences, values, value commitments, personal commitments and so much else are crystallized.

The paradox which seemed to be hidden in our argument was in fact not hiding there at all. MacIntyre was right. In our world there is no fixed 'form' for the modern person to be moulded into. There are no socially given typical moral forms, nor do persons create such forms by themselves. There are different forms of life which shape character to an extent, but they do not shape the modern virtuous character. There are still traditional forms of life which shape characters, virtuous or vicious. Finally, people can move from one way of life to another and dwell simultaneously in many of them without giving them a thought. They let others choose for them. Decent persons are different in so far as they choose, albeit they can choose only certain specific forms of life and not others. Yet they can still inhabit all of them, including those which they did not choose, provided that they conduct their life decently.

We can thus draw our first conclusion: the Aristotelian world order has fallen apart, but it has not taken virtues (and vices) with itself into the grave of history.

And we can also draw our second conclusion. At least within the framework of everyday life, there is no direct link between our virtues (our virtuous conduct of life) and the values we have chosen or to which we are committed. Of course, this is a strong anti-fundamentalist statement and it is meant to be. If one woman decides to have an abortion and another decides against one, both can nevertheless conduct their lives in a decent (or highly non-decent) manner. The same applies to socialists and conservatives, monogamous and pro-miscuous persons, and so on.[11] However, one can subscribe to such a strongly anti-fundamentalist statement only with qualifications. First, the connection between virtues and substantive values can be loose only in everyday intercourse and commitments. Second, all values to which a decent person subscribes must be related by that person to the values of freedom and life. Third, this relation must be established in an authentic manner.

I have termed virtues and vices character dispositions, the very backbone of the conduct of life. Thus virtues, as good character dispositions, constitute the backbone of a decent course of conduct. We have found that it is possible to reconstruct the concept of 'virtue' in a non-Aristotelian manner, and that there is indeed something in modern life which we can term 'virtue', though it is not to be equated with pre-established behavioural patterns, so-called 'forms' into which the 'raw material' of a person may be moulded. The decay of the socially pre-given telos does not therefore entail the decay of virtues (and vices).

The old model of matter–*paideia*–form requires further revisions, this time in relation to the pole of 'matter'. World-views, theories and ideologies nowadays offer a practically unlimited variety of visions of 'human nature'. This alone already makes it impossible to offer a single relevant and strong philosophical statement on the 'human matter' which is supposed to be 'formed'. However, this impossibility can be seen as affording yet another possibility.

When we choose existentially, we choose ourselves, and not merely one or another aspect of our 'selves'. As discussed in chapter 1, we choose all our impulses, feelings, emotions, character traits, and so on. Similarly, we choose our own family, upbringing, social status, our own abilities and disabilities, our fancies and neuroses. We also choose our own understanding of 'human nature', our own world-view, our own vision of the self (in so far as we have any). The formula of the existential choice runs as follows: 'I will become a decent person *as I am*, with all my abilities and disabilities, genetic endowments and social determinations. I take upon myself all my determinations and transform them into assets of my moral autonomy.' In making oneself morally autonomous one does not make oneself completely autonomous. Rather, one vindicates the relativity of one's autonomy (in other words, the relativity of one's heteronomy). In the model of existential choice, 'matter' is as inappropriate a term for the *status quo ante* as 'form' is for the *status finalis*. Since the *status quo ante* includes all that there is in a person's determinations at the time of the existential choice, it makes no sense, or at least it is irrelevant, to sort out which items are 'given by nature' and which are 'given by society'. We choose them all as they are, and equally so. For all practical (i.e. moral) purposes we are wholes, and no other approach but a holistic one will do. If one fails to take a holistic approach, if one does not choose oneself as a whole, then one does not really choose oneself existentially, but chooses only bits and pieces, and this will not do. And a person as a whole can hardly be termed 'matter', whatever matter may be. Applied to humans, the term makes no sense at all. The person who is in the *status quo ante* is already 'formed' (if one must use this term), irrespective of whether one is conscious of this circumstance or not. Existential choice can be made at a very tender age or much later, and the 'instant' of making this kind of choice can come suddenly or be the final intuition in a long chain of reflection and rumination. Thus generalized statements about the *status quo ante* would either be false or empty.

Paideia is the development of a decent conduct of life, of this open-ended enterprise of every decent person. *Paideia* is the learning process by which decent people become decent by practising decency. Decent people do not repress what they discover to be wrong in them, for they have chosen themselves as they are. Yet how can you practise the right things if certain impulses and character traits predispose you to do the wrong ones? This question almost sounds stupid, for everyone knows the answers. First, one can avoid entering into situations in which one's worst emotions will be activated. We know ourselves sufficiently well to guess which situations these are. Furthermore, if the worst impulses are not practised, they will, so to speak, shrink like a member we do not use. Decent feelings and passions can become stronger than non-decent ones, and so carry us further in the business of life – as argued, for example, by Spinoza in the theory of countervailing passions. If one nevertheless does something wrong, one can say, 'I am sorry', and offer reparation. Virtues (character traits which predispose us to do the right things) are, as the definition indicates, really predispositions, and do not determine action. Even if one is predisposed to do the right thing, one can still occasionally do something wrong owing to bad judgement or the strength of contrary impulses. Virtues become our 'second nature' if predispositions are so strong that they virtually determine the course of actions (namely, the kinds of action which go with one virtue or another). This is the end of *paideia*, and not all decent persons actually reach its final stage.

All this is commonplace wisdom, and so is the result: decent persons are not angels. They can be angry, unjust, aggressive, over-sensitive, inconsiderate, jealous, suspicious, quarrelsome, and so much else. Yet, since they have chosen themselves, they also know that they are all this, and know, furthermore, that these character traits and impulses are wrong. They do not castigate themselves for being what they are. They live together with their own shortcomings without guilt feelings, but in the knowledge that they are short-comings. They take no pride in them as if they were virtues and merits. 'Choose yourself' is the modern version of 'know yourself'.

Let me return for the last time to the Aristotelian triad matter–*paideia*–form. My conclusion about this formula is that it has no bearing on the life of the modern (contingent) person. If you believe that the virtues (and their sum total) are the final telos (form) into which our matter is to be moulded, then our modern world is indeed 'after virtue'. Yet why should we subscribe to a formula which was distilled from a structure of morals which is no longer ours? Why don't we rather sound out our new structure of morals? If I am right, we can distil a different (new) triad from the morality of the modern world if we only listen to good persons, our contemporaries. 'Matter' is now replaced by 'the contingency of determinations' as freely chosen, yet the 'instant of the choice' is already the process of *paideia*. There is no 'fixed' end result; the end result is relative, while at the same time absolute and concrete. For it is nothing but the decent conduct of life (where the 'form of life' is the variable). This end result also contains an element of *paideia*, for life experiences are crystallized around the 'backbone' of decent conduct till the end of life. *Paideia* proper (the mediator between the two poles) is the process by which the fundamental virtues, as the backbone of decent conduct, are stabilized.

In the old model there are neither virtues nor vices at the 'beginning', only different qualities and quantities of 'matter'. And at the end there are no vices at all. We encounter the perfect gentleman as the sum total of virtues (which is the same for every gentleman, and the rest is not worth mentioning). In the modern model, virtues and vices are present at all stages. There may be both virtues and vices at the beginning, different kinds of virtues and vices in different stages of stabilization. During the process of *paideia* certain vices disappear or become neutralized, and certain virtues appear that will be constantly practised. However, not all bad character traits disappear and not all possible virtues (in addition to those that form the backbone of a decent modern character) materialize. The end result (if there is any) is that no one becomes the repository of the 'sum total of virtues', and not many will be without bad character traits or serious human weaknesses. Yet everyone will be equally decent in all walks of life. For all people can become decent provided that they choose to become what they are. And everyone does so in a unique way.

VI

Existential choice is a decision which each person makes for himself or herself. Irrespective of whether the choice is made on the spur of the moment or is the final fruit of a long chain of reflection, one is always on one's own in choosing existentially. The instant of choice is the instant of isolation. In choosing oneself one isolates oneself from 'before' and 'after'. The decision is more than metaphorically 'time-less'. In addition, it is not located in space: the world surrounding the subject of choice is blotted out in a manner of speaking. This is why the instant of an existential choice is so often associated with *dying*. We recall Goethe's dictum 'stirb und werde' ('die and become'). Kierkegaard's term is 'the dying-away of immediacy'; Tolstoy's more traditional formula mentions 'resurrection'. After having gone through the eternity of the instant, one *becomes* (what one is), and at the same time the world also 'becomes'. Although one has chosen oneself back to one's own world of 'before', that world becomes a 'world after [the choice]' in so far as one discovers the same world as a possible terrain on which to conduct a decent life. All one's previous relationships and contacts remain 'there'. One will live in the same town, street and house, together with the same people, be exposed to the same kinds of constraint as before, be involved in the same workaday routines as before. And yet everything will become different given the change in one's attitude through making an existential choice.

One chooses oneself as one is, as well as the world (one's own world) as it is. Choosing oneself (and one's own world) is, however, not tantamount to choosing everything in one's world or in one's own self as a value. One does not choose all one's own character traits and impulses or everything that goes on in one's world as valuable. Rather the opposite is the case. The metaphors of 'dying' ('stirb und werde', 'the dying-away of immediacy', 'resurrection') indicate that aspects of the old self die in the choice. The metaphors also suggest that something is born or resurrected. The person after the choice culti-vates the character traits she or he appreciates most, and starts to cultivate associations, friendships, workaday activities which she or he considers valuable while shedding those deemed valueless.

As mentioned earlier, a decent person practises virtues first and foremost for his or her own sake, but practises them in relation to others, caring for others. I described virtues as character traits which predispose persons to promote, support and maintain certain values (common goods). I added that the description must be seen as a very rough first approximation. Yet it was still adequate to the purpose of the previous section, which centred on the refutation of the 'after-virtue' argument. At this stage, however, the description must be further concretized.

Values can be *concrete, abstract and universal*. We need not intro-duce universal values as long as we discuss the activities, attitudes or virtues of a good person in everyday life. Abstract values are always 'common goods', for different groups of people share the conviction that they should be promoted, supported and maintained. (Of course, abstract values are not at the same time also universal values, as not every group will share them.) Abstract values, such as family, religion, constitution, beauty, health, independence, friendship, love, security, progress and science, are different in kind. Most of our common virtues (and vices) are not in a direct, but rather in an indirect, relationship to abstract values. In promoting concrete values (or in protesting against the promotion of one of them) we may enter into the process of argumentation (discussion) in order to justify our decision, attitude or action. It is in the process of justification that we refer to abstract values, deriving legitimacy from our recourse to them or our interpretation of them. In modern life, a process of justification of this kind has gained enormous momentum. In our direct relation to abstract values we by and large choose to mobilize intellectual virtues, as they become manifest in the process of justification, whereas all other virtues will be practised (or neglected) in relation to the concrete values which are to be justified by the abstract ones. Only the civic virtues are exceptions to this rule. The person who makes a good argument for charity is not yet charitable. Sacrifices are made not to an abstraction called 'charity' but to a group of people or to an institution, because one cherishes the common good called 'charity'. This exemplifies why virtues are directly related to concrete values and only indirectly to abstract ones (civic virtues are always excluded).

All socially created, conceived and mediated things, all social, political and personal relations, all states of affairs and so much else become concrete values *if abstract values are related to them.*

Concrete values are communal goods if members of at least one human group share the conviction that one particular good should be promoted, supported and maintained, and they expect each other to promote, support and maintain this particular shared common good by deeds and by practice. In mentioning communal goods, we speak in the plural, referring to '*our* country's constitution', '*your* country's revolution', '*their* country's religious tradition'. If we speak in the singular, we address a person as the member of a community, as someone who lives up (or is supposed to live up) to a common value commitment.

Concrete values are *personal goods* if members of at least one human group cherish similar, but not identical, goods. Property is an abstract value. Our property is a concrete value and, as such, a communal good. My property is a concrete value and as such, a personal good. I promote and maintain my property; you do the same with yours; he with his, and the like. I value friendship ('friendship' is an abstract value); I do my best to promote and maintain *my* friendships, and not the friendships of a stranger.

My values are *my* social relationships, irrespective of whether they are communal or personal goods. I am embedded in the network of personal relationships which are 'mine'. I act for or against, in conjunction with, in the framework of, personal relationships which are 'mine'. If virtues are indeed character traits which predispose me to promote certain values, virtues are then character traits predisposing me to make the best of something that is 'mine'. Mine is, Kierkegaard says, not that which belongs to me but rather that to which I belong. Neither 'my friend' nor 'my people', nor 'my God' belongs to me; it is rather I who belong to them. We should not necessarily follow Kierkegaard's radical reversal of the signs. We may stop in the middle, which in this case is mutuality. The value which I promote is always mine, for it, you, they belong to me; the value which I promote is always yours, theirs, for it and I belong to you, them. In promoting this value I mobilize certain character traits which bind, connect, tie me to you, and you to me. I do not 'have' these character traits. They belong to you, him, her, them, to those to whom I belong. And yet I 'have' them all the same for they are 'mine'.

Character traits (among them virtues and vices) are not like propensities of a thing. They are (human, personal) relations. As such, their practice presupposes *mutual understanding*. Your character traits must be readable, comprehensible, available to others. Otherwise character traits cannot become true virtues; they remain idiosyncrasies. The loss of tradition, the increase in contingency and, as a result, the well-known phenomenon that every decent person is decent in his or her own way make the attempt at mutual understanding absolutely indispensable in the aftermath of the existential choice.

Let us return to the 'instant' of 'stirb und werde'. The moment a person enters the process of 'becoming', something begins to 'die away'. What 'die away' are the unpractised character traits; what is in the process of becoming are the virtues which are being stabilized in practice. It is about these virtues that we have learned something in our short detour. We have learned that they are not personal properties but human relations, and also that one can hardly stabilize virtues before reaching a kind of understanding with people whose own relations such virtues are, and who are as contingent as we are. Even if it comes to the observance of elementary moral principles of orientation, contingent persons can become hopelessly lost if they face other contingent persons, particularly if the relation is close, deep and personal.

Ever since the traditional (triadic) model entered the stage of decomposition, ethical theorists have been directing their attention to this issue. And a category which is far from being of moral provenance – namely, the category of *authenticity* – has become elevated to the centrepoint of this moral discussion.

'Authenticity' is a personality term rather than a moral term. As such, it is multifaceted and heavily overinterpreted. But somehow all interpretations centre on the meaning of 'being real' as against 'being a copy, a fake'. The authentic person is, so to speak, a 'really existing person', whereas the inauthentic person is 'unreal'; such a person *is* but *does not exist*, is alive but does not live.[12] The authentic person is considered to be 'himself' or 'herself', while the inauthentic person is considered to be a shadow, a puppet who does what people generally do (she/he is *das Man*). The authentic person is regarded as 'deep', the inauthentic as 'shallow'. The authentic person cares for the world, whereas the inauthentic person is, to quote Goethe, 'nur ein trüber Gast auf der dunklen Erde' ('only a gloomy guest on the dark earth'). Philosophy thematizes this issue; literature portrays it.

The contrast between authenticity and inauthenticity has gained momentum with the nascent consciousness of contingency as one symptom, and a momentous one at that, of this consciousness. If no social telos is built into one's life, so that one's possibilities become practically infinite, while at the same time empty, one has to pull oneself up by one's own hair (like Baron Münchhausen) in order to avoid being swept away by the tide and currents of all contingencies.

Authenticity is not a virtue; still less is it the sum total of virtues. Inauthenticity is not a vice. Both authenticity and inauthenticity are forms of existence; they are the forms of existence of the contingent person. I have presupposed this dichotomy all along without using the terms 'authentic' and 'inauthentic' until now. I posited this dichotomy in the first section of chapter 1. Similarly, I worked with this dichotomy, without mentioning it by name, where I began to discuss the existential choice. To choose oneself is a sign of authenticity; to let others choose for one is a sign of inauthenticity. But why were these categories not used then, and why are they being used now?

As already mentioned, 'authenticity' is a multifaceted and at the same time heavily overinterpreted personality term. Most interpretations of 'authenticity' are associated with something 'exceptional'. Only a few of us can achieve authenticity; only 'great personalities' are authentic; authenticity requires the mobilization of enormous reflective powers or the mobilization of unique powers. Authenticity tends therefore to connote the 'aristocratic' as against the 'common', the 'patrician' as against the 'plebeian', 'self-isolation' as against sociability. This is why I first had to supply my own interpretation of 'authenticity' before making it clear that I am in fact discussing it.

There are two kinds of authenticity and both are born of an existential choice. Most theories of authenticity have in mind what I have termed the existential choice under the category of difference. Some of these theories assert that everyone has abilities which can be 'completed' and that one can become oneself through choosing one's own abilities. They thus diminish the aristocratic connotations of the term 'authenticity'. People cannot be enjoined to become authentic in the above terms, for it is the difference that is intended in this type of existential choice.

I made the case earlier for an existential choice under the category of the universal. One need not be an exception to choose oneself in this fashion. The authentic moral choice is open to all. It has no aristocratic connotations; it does not require the mobilization of immense reflective powers. The existential choice under the category of the universal is one's choice of oneself and thus it results in authenticity. A person who conducts a decent life and becomes what she or he is is by definition 'authentic'. Yet authenticity of this kind does not isolate. It is 'sociable'; it does not go with the practice of 'technique of the self', but rather with the practice of certain virtues, the very backbone of good conduct. People who become authentic in such terms can be addressed by others as well as address others. All men and women who have chosen themselves as such have chosen themselves as *public–political beings* and not as practitioners of a particular technique, whether or not they are aware of this aspect of their choice.

The term 'authentic' has certain as yet unmentioned important connotations. It refers not only to the personality, its attitude and its actions, but also to the person's knowledge – particularly to the person's knowledge of himself or herself. Authentic persons know themselves (as far as this is possible) and act and behave in accordance with their deeper selves. And, although they need not disclose this knowledge of their selves, they normally do so – to other authentic human beings. Thus, authentic human beings communicate with one another in mutually disclosing their respective selves to one another (becoming relatively transparent), though they do not as a rule disclose themselves to inauthentic beings (in this respect they remain within an incognito). Mutual understanding is the mutual understanding of authentic beings. If, however, an authentic being communicates with an inauthentic one, the result is mutual misunderstanding. For authentic beings it is preferable to shun contact, particularly intimate contact, with inauthentic beings. And, if they cannot avoid them, they have to contend with mutual misunderstanding, and suffer from it within the walls of their incognito. They also sometimes have to endure cutting a comic figure.

'Know thyself' is the moral injunction for which all philosophies of authenticity make room. And they also articulate the immense weight of such an injunction. One has to live up to this injunction to the same degree as ever, yet, the more contingent one becomes, the greater are the difficulties one encounters in knowing oneself.

In ethical terms, we need to know which situations to avoid and which to enter into, so that our worst impulses remain barren and thus die away, shrink, disappear, and so that our best impulses are mobilized and thus develop until they become 'second nature'. However different and contingent we are, we need to know the other(s), for it is only thus that we can find out which character traits to stabilize or which virtues to mobilize if we act on behalf of or towards or together with another. Indeed, 'know thyself' but also know the people close to you as if they were 'thyself', and help them so that they too can know you.

That the source of self-knowledge is action and that others sometimes know you better than you know yourself is ancient wisdom, as ancient as the injunction 'Know thyself.' Candour, truthfulness, trustworthiness and sincerity are, equally, age-old virtues. That mutual understanding gets shipwrecked if truthfulness is wanting, or, to speak with Habermas, that truthfulness is one of the three conditions of rational speech aiming at mutual understanding, is wisdom which summarizes several thousand years of theorizing moral knowledge and experience. That all these virtues are of crucial significance also for the decent person in our time is not astonishing. What is astonishing is, rather, the fact that theory has paid so little attention to such matters (though creative writers, Ibsen and Dostoevsky in particular, knew everything about them). To these questions I shall now turn.

One cannot be a decent person

(a)   if one does not show what one is (or believes oneself to be) – if one's 'essence' never 'appears';

(b)   if one never discloses oneself to any human being, never even tries to make oneself transparent to a single 'other';

(c)   if one habitually conceals the motives for one's actions and attitudes;

(d)   if one acts or behaves with pretence (other than to avoid evil consequences);

(e)   if one does not trust anyone;

(f)   if one habitually suspects others and attributes bad motives and intentions to them;

(g)   if one habitually withholds knowledge or information from others;

(h)   if (other than to avoid evil consequences) one withholds knowledge or information from others, so as diminish their autonomy;

(i)   if (other than to avoid evil consequences) one makes promises without intending to keep them;

(j)   if one habitually makes promises without considering whether or not one can keep them;

(k)   if one does not keep a crucial promise, although one could;

(l)   if (other than to avoid evil consequences) one discloses confidential information.

The candid, truthful, trustworthy person is one who does none of those things. In addition, such a person is supposed to have confidence in (certain) others in the expectation that they too are candid, truthful and trustworthy. Although candour, truthfulness and trustworthiness seem to be 'one-way' virtues' ('*I* am candid, truthful and trustworthy'), in fact they are 'two-way' virtues, for we simply cannot practise them without attributing similar virtues to (certain) others.

Everything in the above list is common sense: everyone knows that decent (good) persons do not commit such acts. Since I am still following the course of the decent person who is 'possible' since she or he exists, I am not trying invent new virtues and vices or to construct new formulas. I am keeping strictly to what good persons are already doing and thinking.

But what is the reason for formulating the decent person's *modus operandi* in a negative way (that is, what such a person does not/ should not do)? And, if this is my approach, why are the traditional strictures ('Do not lie', 'Do not cheat', and so on) missing? The answer is that I have formulated only restrictions, not inhibitions. Indeed, only point (l) could have been formulated as a straightforward stricture ('Do not betray a confidence').

Decent persons, our contemporaries, seek orientative rather than strictly prohibitive norms. Although in extreme cases they do subscribe to prohibitions ('Do not murder', for instance), they are reluctant to conduct their lives in a dense *Sittlichkeit* with a broad variety of prohibitions. A 'conduct of life' is only conceivable if the modern decent person can be decent in his or her own way. This applies to all matters of moral relevance, but particularly to subtle issues such as immediate interpersonal relations or attachments. Although the virtues belonging to the group 'truthfulness' radiate far beyond the realm of immediate relationships and attachments, it is in such relationships that they are most commonly present, practised and expected. The stricture 'Do not lie' is certainly right. However, one does not lie only by making a statement one knows to be untrue. One can also lie by not showing what one is, by making no effort to make oneself transparent, by acting and behaving with pretence. Lying is a very complex matter which no stricture can simply 'prohibit'. On the other hand, who has not lied in trivial matters? Is there anyone among us who has kept all promises? Therefore, when it comes to the virtues of truthfulness, it better suits the modern person to know roughly what are the limits that may not be trespassed, within which there is still 'more' and 'less', 'this kind' and 'that kind', 'better' and 'worse', 'fully' and 'not quite fully'. These qualifications are not concessions to our 'human weaknesses', nor are they so many allowances made to our 'sinful nature'. They are proper yardsticks in the open space where the choice of ourselves (as we are) can be made good. *All positive formulations of the virtues of truthfulness are by definition fundamentalist.*

The kind of virtues which I have termed for simplicity's sake 'virtues of truthfulness' are, as mentioned, 'two-way' virtues. As such, they are commonest in immediate (person-to-person) relationships, in particular in personal attachments. It has also been mentioned that, as contingent persons, we can only develop virtues in constant interplay with the expectations of others. For in the absence of such an interplay one could cultivate idiosyncrasies, but not virtuous character traits. The two propositions can now be linked.

To invoke the injunction 'Do disclose yourself to at least one person' would be silly and superfluous, because self-disclosure is a general and deep-seated need. Normally we long to disclose ourselves to at least one other person. The need for self-disclosure is a fairly complex one. It may include the need to be seen, the need for intimacy, the need to share one's self-pity or self-indulgence with someone else, or, finally, the need to talk about oneself – a foremost topic for so many people. It also includes the need for recognition, empathy, sympathy, self-understanding, self-clarification, and so much else. This long catalogue appears to reveal that the first two points in my list are superfluous. Why mention the need to disclose oneself when people do it anyway and with such gusto?

Whatever has been stated about self-disclosure is meant to denote an *authentic* kind of self-disclosure. Narcissistic people do not want to know themselves; they stand 'before the leap' (and will in all likelihood remain in this posture without ever leaping). The narcissist does not want to know the other either, and cannot establish an authentic attachment. Inauthentic disclosure is either narcissistic or instrumental or both combined. This feature, so frequent among his protagonists, was termed by Dostoevsky 'inordinate [inauthentic] repentance'.

All those who have chosen themselves existentially (who have chosen to become what they are) are authentic persons.[13] Men and women who have chosen themselves under the category of difference are also by definition authentic. Yet people of this kind are, unless they also choose themselves as decent persons, haughty in making an exception of themselves. They are full of contempt or indifference toward their fellow creatures. Typically, persons of this type do not disclose themselves to anyone; they do not want to become transparent for others. On the contrary, they keep their 'selves', their good as well as their evil impulses, their feelings as well as their lack of them, 'close to their chests'; they cherish them as secrets. To use Kierkegaard's term, they stand in a 'closed reserve'. It was not philosophy, music or literature that created 'incognito'. Rather it was the men of incognito, contingent persons who chose themselves under the category of difference and stood in 'closed reserve', who served as models for Johannes de Silentio, Lohengrin and Stavrogin, as well as for all the petty Peer Gynts who made the same choice but whose choice did not come off. It is precisely against this backdrop that the principles concerning self-disclosure gain significance. Peer Gynt's maxim that for a man it suffices to be himself is insufficient for the decent person. For the decent person cannot be himself or herself (decent, that is) without 'being for the other' and without 'others being for him/her'. If one discloses what one knows about oneself to another person, the act of self-disclosure makes one know oneself better than before. And in the process of mutual disclosure the persons involved will know themselves, as well as each other, differently.

Mutual self-disclosure is unlike confession, and is not an 'outpouring of souls' – *it is practical hermeneutics*. Exposure of the soul can also happen in a silent prayer, but only another person can engage in a process of practical hermeneutics with you. It cannot be repeated often enough that no person is completely transparent, either to himself/herself or to another.[14] Moreover, as is usual in all kinds of hermeneutical practices, however much is understood there remains much that is not understood. Beyond all transparency there will always remain opacity. Misunderstanding too is inherent in understanding. Yet the search for human decency is not a quest for the absolute. If what you know about yourself is enough to enable you to develop fundamental virtues and to prevent you from committing grave moral blunders, it will suffice.

Needless to say, practical hermeneutics can be total or partial, and it can be the latter to different degrees. Total practical hermeneutics makes its appearance felt in the most intimate relations and attachments. It is either preceded or established by basic trust. Every child knows that total disclosure creates friendship, although children do not yet distinguish between practical hermeneutics, confession and the outpouring of the soul. One learns this distinction through a series of painful experiences. Inauthentic persons will never learn the difference, and thus they either lose their sense of shame or they are constantly embarrassed afterwards. Authentically decent persons can of course also blunder, although probably not so much in their own acts of disclosure as in their judgement of the other who discloses himself or herself to them. At any rate, close attachments are rare in anyone's life, and not even all close attachments leave room for total practical hermeneutics, or are established by a total practical hermeneutic. Too much would be too little anyway. For total practical hermeneutics is not a 'happening' (while confession or 'outpouring of the soul' can be); it is rather the relation of mutual understanding among equals attached to one another, and it is an ongoing process. The term 'ongoing process' should not be misinterpreted as 'something which happens each and every day' or as 'one analytical session every day'. There may be only one such session, or there may be none for many years. And yet the relation is and remains one of total practical hermeneutics.

Partial practical hermeneutics does not require either close attachments or intimacy. It can be practised in any face-to-face relationship. What it requires is openness and sincerity. If you want to avoid misunderstanding, you begin a 'discussion of clarification' or pay attention to others who initiate such a discussion. Inauthentic persons subject themselves to public opinion. Person who have chosen (destined) themselves under the category of difference normally despise public opinion. Decent persons do not subject themselves to public opinion, for they do not let others choose for them – but they do not despise public opinion either, for after all public opinion is also an 'opinion of others' to which they pay attention. This is how decent persons enter the relationship of practical hermeneutics. They address the repositories of public opinion and call for clarification. They open themselves up to comments, criticism, approval just as much as to disapproval. In this kind of discussion, mutual understanding can either succeed or fail. But decent persons try hard to arrive at mutual understanding. In a way, partial practical hermeneutics is an even more delicate matter than total practical hermeneutics. The gesture of opening up a discussion of clarification might be rejected by the other as an 'invasion of privacy' or with the retort 'This is none of your business.' Decent persons would never complain about an 'invasion of privacy', or retort, 'This is none of your business', unless total practical hermeneutics were initiated without previous intimacy or encouragement. They would not mind 'poking into another person's business' if they feared that the unclarified might carry dangerous consequences. Yet, if the matter were of no great importance, it would be prudent not to initiate the process of partial practical hermeneutics before a readiness to enter into such a process had been made explicit by the other party.

Practical hermeneutics accomplishes the 'tuning-in' of our virtues of truthfulness. I have already discussed the reasons for formulating the principles of these virtues as *restrictions*. Within the limits of restrictions, there is still 'more' and 'less', 'this kind' and 'that kind', 'better' and 'worse', 'fully' and 'less fully'. This is the open space in which the choice of ourselves (as we are) can be made good. Further- more, sincerity, truthfulness, trustworthiness, confidence, candour and the like are, as already stated, not 'one-way' but (at least) 'two-way' virtues. Finally deep-seated preconscious elements (affects, patterns of temperament, and the like) enter into the practice of all these virtues. We choose all these preconscious elements in choosing ourselves; we choose them for we choose to be decent in our own incommensurable ipseity.

Because of this complex and idiosyncratic psychological back- ground, persons may be prepared to practise one kind but not all kinds of sincerity; they may shun all or perhaps only some kinds of secrecy while being convinced that this is the way all men and women are 'by nature'. If one enters into an attachment with another person or initiates any process of practical hermeneutics with him or her, this is the kind of misunderstanding, among all other kinds, that must be clarified first, unless the psychological make-up of the 'hermeneuts' is remarkably similar. It is in the process of practical hermeneutics that people learn to understand what sincerity, truthfulness and trust mean to another person. And it is thus that they become 'tuned into' one another, that they become 'tuned into' a particular relationship. In the process, they reach a rapprochement over the way they inter- pret and practise the virtues of truthfulness. Without such a recipro- cal process of 'tuning-in', they would be unable to catch the waves transmitted by the other.

Understanding another is catching the waves transmitted by the other in the process of 'tuning-in', and, since the process is meant to be reciprocal, understanding is mutual. It is on the grounds of such a mutual understanding that men and women can act towards one another. However, since 'tuning-in' does not result in identity – that is, in interpreting and practising the virtues of truthfulness in exactly the same way – mutual understanding is not tantamount to consensus. Nor is consensus the condition of mutual understanding. Consensus may be the result of the process but it is not the specific goal. For trying to arrive at a consensus in matters which are beyond the scope of justice is at cross-purposes with the general principles of moral orientation ('Care for other persons' autonomy').

Very few decent persons are without character deficiencies. However, there are four character deficiencies which cannot be combined with decency. These are envy, vanity, resentment and cowardice. People choosing themselves can choose to be cowards, resentful, vain and envious. But these character traits are put out of use and die, so to speak, in the aftermath of the existential choice of goodness. Aggressiveness, jealousy, haughtiness, self-righteousness, intemperance and so many other blots on the character can on occasion incapacitate one from doing the right thing. Yet envy, vanity, resentment and cowardice are such pervasive character deficiencies as to make one regularly incapable of doing the right thing. They prevent a person from making the first move in establishing a relationship of mutual understanding. They block the person's road to self-understanding. They also make it impossible for one to recognize one's own moral blunders and thus correct one's failings. Vices are not quantifiable. Yet, if they were, everyone would agree that that cruelty is a graver vice than envy. Decent persons cannot be cruel as a rule. If only they observe the principles of a general moral orientation, they will not be cruel. However, whether or not we act cruelly does not depend exclusively on us. Sometimes it is others who force cruelty upon us (as, for example, when they do not care for our autonomy). At other times, it is justice that cannot be done without acting cruelly. It is almost a commonplace to state that on occasions one can act cruelly without being cruel. But envy, vanity, resentment and cowardice are all-encompassing vices. Although 'lesser evils' in themselves, they are potentially the gravest of them all, in so far as they predispose people to do all the wrong things.

This was not always the case, but it is certainly true in modern times, when we discover rather than are presented with norm interpretations, when the code of mutual understanding is not settled once and for all by an inherited and traditional background consensus, when knowledge of character acquires primary importance, and, finally, when mutual understanding requires an authentic readiness to 'tune into' the waves emitted by others. A vain person who is titillated by flattery lives in a dream world of inauthenticity. An envious person also lives in a dream world, except that she or he has bad dreams.[15] Self-complacent vanity, although invariably inauthentic, is rarely evil. However, vanity reinforced by envy can unleash the demon of destruction and self-destruction. Resentment, the offspring of envy and hatred, has gained prominence as a character trait (and not as an undefined feeling) in modern times. Resentment absorbs ideologies, or rather their undigested chunks, and it combines hatred and envy with the aid of ideologies. In the main, resentment unleashes its own demons in the political sphere. However, the resentful person, who is in the final analysis an everyday actor like anyone else, will be as incapable of enjoying authentic human relationships, of practising the virtue of truthfulness, of developing the readiness for mutual understanding, as the envious or the ordinary vain person.

We were once told that our sins were the sins of the flesh. Today we are told that the human race is aggressive and destructive by nature. Yet, if we only looked around and relied on our own experience, we would see that half of all human crimes are committed out of cowardice, and that a good many others could be prevented if those able to prevent them did not behave in a cowardly fashion.

Have courage, be brave.

Existential choice is a matter of courage. To live up to this choice is also a matter of courage. To live a decent life is no less a matter of courage. To live a good life is similarly a matter of courage. Have courage, be brave.

Ultimately, it is simple to be brave. Once one sees what the right thing to do is, one does it. Seeing what is the right thing to do is, in Kierkegaard's phrase, to be in an instant: there is no 'before' and no 'after'. One ceases to consider losses and gains; one stops imagining what is going to happen to oneself. In the 'instant' there is only the person and eternity. You close your eyes, take your hand off the rail you have been grabbing, and – there you go. Once in the water, you will swim. Have courage, be brave.

A decent person requires courage when it comes to doing the right thing (and avoiding the wrong thing). One can appropriate the 'gestures of bravery' in matters of no moral relevance as well as, for example, in swimming – to read the metaphor non-metaphorically. Since the virtue of courage is so crucial to upholding important values, it is better to make courage a habit, although psychological courage is far from being the permanent condition of decency. (Persons who are otherwise timid can be as brave as lions if moral matters are at stake.)

If one knows that *this is the moment when something should be done*, and if one knows *what* it is that one should do, then, if one has courage, one does it without hesitation. What then holds one back from doing what should be done?

The virtues of truthfulness and the virtue of courage are different in kind, yet they are intrinsically interwoven in the personality of decent men and women. Authentic persons try to know themselves. They are neither afraid of knowing themselves nor frightened of disclosing/ exposing themselves to the scrutiny of friends, the one they love, or 'others'. Truthfulness, sincerity and trustworthiness all require courage, in the same way as moral courage requires truthfulness, sincerity and trustworthiness. This connection has developed in modern times. This is why it was not addressed in Aristotle's comprehensive discussion of courage and of all similar character traits.

To return to the metaphor of swimming, or that of letting go of the rail, we may refer to Aristotle's dictum that a person is courageous if she or he is ready to use this quality when it needs to be used. Given that values are heterogeneous in character, and that they are different in kind even within one sphere; given, further, that in society as well as in the way of life of a single individual there is a distinct hierarchy of values – the virtue of courage is seldom an 'all-round' one. One is not required to take one's hands off the rail, suspend one's memory and imagination, forget one's past and bracket one's future in actions which are related to values that are of no great relevance for others. Courage is always commendable, but the need for it becomes pressing only when there is the right thing to be done, to be done now and specifically by you. You, together with others, must figure out when you are needed or obliged to act courageously. To this question I shall return in chapters 3 and 4.

When the evils of the world are discussed, and the topics of our original sinfulness and natural aggression have already been exhausted, the next trump card will certainly be our inborn self-centredness. People follow their own interests; they do what benefits rather than what harms them. This is indeed so, but there is nothing evil in it.

Let us once again return to the 'instant' of a concrete moral decision. This is not the instant of choice, for we already know what is the right thing to do. And, since we have chosen ourselves as decent persons, we have thus chosen to do the decent thing. Thus, in the 'instant' of decision, there is no choice left whatsoever. The choice has already been made long ago. The 'moral decision pattern' is different from the 'moral choice pattern', and both are different still from the 'existential choice pattern'. In existential choice, the person isolates himself or herself: the instant is one of eternity, for it is the instant of self-choice ('stirb und werde'). By contrast, all moral choices happen in the process of communication, discussion, reflection. This kind of choice is theoretical, not practical, in nature: I figure out what would be the best thing for me to do; we figure out together what would be the best thing for me to do. Let us assume that I know what is the right thing to do. If this is so, then I should just shut my eyes and let go of the rail. This particular act of decision, the act of courage, is unlike the pattern of 'finding out what the right thing is'; it is also unlike the 'existential choice pattern'. I isolate myself from my past and future because I act no matter what may be the consequences of my actions for my own life. (*Nota bene*: this is one of the definitions of the decent person.) I thus set myself free from all determinations which lie in the past, and from everything that I have achieved so far and which has been supporting me in life (the 'rail'). Yet I do not isolate myself from the world. On the contrary, I turn towards a value passionately. I let myself go *in order* to swim *towards* something. The 'thing' towards which I swim could be a very concrete thing; it could also be my honour and dignity. But, wherever I swim, I always swim towards the best possible moral world. What follows may sound a ludicrous travesty of the categorical imperative, and yet I would commit it to paper: decent persons are those who let go of the rail, shut their eyes and swim as if everyone were swimming along with them, as if everyone accompanied them in their passionate commitment to the best possible moral world. They need not be aware of this commitment. We humans are much too prosaic to think big, yet everyone who lets himself or herself go in such a way has done so in passionate commitment to the best possible moral world.

The gesture of moral courage is *not* identical with the gesture of self-sacrifice. It could go with the latter but this rarely occurs. Short of the certainty of violent death, nothing can be termed 'sacrifice proper'. For in making a moral decision, in letting oneself go, one is aware of what exactly one leaves behind, but one cannot know for sure what one is going to gain or lose in the future. After all, it was when he went after his father's donkeys that Saul won his kingdom. In this respect, making a moral decision is like making any other crucial decision. Courage is courage, whatever is at stake during the decision.

In the case of a non-moral decision pattern, it is apposite to mention 'taking risks'. One here engages oneself in the gamble of life; one is well aware that one may either lose or win while invariably expecting to win. No one would say that in taking risks and engaging in a kind of gamble, people sacrifice their own interests for the sake of something higher or nobler, or that they practise courage against their best interests. However, in the case of the 'moral decision pattern', the pattern is subjectively different. Although one is normally aware that one takes a risk, one does not gamble. One does what one does because one believes that this is the right thing to do, irrespective of gains or losses. Yet, if we disregard the subjective motivation, that of *morality*, and look at the matter objectively, we shall see that in such a case one is indeed engaged in a gamble. One can lose everything, can regain everything that has already been lost, can win more than one has lost, can win, like Saul, a kingdom. One does what one does not in order to win, perhaps not even expecting to win – although one certainly does not expect to lose either; one contains one's imagination instead of unleashing it. One is then, to quote ancient moral theorists, the kind of person who has neither hope nor fear. And yet, since both patterns have the same objective structure, since, objectively speaking, one takes a gamble in both cases, is it not then the 'retracting force of interests' which prevents people from doing the right thing when they do not do it? But how can they know where their interests lie? Admittedly, they can 'know' their past, but they are certainly in the dark as far as the outcome of their decisions is concerned. And, indeed, it is not their 'self-interest' which pulls men and women back, which makes them cling to the rail, stay put and avoid all the good things they should or could do. Rather, it is cowardice, pure naked fear, which does the job. It is the fear we humans have of losing everything we have achieved, be it wealth, position, reputation, conviction, faith, someone close to us, or something else. We tremble in our boots as we contemplate what will happen if in a gesture of goodness we lose a certain thing without being compensated, without having the time to gain it back, for life is short. If we only knew that things would not turn out too badly, that we would be compensated, that we would at least gain the respect of the world, that we would survive – but we don't. So we imagine the worst and keep holding onto the rail.

VII

In the modern world, where the functional division of labour has become dominant, men and women enter the 'social system', the cycle of social reproduction, as performers of certain functions. Both the preparation for practising such functions and the practice itself happen within the framework of particular institutions which can also be termed subsystems – schools, workshops, universities, factories, department stores, banks, planning institutions, government offices, and so on. In the main, the workplace has been separated from the household, and the central institution of everyday life, the family, has increasingly been transformed into the venue of private consumption and the locus of intimacy. Even if, for most people, work (narrowly defined) devours less time than ever before, the circumstance that it is practised in institutions (alias subsystems) transforms such institutions into a 'secondary habitat'. The term 'secondary habitat' denotes a place that one truly inhabits, less than a dwelling but more than a space in which one just happens to spend some time (a cinema, for example). A 'secondary habitat' is an institution of learning or working which one voluntarily enters (for one can leave one and enter another,) and which makes demands on its members. Entering an institution entails taking up obligations. Whether one loves or hates one's work or study, one is obliged to do it as long as one remains a member of the institution. This aspect of the ethos of institutions does not concern moral philosophy, so long as human interaction is not involved in it. Yet, if the norms and rules of a particular institution extend to human behaviour and interaction, if in observing or infringing such rules and norms human beings do something for or against other human beings, deal with or are dealt with by them, co-operate with them or behave disruptively – if, that is, the decent person has problems, and seeks answers to the question 'What is the right thing for me to do?' – then this is already the domain of moral philosophy.

In the previous sections we have been following the path of decent persons in situations of symmetric reciprocity. It has been stressed that, whatever their institutionalized relationships may be, decent persons construe their relationships with others as ones of symmetric reciprocity outside the institutional framework. Yet can the same reciprocity be achieved by them while performing their functions within institutions? The functional division of labour has both horizontal and vertical dimensions. On the horizontal level, relations are symmetrically reciprocal, while on the vertical level they are not. Even if the office in question is not organized on the model of the army – which is to say, on the vertical relation of command–obedience – a stricture of giving and receiving instruction is normal. The character of vertical relations remains asymmetrical even if they are decorated, and thus to a degree palliated, by polite ceremony, with one 'requesting' and another gracefully accepting the 'request'.

A person who in all his or her freely chosen relations enters only into ties of symmetric reciprocity will obviously be ill at ease within such an institutional framework, where asymmetric reciprocity would seem to be inevitable. Or is it?

Let us assume that our decent person is a woman in a subordinate position. Can she or can't she establish the relationship of symmetric reciprocity with her boss *within* the institution while remaining decent? Justice requires that all subordinates (belonging to the same cluster of subordinates, among them our 'decent person') should be treated equally. In establishing a symmetrically reciprocal relationship with her boss, our decent person creates a prerogative for herself. Thus she is guilty of doing others injustice, of hurting the feelings and, more importantly, the chances of others. In addition she may, and in all probability will, elicit the worst kinds of feelings in her colleagues: jealousy and envy. Let us now assume that our decent person is in a superordinate position. As a boss, she establishes relationships of symmetric reciprocity with her own subordinates, whereas none of the other bosses on the same horizontal level do. However, such symmetrical relationships will only apparently be symmetrical. Given that the boss (our 'decent person') institutionalized her democracy as an exception, and she could do this only because she was a boss, the relationships within the particular group will be tribal in nature and the boss in question will by definition be a chieftain. Paternalism (or maternalism) in a group creates informal dependency.

Whether our decent person experiments with establishing symmetrical reciprocity within an institutional framework as a boss or as a subordinate employee, she will inevitably come to the conclusion that *the private personal elimination of asymmetrical relations within institutions based on a vertical hierarchy is better avoided.*

The obligation to observe the rules of institutions emcompasses both symmetric and asymmetric relations of reciprocity. A completely democratically run institution is no less rule-governed than a quasi-autocratically run one is; indeed, it is more rule-governed. Institutional rules are set for requirements, obligations, rights and procedures. They prescribe what one can expect from someone else (nothing else, or more, can be expected). They also prescribe what one should offer another or others (nothing else or more is to be offered). All 'offering more or else', all 'expecting more or else' should happen outside the framework of the institution. Suppose that X does Y a favour and that Y reciprocates the favour within the framework of an institution by arranging for Y to get a prize ahead of more deserving candidates. The form of the reciprocal gesture seems to be in perfect harmony with the moral norms of giving–receiving–reciprocating. And yet we all know that, despite the formal harmony, the given act of reciprocation is wrong, even indecent, because it is unjust. It is unjust in so far as it infringes one of the basic norms of the institution: if excellence is the basis of prize distribution, no other criterion should interfere with the principle. It is the most excellent who should get the prize. Once decent persons have made the transition from the daily to the institutional framework, they will come to the conclusion that *institutional norms are stronger than the everyday norms of giving–receiving–reciprocating. If there is a collision between these norms and the institutionalized rules, the latter have priority over the former within the framework of the institution.* For traditional families, this priority looks unsound, because in families it is expected that everyone will do a favour for a member of his or her own family, giving preference to tribal rules as against the rules of institutions. And yet for the contingent decent person the strict observance of the priority rule will certainly appear as the precondition of democratic institutions. In addition, we are dealing here with a *priority rule proper*, since the rule comes into effect only in the case of conflicting loyalties and allegiances. If there is no such collision, everyday norms of reciprocating remain in force also within the institution.

The strictly functional division of labour within modern institutions does not transform the sum total of human interactions (and relations) into functional ones. An institutional unit can be described as a system or as a subsystem of a system. Yet single individuals, even if one comprehends them strictly as members of subsystems, can never be adequately described as the indivisible and smallest subsystems within the broader context. Sometimes 'organization man' is characterized as the 'cog in the machine'. The rhetorical exaggeration none the less carries an important message: human will and reason should not be subjected to systemic constraints. Unintentionally, the slogan also offends those in the name of whom it lodges the protest: human beings, concrete individuals who are never mere cogs in any machine. They remain responsible subjects within the framework of every institution. True enough, as far as their performances are linked together by systemic mediation, they serve each other as mere means. However, in all face-to-face contacts, those of direct reciprocity, be they co-operative or conflictual in nature, they relate to each other not simply as to functions but also as to persons. Or, at least, they *can* relate to one another in such a fashion. Not everyone in every face-to-face situation is capable of relating to any other as to a person. Certain persons are invariably regarded as mere repositories of a function. Yet in the main, person-to-person relations are possible within institutions, and the institutional–functional framework does not prevent men and women from living up to the substantive formula of the categorical imperative, the one which suggests that a person should serve another not merely as a means but also as an end (in his or her personhood).

It follows from this that institutional–functional relations do not prevent anyone from observing the orientative moral principles or from practising all the virtues which have been previously discussed. As mentioned earlier, even the norms of giving–receiving–reciprocating can be heeded unless their observance collides with the rules of the institution themselves. When we turn from the everyday to the institutional context, it is not the *kind* of norms, principles and virtues (or vices) involved that alters, but rather the *interpretation* and *application* of principles and the *way* in which and the *intensity* with which certain values are actualized. Since people do not meet each other within institutions in their 'wholeness', but rather only 'touch' each other in one or another aspect of their existence, they cannot turn towards each other with the normal intensity of direct personal attachments. In fact, it would be rather ridiculous if they did. I would have been downright ashamed of even mentioning such a commonplace, if only philosophers, social theorists and critics knew what everyone else does. But they discuss 'cogs of a machine', mere functions or role-players whose self hangs like a coat on a peg. It is because of them that one has to dwell on the obvious.

It has been mentioned in section III that the universal orientative principle of morals ('Care for other human beings'; 'Do not harm another human being on purpose') cannot be waived, although certain concrete interpretations of the principle can, in so far as they collide with institutional rules. (It has also been mentioned that the principle can be waived if its observance collides with universal maxims, norms and laws.) If we cast a second brief glance at the catalogue of interpretations of the universal orientative principle, we see that actually very few of the concretized principles can, incidentally, collide with the observance of institutional rules. For the most part, we rather notice that the strong principles become weak, and the intensive ones less so, at a lower level of involvement, engagement and emotional commitment, and where the matters in which we need to achieve mutual understanding are less pressing or important. One should have proper regard for the other person's vulnerability within the institutional framework as well as in extra-institutional personal contact; the difference lies in how one shows that regard. In both contexts one should not put to shame and ridicule another person, or show contempt for another person (unless morally justified); and in both, too, should help the other person to 'save face'. In neither situation should one manipulate others or keep others in tutelage. Yet the principle guiding us on how to respond to another person's need for us as whole persons is out of context within institutions, whereas the principle which advises us to learn to express our feelings can apply only in a very low-key manner. (For example, one should not, for the sake of benefits, show admiration for persons whom one does not admire.) Proper regard for the other person's autonomy is as decisive within institutions as outside them. And yet again, as applied to most institutions, a few concrete interpretations of the principle sound odd or are out of context (for example, the advice to let a person go even if parting causes pain). Finally, irrespective of whether we are brought together by accident or choice, whether we intend a full or only a partial mutual understanding, or none at all, whether our relation is permanent or temporary, we are still, in all such cases, informed by the universal orientative principle of morals. In another, clearer formulation, those who choose to be decent persons will heed the principles of general moral orientation also within institutional- ized frameworks – *piano* rather than *forte*, perhaps, but they will still heed them.

The *piano* version of heeding the general principles of orientation is termed 'civility' or 'urbanity'. Courtesy and politeness too are modes of smooth and inoffensive human interaction, but they do not include the *modern* element. Civility and urbanity are virtues pertaining to all kinds of human encounters, interactions and communications, for they are centred around the *due respect* which persons should pay to each other's 'personhood'. The 'modern element' of the attitude is precisely that respect/recognition which is due to everyone's 'person- hood'. Urbanity and civility thus entail the essential constituent of symmetric reciprocity: persons with self-esteem respect the person- hood of other persons with self-esteem. The general principles of orientation permit and suggest far stronger interpretations. Practices guided by stronger interpretations involve many virtues in addition to those of civility and urbanity. If the general principles of moral orientation guide practices exclusively in the *piano* version, one will behave in a civil manner without entering into any relationship which would require more than that. An all-round civil and urbane person observes the principles of moral orientation. However, she or he by no means necessarily has active interest in, or a deep relation to, any other human being.

A decent person relates to other persons in an urbane and civil manner. Within an institution, no more is required; attempts at more sometimes end up with considerably less. And yet, urbanity and civility are not exhausted by a few gestures or figures of speech which one keeps practising without paying any attention to them. Putting on the proper mask or rehearsing the proper role does not make anyone genuinely civil or urbane, for no mask covers the face properly and the routine smile expresses indifference. Genuine friendliness cannot be rehearsed, because it changes its toncs and shades from person to

person. Advertising agencies are more aware of such elementary
human facts than many sociologists. They know that we cannot be
cheated by computerized gestures of urbanity, so instead they cheat
us by pretending that they are turning to us as unique persons. Since
institutions are based on the functional division of labour, the gesture
of 'paying attention to' is not deep in them, but the lack of depth is
not tantamount to impersonality. I address you, and I address you in
a civil manner, and in a way which is different from the one in which I
address another, and I shall do it again in a different way tomorrow,
depending on the matter in hand, your mood or state of mind, and the
like. This sounds very demanding, but it is not. It may be more
demanding to wear a mask and make sure that it does not fall off than
to pay genuine attention to another person for a minute, even if not
necessarily deep attention.

Hence all norms and principles of everyday life remain valid within
institutions. This is also true about the norms of giving–receiving–reciprocating. The norms of reciprocating are valid even if certain acts
of reciprocating are banned from the institutional framework by the
priority rule. The first general norm of reciprocity in giving and
receiving suggests that, except in the case of retribution, one should
not initiate the interruption of a relation of reciprocity in giving–receiving unless the expected kind of reciprocity or the relation of
reciprocity itself is unjust or evil (or both are). The priority rule
applies if the relation of reciprocity (the act of reciprocating) is unjust.
The priority rule is thus not at cross-purposes with the general
validity of this norm. The second norm of reciprocity (in giving–receiving) was initially restricted to everyday life (to non-functional,
extra-institutional forms). However, several interpretations of this
norm retain their normative power within institutions as well.

That the 'sum total of virtues' is not mobilized in an average
institutional setting is a truism which does not need to be elaborated.
Certain virtues, although sometimes mobilized, are not constantly
practised. One can be generous in the office or on the shop floor in
teaching skills to young persons without specific remuneration. More
can and should be said about the virtues of 'truthfulness'. In section VI
I enumerated the typical patterns of gross violation of the virtue norms
of candour, truthfulness, trustworthiness, and the like. I also illustrated the lack of the 'personality value' of authenticity. In order to
avoid fundamentalism, I recommended restrictions (the borderline,
the limit one should never cross); and I have avoided both strict
prohibitions and commandments (even recommendations). Although
the aforementioned restrictions address 'human persons as wholes'
(in all of their human relations), some of them are fully relevant in

institutionalized situations. Here are some examples. A person who habitually withholds knowledge or information from others (contrary to the rules of the institution) cannot be decent. Nor can a person who makes promises without intending to keep them, or a person who acts and behaves with pretence, or a person who is habitually suspicious of others' motives and intentions, attributing only negative ones to them. Vanity, resentment, envy and jealousy, those commonplace vices of everyday life, are even more dangerous and destructive within institutions than in everyday encounters. The constant comparison with others, that well-known fuel of envy (and sometimes also of jealousy), is most at home here. This is so since the rules of institutions themselves invite constant comparison by ranking people hierarchically by function.

Purely personal jealousy, envy or resentment can remain fixated on one person or a few. But the kind of jealousy, envy or resentment which is initially impersonal, functional, because rooted in the (institutionalized) practice of comparison, is all-round and non-fixated. It very rarely erupts, but rather is sedimented as a character trait of constant rancour which literally consumes the healthy and decent kernel of the human character. Merely base feelings concerning petty issues can attain demonic dimensions once they become constant. In section V of this chapter I mentioned the well-known 'technique' of decent persons. They avoid situations in which their worst emotional dispositions would be activated. If they avoid them for a long time, such dispositions begin to 'shrink' in the absence of practice; in the end, they will become unsymptomatic. Situations which create envy, jealousy and resentment can hardly be avoided within an institution. Thus the decent person develops a kind of 'mnemo-technique in reverse'. Mnemo-technique teaches us how to memorize things which are difficult to memorize. The obverse technique teaches us how to drop issues from our memory which would otherwise stick, persevere and poison us from within. Finally, authenticity is of great assistance in dissuading us from constant comparisons. For authentic persons are not particularly inclined to compare themselves with others: they are what they are.

Courage is half of all virtues. It is a virtue on its own and it supports the practice of all others. Provided that an institutional framework is accepted, one must see to it that the norms and rules are applied consistently and continuously, for justice should be done. Every time the application of norms is flawed, the decent person stands up to protect the cause of justice. And she or he needs to be courageous in order to do so. Sometimes she or he must be very brave, for acts of protest in the cause of justice may carry social sanctions – particularly if people at the top are the source of injustice.

So far we have traced the footsteps of decent women and men who, like everyone else, spend their working days far from their homes, in a different setting, within institutions where they perform a function like everyone else. On this general level, all institutions require just that. Yet there are decisive differences between institutions as well as between the functions performed in them. Furthermore, the performance of certain functions goes with membership of other, related institutions – be they social, political or religious organizations, clubs or unions, or anything else.[16] Whatever the character of such affiliations, the fact remains that one gets entangled in yet another institutional framework with another set of rules which in turn can be applied in a just or unjust manner. There are, in addition, transfunctional organizations with their own, loose or tight, sets of rules. Even if not all primary institutions (of work) are permeated with a kind of ethos (although Galbraith warns us that they normally are), both function-related secondary institutions and transfunctional ones require a certain kind of loyalty to the rules, principles and ideas which they promote or pretend to promote. If someone perceives an inconsistency between being a member of one institution and performing a function in another, it is normally not the two sets of rules which seem to collide, but two different kinds of ethos, or the overall ethos of one set of rules seems to be in conflict with the other set of rules. Whether the ethos is tightly knit or loose is of no relevance in such a conflict.

Conflicts arising out of membership of two institutions can be imposed on a person. But, if they are not, it is a matter of perception whether they arise at all. Persons who have not chosen themselves but who let others choose for them will in all likelihood remain unaware of such conflicts. Strictly speaking, there will be no conflict for them. They will become role-players who learn to play it safe in every institution and thus lose their selves. Certain qualities of their moral make-up will make decent persons sensitive to such inconsistencies. These qualities are sincerity, self-knowledge and above all the readiness to ask the decisive question 'What should I do?' or 'What is the right thing for me to do?' Furthermore, they will seek an answer to this question.

If the question is morally motivated (although not morally raised), several options are opened up for decent persons. They can of course leave one of the institutions. In so doing, they would certainly eliminate the moral inconsistencies. Suppose they can leave both: which one should they choose? Let us further assume that there is nothing wrong with the ethos of either institution, but that one simply cannot follow both types of ethos at the same time. If this is the case, the decision will be pragmatic, not moral, in nature: one follows one's own taste, interest and the like. But, for this to be so, one has first to find out whether this is really the case, whether there is really nothing wrong with the ethos of one of the institutions, or perhaps with the ethos of both of them.[17] If it turns out that there is indeed something wrong with the ethos of one of them, the decent person's decision would not be in doubt, irrespective of so-called pragmatic considerations. But what if something is definitely wrong with both of them? Should the decent person quit one or quit both? How can one solve this predicament?

Our decent person has a second option: to decide to stay in both institutions, but defy certain rules in one of them and thus eliminate the moral inconsistencies (by 'privately' waiving the asymmetrical character of vertically divided institutions, disobeying orders or re-fraining from giving orders). Since this attitude involves the moral risk of violating rules, it becomes far more important than in the first scenario to find out which of the institutional norms are morally problematic or wrong. But what are the criteria of 'right' and 'wrong' in the case of institutionalized norms and rules? How strong are they if they exist at all?

There is yet a third option. Our decent person may come to the following conclusion: 'I will not disobey; I will not refrain from giving orders; I will not try "privately" to waive institutional hier-archic rules. But I will turn to those who are in a position similar to mine (an act of symmetric reciprocity) and try to persuade them of the need for collective action.' However, our decent person should find out in which of the two institutions she or he should call for collective action in order to make a right decision. For disobedience is just in the case of an institution whose institutional rules are unjust, and unjust if the rules are just.

This third option can carry both the smallest and the greatest moral risk. The justice or injustice of rules or norms depends largely on the perception of the actors who live according to those norms and rules. If the response to the call for collective action is enthusiastic and wide, and particularly if others had already challenged the justice of the rule in point, then there would be practically no moral risk involved. By contrast, if collective action is urged against a rule the rightness of which had not yet been placed in doubt, and if the initiator of collective action makes efforts to recruit others for partici-pation in a collective action which they had not really intended to launch, then the moral risks are enormous. Acts or initiatives of this kind are in blatant contradiction to the general principle of moral orientation ('Care for the other person's autonomy').

There is, finally, a fourth option. Our decent person will not leave either of the institutions, or violate the norms of either of them privately or by initiating collective action. Rather, she or he will turn to the public and make a strong case against a particular set of valid norms and rules, suggesting that they need to be changed as well as indicating the direction of the called-for change. She or he will present good arguments to indicate (to 'prove', in the broadest sense of the verb *probare*) that the valid norms are unjust, or even morally evil (which is worse than unjust), and that they should be changed and replaced by alternative (just and good) rules and norms.

This is the way in which Immanuel Kant addressed the issue in his celebrated essay 'What is Enlightenment?' As is well known, Kant distinguished between the private and the public use of our reason. Within an institution, Kant argued, we are in a 'private' sphere which puts limitations on the use of our reason. We must not violate the norms of the institutions whose members we are, even if we are convinced that the rules are unjust and wrong. What we should rather do, unless we leave the institution of our own free will, is to turn instead to the public and argue for changing the rules. Of course, Kant assumed that everyone is familiar with the criteria of a proper moral argument. But our protagonist, the decent person, has not yet arrived at this stage. She or he only knows that such criteria should exist, otherwise one would not be able to conduct an argument and make a persuasive case for the devalidation of an unjust (or morally wrong) rule and for the validation of right and just ones.

The inventory of the options open to the decent person has convincingly shown that the conclusion of all his or her searches for practical options invariably ends with the question 'What should I do?', the very question that she or he raised at the beginning, on becoming aware of the inconsistencies between different sets of norms and rules from the moral point of view. Decent persons in that situation face a variety of alternatives, including ascertaining which set of rules is 'better' than the other and which of them is more just. In addition, they have to figure out whether the norms of giving–receiving–reciprocating should really be waived each time they collide with institutional rules. They have to find out whether they should observe institutional rules on every occasion or whether there are some occasions when it is better to violate them than to observe them. They have to find out whether it is better to violate unjust norms with a private gesture or in collective action, as well as *when* they should choose one of these options. They have to find ways of formulating the most rational argument to prove that certain norms are unjust and to demonstrate which alternative norms would be right and just. These problems are heterogeneous: they arise at different junctures and are formulated at various levels of generality and concreteness. A crutch is needed to support us in our efforts to move in the right direction.

The rule of thumb is of no help here, for one must first have the right direction. So the decent person may turn to the general principle of moral orientation for guidance (with all its more or less concrete interpretations). Since the principle is general, it provides guidance for all possible cases, all possible junctures of moral relevance. Yet the circumstance that the principle is orientative must caution the actor reaching out for a moral crutch: orientative principles do not qualify as universal yardsticks, for we cannot apply them to *determine* which norm or action is right and which is wrong. 'Care for other persons'; 'Do not harm another human being on purpose.' If you are a participant in an action whose purpose is evicting people from their homes (provided that this is your job), you can still care for others (even for those you evict), and you can still appease your conscience by saying that you did not harm them on purpose. Alas, you did what you had to do and they did what they had to do. The general principle can thus still orient you, albeit in a subdued, *piano* version. However, it does not follow from this that evicting people is right and just, or that you should not have misgivings about it or ponder whether the rules regulating housing as well as housing distribution are just or unjust, right or wrong, better or worse than possible alternatives.

Furthermore, the orientative principles are formulated with provisoes to the effect that one should not do X or Y *unless morally justified*. This makes sense since there is more than one orientative principle relevant to any given situation. The plurality of principles can lead to dilemmas – for example, in the case of 'showing contempt'. One should not normally show contempt for another person, but on some occasions it is morally justified and hence unavoidable; so one has to weigh the situation and choose. The principle, which is just one party to the choice, cannot serve simultaneously as the yardstick which determines priority.

In section III, where a few orientative principles were enumerated, we came across certain principles which also served as *general norms* and, as such, were not orientative but rather *constitutive* in nature. I assume that, when a decent person begins to search for more general yardsticks, she or he will pinpoint exactly those well-known interdictions

('Do not murder', 'Do not rape', etc.), and especially the only constitutive principle derived from several orientative ones. This states, 'Do not violate another person's body or soul; do not manipulate others or keep them in tutelage because of their race, sex or membership of other human groups.'

We have left the good person in a state of embarrassment. She or he felt, even knew, that there was a kind of inconsistency in being a member of two institutions with different kinds of ethos, each at cross-purposes with the other. In the quest for a solution she or he came to understand that the first thing to do is to find the answer to the question 'What is the right thing for me to do?' This question could not be answered by relying on the moral arsenal of everyday life, the rule of thumb or the general principles of orientation. Everyone who is familiar with decent persons is also familiar with the fact of how good their moral intuition is. Some of them therefore might make the right choice in such a conflict simply by relying on their intuition. Yet even the best intuition can fail or err amidst unforeseen circumstances or within brand-new institutions about which no one has yet obtained everyday or non-everyday experience. Intuition is good if it is backed by life experience. Otherwise it falters. Decent persons who know themselves as contingent and who are aware of the contingent character of modern society will certainly not dare to rely on intuition alone. So they will come up with the only solution which presents itself so far. They will come to the conclusion that they should use the only universal yardstick, the single constitutive moral principle at our disposal: 'Do not violate another person's body or soul; do not manipulate others or keep them in tutelage because of their race, sex or membership of other human groups.' How far one can go by relying upon this crutch remains to be seen. Yet if it proves to be a reliable crutch, then decent persons will use it. Practice is experience: the more one learns to apply a yardstick, the more one applies it, and the more experience is collected. Out of newly gained experience, the intuition of the decent person may arise once again and be as good a guide as it has proved itself to be in everyday matters and situations.

VIII

Philosophy is a city ruled by philosophers. A city of imagination is easy to rule: what one dreams can be dreamt of as perfect. But imagination feeds on experience; so does philosophical imagination. As Hegel remarked, the clue to Plato's *Republic* is Greek *Sittlichkeit*.

As a rule, pre-modern moral philosophers took the position of the righteous (good) person of their own *sittlich* world. Modern moral philosophy can continue this tradition and, at the same time, break ground on a new path: it can address all contingent persons, whatever the *Sittlichkeit* to which they belong. Much has been said in chapter 1 about the consequences of such an attitude. At this point, some new ideas should be added.

In modern moral philosophy, contingent persons address other contingent persons. It is for this reason that the famous 'problem of authority' can be eliminated. But not everyone who shares the globe with us is a contingent person. Many – but not all – things which have been said here about the decent and contingent person will also ring true for the decent and non-contingent person, irrespective of his or her own particular *Sittlichkeit*. What will be endorsed in one such tradition may well be rejected in another. Yet I expect that everything said here will ring true for the modern, contingent and decent person. This is not a statement about the general endorsement of this moral philosophy. But I expect all contingent and decent persons to share my belief that the sort of person I have been depicting is *good* (*decent*). They may still reject this philosophy as boring, much too commonplace, maximalist, minimalist, naïve, ambitious or anything else. *Yet it is not consensus which I seek in my philosophy* but rather endorsement of my claim that the sentence 'Good persons now exist' is true, and of the truthfulness of my answer to the question 'How are they now possible?'

In all my statements about the decent person I have presumed that our person dwells in a *modern* world of *Sittlichkeit*. I have thus presumed that *Sittlichkeit* (the shared values, and all norms and rules of proper conduct related to them, including virtue norms) is not homogeneous, but, rather, differentiated and sometimes fragmented. I have also presumed that it can be loose or tightly knit, or loose in one sphere and tightly knit in another; and that our person has the choice of shifting from one *Sittlichkeit* to another, or can dwell in several *Sittlichkeiten* at the same time. I have finally presumed that conflicts may arise between the different *Sittlichkeiten* in the life of contingent persons, who are all in the position to choose, accept, reject and change. In order not to confuse the issues and to preserve the quasi-narrative style of discussion, it was only in discussing such conflicts that I first presented the decent person in the *position of moral reflection*. However, decent persons adopt the position of moral reflection even in the most elementary settings of daily life. This circumstance has been presupposed all along, as must have become obvious from the many provisoes added to the interpretations of the general principle of moral orientation. To find out whether or not such provisoes apply requires moral reflection. In taking one more step backwards we arrive at the existential choice of goodness: choosing oneself is knowing oneself; self-knowledge is self-reflective and, in this case, also moral. Self-reflection belongs to the intrinsic essence of a decent human existence.

Reflection (and self-reflection) is rarely divorced from action. It can precede action, it can accompany action or it can appear as an 'afterthought'. Provided that reflection is carried out within the framework of one particular *Sittlichkeit*, it is so thoroughly linked to intuition that no theoretical scissors could divide them. However, if it comes to a conflict between two *Sittlichkeiten*, reflection cannot have recourse to one or the other *Sittlichkeit*. Moral reflection must thus be divorced from intuition; action itself should be suspended for the duration of reflection.

Once we have conflicting preferences (because we cannot take both of two courses of action simultaneously) or we are entangled in a moral conflict proper (there is a degree of good on both sides but we cannot choose both simultaneously), we seek a *standard of comparison*. We need a yardstick to decide which option is better – pragmatically, morally or otherwise. In the case of moral conflicts, the yardstick must be on the level of greater *generality*: two concrete norms can be compared by using an abstract one (or more than one abstract norm); two abstract norms by using a general one. The more general one is, for such purposes, the 'higher'. In the case of a conflict (be it moral or other), one tries to make a decision on fairly rational grounds. Either someone else tells you what you should do (in which case you have no choice) or you are not instructed by a superior and are free to choose for yourself – but then you need a yardstick that stands as 'high' as the hypothetical superior or at least stands higher than yourself. It is the impersonal 'higher one' which enables you to make a decent choice.

'Higher' norms (general, universal ones) do not give us the freedom to decide (for their existence is rather the result of such freedom). Instead they provide us with the opportunity of establishing a proper *priority* in cases where moral priorities can be established. Since the problem which arises when no moral priority can be established will not be discussed until chapter 4, we shall limit the discussion to cases in which comparison may, or does, result in establishing such a priority.

Modern men and women have invented a few general (universal) norms, maxims and principles as the highest (impersonal) authorities in moral decisions, as well as in those socio-political decisions in which a moral aspect is inherent. They have invented them because they need them, because they need to choose from a broad spectrum of values, virtues and norms, and because they have to find out which of them should be given priority. They have invented general–universal norms because, faced with competing sets of norms (social, political, legal) they need to find out which is best or most just. They have invented them perhaps because they had already made up their minds about giving a particular set of values priority over others and wanted to prove that they had made the right and true decision, that their priority was rationally founded. They needed those universals for they had already rejected certain traditional norms as inferior, unjust, flawed and faulty. And finding the higher norm (the standard of comparison) seemed to be the way to prove that this prejudgement was right, just and true. There is no ontological–metaphysical ground for labelling the general or the universal as standing 'higher' than the particular or the individual. They are higher in so far as they are higher *for us*, because as moderns we need them to be higher in so far as we need some kind of a yardstick. We do not need a *Führer* who in his capacity as a singular (and not universal!) person would represent a commanding authority for us. Placing the universal 'highest' can indicate a position in rational argumentation. We employ universal and general assertions in precisely this sense, and it is we who use them. In our absence, there would be nothing in them which would make them inherently higher than anything else. It even sounds silly to ponder whether humankind is 'higher' than a person: on what grounds can one compare them? General (or universal) terms, categories, norms and maxims serve us in their capacity of making other categories, norms, rules or values *comparable*. The aim of comparison is to obtain an answer to the question of priority (this is, one should remember, the problem of the decent person). Yet, if one compares one general norm to a particular and a concrete norm, or one universal concept to a particular or 'individual' concept, the comparison becomes meaningless – moreover, misleading. It cannot result in a decision concerning moral priorities, which is, after all, the point of comparison.

To sum up: modern men and women have invented certain universal norms, maxims, rules, principles and much else because they need them. In fact, everyone needs them, but decent persons need them more than others. For they cannot remain decent unless thay can rely on the judgement of universals and maxims if a conflict arises in which neither the valid norms and rules nor the intuitions of the good person suffice to establish priority.

Philosophers, who arc after all modern men and women like

everyone else, share this need and experience. It is for this reason that they have made a case for the universality of the value 'freedom' and the value 'life'. It is thus that they have 'found' – rather, proposed – universal maxims, rules and similar yardsticks of comparison. They have not 'invented' those universals; the invention was a collective act. However, they have formulated them in a lucid fashion and their formulations have become the trademarks of different philosophies. Modern *Sittlichkeit*, to which universalism in the above sense certainly belongs, has been transformed into philosophical systems and propositions. All of the pieces have been fitted together in a variety of marvellous jigsaw puzzles. Yet there is a problem with such jigsaw puzzles when it comes to ethics. Universals, maxims, even universal values such as 'freedom' and 'life' are *our images* and *our life forms* which are supported by modern men and women and concretized via their actions and creations. Philosophies have become too exalted about them. Universals are worshipped and treated as ontological entities. They are put on pedestals, and we, single individuals or particular causes, are supposed to bow to them. General norms and maxims are construed as a kind of court of appeal, not as man-made supreme arbiters in human matters. This song-and-dance around universals has, of course, created some suspicion and triggered some vitriolic remarks about people who, in their ultimate commitment to world history and humankind, could never bring themselves to help, respect or love a single human being. Modern men and women, who have elevated and abstracted norms and values and made them serve as universal standards (of comparison), are not prepared to be dissolved in abstractions themselves. Nor are they willing, in so far as they are decent, to dissolve others in such abstractions. For decent people always keep in mind the general principle of moral orientation as well as all the concrete orientative moral principles. And one cannot respect the sensitivity of an abstraction, alleviate the suffering of an abstraction, trust an abstraction, pay attention to the vulnerability of an abstraction, be kind to an abstraction, help an abstraction save its face. And yet one needs all those abstractions. For without them one could hardly tell good from bad in the most difficult (and sometimes the most decisive) situations of choice.

Apart from the eventual reification of universals, the philosophical jigsaw puzzle has a second suspicious feature. This feature is at the same time its forte: in the jigsaw puzzle all pieces fit, for they are fitted together. Good philosophies are holistic and totalizing; they are supposed to rest on their own foundations. No *complete* philosophy can be satisfied with less. It belongs to the language game termed philosophy that it must present the universals as system-immanent abstractions. The universality of universals, be they values, norms or maxims, should be proved. It is a serious offence against the genre to assert that universals have been formulated by us, that they are handy yardsticks which we can simply go by (as we certainly do). The universals must be *transcendentally deduced*, in their capacity as the 'moral law' which we *discover* but which we do not legislate ourselves, as the transcendental conditions of human speech, human action, human creation – depending on the paradigm one invents. Contemporary neo-neo-neo-Kantian ethics is extremely ingenious in inventing universal maxims and norms; and I have played my part by proposing at least five universal principles, several general norms, and the like.

To repeat the initial statement of this section: every philosopher rules his or her own city (his or her own philosophy). Therefore, if the philosopher so wishes, she or he can deduce universals within the particular system, consistently and lucidly. Such deductions are important in a philosophical system: in so far as one plays a (language) game, one is bound to observe the rules. Philosophy is a magnificent language game; it also challenges us to put the pieces of the puzzle together in our own way. Yet, as far as the universals (maxims or universal norms) themselves are concerned, *it is completely indifferent whether they are indeed transcendentally deduced or simply 'declared' or 'pointed out' (empirically)*. If they are versions on the theme 'Let us propose universals and maxims as standards by which to compare alternative sets of rules or patterns of action in order to find out what would be the better or the best thing to do', then one universal formula is as good as another. In using these universals, we could even forget about the philosophies from which they were originally drawn, to be polished up, absolutized and worshipped. There is only one exception: the substantive formula of the categorical imperative. If he had formulated nothing else, Kant would remain the greatest genius of modern philosophy. He found the fundamental maxim (or imperative) from which all others spring. One can fully subscribe to this formula without knowing anything at all about Kant's philosophy. One need not understand its philosophical foundations in order to endorse the *simplest*, the most radical, the clearest and most sublime universal maxim one can dream of, which prescribes that one should never use another person as a mere means but also as an end.

The best maxim is also the best exemplification of the importance of a philosophical formulation. The substantive formula of the categorical imperative was not 'invented' by Kant but by modern men and women before him. Richardson's heroine Clarissa had already formulated it, and Richardson himself had perhaps learned it from one of his confidantes who opened up to him women's fate, concerns, virtues and hearts. Kant supported this formula with a whole system. He deduced it transcendentally, he used it as an explication of the main formulas of the categorical imperative, which are too formal to serve modern men and women as a good guide – and this is how he impressed it on the mind of those studying his philosophy. The latter, for their part, preserved and disseminated the formula while other maxims and universal imperatives were forgotten or became marginalized. *The 'means–end' formula is the universalization and the simultaneous absolutization of the constitutive moral principle, which itself derived its legitimacy from serving as the prohibitive version of a few orientative principles concerning the other person's autonomy.*

Although, for me, the Kantian formula seems to be the unsurpassable universal maxim, because it encompasses all others in one way or another, I would not suggest that we endorse it as the *sole* yardstick of comparison or as the sole guide to a particular 'action choice'. Odd as it may sound, even the universal maxims need to have their *use* specified. 'We should never *treat* (use) a person as mere means but, simultaneously, always as an end-in-itself', the maxim tells us. But we may ask, *when* actually do we *treat* (use) a person? Do we 'treat' a person in a department store when we buy a pair of socks from a salesgirl? We certainly use the salesgirl as a mere means for our own end (to get a pair of socks), for we could safely buy socks from an automat. One can contend that, in buying a pair of socks from the salesgirl, one does not *treat* (use) this girl at all – in other words, one can treat her neither as a means nor as an end. Furthermore, what does it mean to treat someone 'as an end'? If we interpret 'end' in terms of the orientative principles concerning autonomy, both negative and positive formulations will seem too strong to make sense in such situations. In buying a pair of socks, I cannot possibly, in the normal way of things, inflict bodily harm, humiliate, withhold vital information, exert influence over the other, use my charisma, make the other financially dependent, keep the other in tutelage, and the like. In addition, the orientative principles by definition leave the assessment of the situation to our discretion, something which absolutist formulations should not do. And yet, in this case, it is the 'means–end' formula which requires our discretion in its application, rather than the orientative principles concerning autonomy. A weak definition of 'treating someone as an end' can also be offered. In this understanding, every person is treated as an end who is considered a rational agent and an independent person (as the salesgirl indeed is). However, such an interpretation makes the formula too weak – so weak, in fact, that it could be used to authorize almost every action and human relation, with the exception of slavery, serfdom and outright political tyranny.

All this is not a rejoinder addressed to Kant, who was acutely aware of this quandary. In order to avoid it, he proposed the empty and formal versions of the categorical imperative, and advocated non-contradiction as the sole and complete criterion of the rightness of our maxim. As far as I am concerned, I would rather meet the challenge of the 'means–end' formula head-on. *I recommend the acceptance of the means–end formula as the universal maxim.* What I suggest is we should all keep this maxim in mind whenever we wish to find out whether this or that particular course of action is right or wrong; whether this or that institutional rule should have priority if a conflict arises; whenever we reject or devalidate existing rules and norms as unjust or wrong and recommend alternative regulations instead as just (more just) and right. *And yet I recommend the acceptance of the 'means–end' formula as the categorical and orientative universal maxim.* The qualification sounds anti-Kantian, aphilosophical and inelegant, and perhaps it is. However, my motive in offering such a bastard formula was neither elegance nor philosophical sophistication. I have still been keeping in mind those good men and women who want to find out how they can become what they are: decent persons. I am fully aware of their predicament. They live in a pluralistic moral universe and, as contingent persons, need to find out which course to take. This is why they look for a crutch to support them in their efforts to move in the right direction (if such a direction exists at all).

The 'means–end' formula serves well as a universal crutch, but only with the proviso that the interpretation of the act as 'treating' and as 'treating someone as an end-in-itself' is left to the actor's discretion (which is what makes the maxim orientative). The actor can, if she or he so wishes, give a very strong interpretation to the maxim. The strongest interpretation will presumably prevail in human contacts and attachments. But, if the optimal choice is an action requiring the weakest interpretation, it is permitted to choose a course of action (or institution) to which the weakest interpretation applies. This is far from hair-splitting. Absolutism in choices which are political or social in nature may invite disaster. Someone who allows only for the strongest interpretation of the maxim will be unable to compare institutions according to the degree of autonomy they offer. I will discuss in the next chapter how, without a dose of relativism–pragmatism, political practice becomes impossible. To accept the absolutist version of the 'means–end' formula would in practice entail such heavy qualifications to its categorical claim as to devalidate it completely. For there is indeed a categorical claim in the formula: it *absolutely forbids* committing acts which violate the maxim in its weakest interpretation, or accepting such institutions, organizations or sets of rules as, by definition and *ex principio*, instrumentalize people. The decent person can comfortably rely upon this crutch. On the other hand, the one which was carved out in the workshop of philosophy to perfection and with so much elegance will crack in use, for it is too refined for common applications.

We should never treat other human beings as mere means but also as ends-in-themselves: decent persons keep this maxim in mind in the process of *moral reflection*. Moral reflection is not a solitary business (like the existential choice of goodness). Men and women discuss the issues on the agenda; they consult one another, they seek advice. Whether a strong, or perhaps the strongest, or alternatively the weakest, interpretation of the categorical orientative universal maxim is warranted in a particular situation of choice is normally not decided by a particular actor, a social monad, alone, but rather through a process of collective or quasi-collective deliberation. In the course of such deliberations men and women formulate a few general guidelines and principles which can be regarded as interpretations of the categorical–universal orientative maxim. In a more cautious formulation, it can be stated that not all of these guidelines will qualify as such, but some of them will. Philosophers will, if they so wish, be able to deduce them (logically) from the categorical–universal orientative maxim, to relate them (without contradiction) to this maxim, and to demonstrate that they are nothing but interpretations of it. Decent persons (real human actors) do not often make an attempt at arriving at philosophical consistency. They rather have a 'feel' for the principles that will serve as reliable guidelines and prevent us from instrumentalizing other human beings in one or another situation while addressing one or another political or social issue.

Decent persons are perfectly well aware that one could subscribe to the most wonderful and perfect principles, but to no avail in the absence of resolve and ability. Resolve and ability require virtues in all moral matters. The development of virtues requires the presence of certain virtue norms and other moral norms. Thus the decent person will reflect upon this issue as well. The universal maxim can be observed, and thus kept alive, if certain virtues which keep the attitude of autonomy alive are also universalized. The decent person will mobilize his or her imagination in order to find those virtues which should be universalized so as to keep the universal maxim alive.

In what follows, I shall recommend certain maxims for universal acceptance. Before venturing on such an immodest proposal, how-ever, I would first like to clarify what I mean by 'I recommend', 'certain maxims' and 'universal acceptance'.

In so far as I recommend something, I do so as a contingent person who has entered into a discussion about modern *mores* with other contingent persons. All that I know about morals has been learned from my father and from other decent persons whom I have known – not from books on philosophy. The latter only helped me to formu-late better what I already knew. A host of contingent persons think in the same way as I do – this is my life experience. I have not invented the maxims I am going to list; I have taken them over from others. Some of them were first formulated by Kant, although he did not invent them either. Others have been distilled directly from the practice of decent persons.

I recommend *certain* maxims; I do not recommend maxims in general. If one believes that there is an *eternal moral law* as *the* absolute, which can or cannot be discovered but which can never be modified or changed, and if, further, one believes that all maxims can be deduced (logically) from such an eternal moral law, then one can rightly claim to have presented all the moral maxims. However, if one believes that universal maxims are invented by good persons who have chosen themselves under the category of the *universal*, who require them because they want to become what they are, namely decent, both in spite of and as a result of their contingency, then one cannot claim to have presented all the universal maxims. One would rather invite other contingent persons to add their own recommenda-tions to the list, or to query the universal claims of maxims elaborated by others. Since I belong to the second group, I recommend the acceptance of only certain moral maxims. No one knows, and no one will ever know, whether hidden behind the veil of *our* ignorance there exists an eternal and absolute moral law of which we can only occasionally catch a glimpse. However worthy a task it is to speculate upon this idea, it does not add one iota to the decency of contingent persons. The greatest moral ambition of contingent persons is *to recommend such universal maxims as could, if an eternal, absolute moral law existed, be deduced from that law.*[18]

By 'universal acceptance' I do not mean that every human person accepts the validity claim of the maxims. Within the framework of a moral philosophy, 'universal acceptance' is a far more modest idea. Since the need for universal maxims has grown out of the moral situation of contingent persons, their acceptance by the contingent persons alone would amount to universal acceptance. Universal maxims generalize the practices and norms of modern contingent persons. They generalize them to such a high degree that these universal maxims can take the 'highest' place. To claim universal acceptance of universal principles is but to repeat the *gesture* made at the beginning of this moral philosophy. A moral philosophy answers the question 'What should I do?', 'What is the right thing for me to do?' It can only address the person who is ready to ask such a question. To all other persons, among them those who mock morals as a dress out of fashion, moral philosophy turns with a single gesture: choose yourself! Choose yourself as a decent person (under the category of the universal). The claim to 'universal acceptance' rephrases exactly this initial gesture.

One may feel uneasy about the term 'universal maxim', for how can one mention universal maxims if such maxims are not universally accepted even by all contingent persons? One should therefore add in clarification that the term 'universal' does not stand here for 'by everyone' but for 'towards everyone'. And, indeed, decent persons live up to universal maxims in their relationship to everyone, be they other moderns or pre-moderns, decent or indecent. One cannot be true to the orientative principles of autonomy without relating to everyone as if they were indeed autonomous beings, or at least as if their becoming autonomous were dependent upon us. Whether the maxim would in fact be universal if only a single person formulated it and claimed universality for its empirical universalization is an academic question. Actually, there is a host of decent persons who make such universal maxims good.

After this necessary detour, I shall, as promised, set about recommending certain maxims for universal acceptance. I have already recommended acceptance of the 'means–end' formula as the categorical–universal orientative maxim. Other universal maxims can be regarded as *explications* of the 'means–end' formula or concretizations thereof. By 'concretization' I do not mean that the maxims are concrete (this would be nonsensical), but that they may be of crucial relevance for one particular sphere or segment of life and less relevant for others. The fact that single maxims can be seen as explications of the 'means–end' formula reflects the circumstance that all maxims (the means–end maxim included) are generalization / universalizations of the elementary norms, virtue norms, principles which are normally practised, observed, invented, embellished, modified and particularly cherished by decent persons in their daily life. This also works the other way around. The 'universal maxims in the making' are embedded in daily life; they shape and modify the norms and moral practices in this life. Universal maxims in the making allow the contingent person to follow certain principles in his or her daily life, and to distil out of the tradition the kind of virtues and norms which fit into the modern framework whilst letting others vanish in oblivion.

I distinguish between *maxims of the first order* and *maxims of the second order*. Maxims of the first order are (a) of a *prohibitive* nature and (b) of an *imperative* nature.[19]

Prohibitive maxims

1 Do not choose maxims (or norms) which cannot be made public.
2 Do not choose rules (or norms) the observance of which involves in principle the use of others as mere means.
3 Do not choose *moral norms* (binding norms) the observance of which is not an end-in-itself.

Imperative maxims

1 Give equal recognition to all persons as free and rational beings.
2 Recognize all human needs except those the satisfaction of which in principle involves the use of other persons as mere means.
3 Respect people only according to their (moral) merits and virtues.
4 Maintain your dignity in all your actions.

Explication of the prohibitive maxims

Maxim 1   This maxim derives from, or is most closely connected with, the second cluster of orientative moral principles ('Have a proper regard for other persons' autonomy') and the virtues of truthfulness (sincerity, trustworthiness, candour). The second cluster of orientative principles contains the *prohibition of manipulation* ('Do not withhold information (do not lie) in order to make others do something which is for your own pleasure or benefit, even if the act is good'). Norms related to the virtues of truthfulness are also restrictive: for example, 'One cannot be a decent person if one habitually withholds knowledge or information from others'; 'One cannot be a decent person if one habitually conceals the motives for one's actions and attitudes.' No wonder that a maxim which has been distilled and abstracted from prohibitive principles and norms is similarly prohibitive (and not imperative) in nature.

'Do not choose maxims (or norms) which cannot be made public' is a *weaker* prohibition than the ones we have met previously. It has to be weaker because of its generality. The maxim had to be formulated such that it would be valid in face-to-face relations, in institutionalized encounters and in the public sphere, able to qualify as a guide for direct, communicative and judgemental actions alike, and thus able to serve us in the capacity of a high court of appeal where institutional rules or inter-spheric norms collide with one another. In such a general context, a *strong* prohibition on not disclosing our motives would strike us as fundamentalist. By and large, a person can be completely decent if she or he does not fully disclose motivations – as, for example, when it comes to particular decisions in an institution or in the field of politics. Habitually to withhold knowledge and information is generally wrong, but here too there are exceptions. In wartime, for example, decent persons will make it a habit to withhold information and knowledge from the enemy. On the other hand, it is absolutely wrong to conduct a war in such a way that the maxims governing its conduct could not be made public. For, if a war is just, the maxims governing the conduct of that war can by definition be made public.

Maxim 2   I have recommended the acceptance of Kant's 'means–end' formula as the categorical–universal orientative maxim. All first-order maxims are explications of that maxim. This is most obvious in the case of the second maxim. Yet this maxim is not orientative, because it states exactly what one should avoid. Before entering an institution, one should first figure out whether the norms and rules of the institution themselves require or prescribe the use of persons as mere means. If a person resolute to live up to the categorical–universal orientative maxim joins an institution (for example, a totalitarian party or a secret-service organization) which uses people as mere means *ex principio*, that person gets entangled in the gravest of moral conflicts. As already noted, moral maxims have been invented (formulated) as supreme guidelines or courts of appeal for decent people who want to conduct a decent life. Maxim 2 offers such a guideline, and it also serves as such a court of appeal. It suggests that one should take care before entering an institution voluntarily. One should refrain from joining it if the norms and rules of that institution require the violation of the categorical universal maxim. Maxim 2 also suggests that, if one discovers that an institution of which one is a member requires, in principle, the use of other persons or groups of persons as mere means, one should leave it immediately.

The rules and norms of certain institutions *permit*, but *do not require*, the use of other persons as mere means *ex principio*. Maxim 2 does not prohibit us from entering such institutions. Such an interdiction would be unduly fundamentalist given that most institutions permit, even if they do not require, the use of others as mere means. An interdiction of this kind would simply defy common sense. In addition, the decency of such maximalism would also be questionable. In formulating maxim 2 as I have done, I have implicitly taken sides in a 200-year-old debate. It was Rousseau who devised the model of the modern hermit, of the person who preserves his goodness and maintains his purity by keeping out of the 'tumult' of socio-political life. And it was Diderot who sensed the unsavoury character of too much moral indignation, and who retorted that someone who shuns the society of other human beings cannot himself be decent.

That maxim 2 supports Diderot is completely consistent with the general orientative principle: 'Care for other persons.' A few of the concrete orientative principles advise us against being contemptous or showing our contempt towards other human beings (unless it is morally justified). A decent person, like everyone else, chooses to enter at least one institution. But the recluse, who does his or her work without communicating with anyone, who spends all his or her time alone or in non-committal encounters, does not conform with the usual image of the decent person. By associating with others one undeniably risks exposure to the company of indecent, as well as decent, persons, and to institutional settings in which the rules can be used for instrumentalization. However, to shun other people because of this mixture of the decent and the indecent is the clearest proof of misanthropy, of contempt for other human beings. Contempt is never morally motivated unless the other person deserves contempt. Participation in institutions which do not require the use of other men as mere means, but only permit a use of this kind, is not a moral transgression, and it does not deserve contempt. If one participates in such an institution, but does not use others as mere means, the universal principle of orientation *and* the categorical–universal orientative maxim are observed in concert.

Maxim 3   In contrast to maxims 1 and 2, maxim 3 does not refer to norms in general, but only to *moral norms*. It thus cannot be extended to encompass social and political norms and rules. For example, one can accept majority decision not as an end-in-itself, but as the best rule, the most just procedure (means), in deciding matters of common concern. Moral norms are transclusteral in nature: that is, they do not constitute social clusters. Furthermore, they are norms which should be observed irrespective of pragmatic consequences. This circumstance is one of the *definitions* of moral norms; the expression 'Moral norms are binding' is but a shorthand version of this definition. It should become clear from the definition that the observance of moral norms is an end-in-itself, for only if an act (or a series of acts) is to be regarded as an end-in-itself can and should one embark on it irrespective of consequences.

Modern men and women are born into a network of moral norms. They choose again some of them, while dismissing or disregarding others. It would be maximalism to require them to observe moral norms under the condition that the observance be an end-in-itself. Children of pious parents observe certain religious–moral norms only as long as their parents live, and therefore *not* irrespective of certain consequences. For them, observance is not an end-in-itself, but rather a gesture of love; it is performed for others' sake. Needless to say, decent persons can act in this fashion if they do not infringe the categorical–universal orientative maxim by so doing. Orientative principles sometimes advise us to act exactly in this fashion.

Maxim 3 excludes from the republic of moral norms (Kant would say, from the kingdom of ends) all substantive goals and goods. One should not subscribe to a norm as a *moral* norm if it enjoins actions *because they realize* goals which are also regarded as goods. It makes *no difference* whether the end state is the greatest happiness of the greatest number, the victory of socialism, the might of our country, or anything else. No substantive goal whatsoever can generate moral norms whose observance is an end-in-itself. There is only one end implicit in moral norms proper: the best possible moral world. This world is not a substantive goal, for it is precisely in moral action, practised as an end-in-itself, that the promise of the best possible moral world is kept alive.

Thus the third maxim excludes utilitarianism as a moral principle and, as a result, all utilitarian maxims in their capacity of generating moral norms. However, the maxim does not exclude the utilitarian principle in its role of generating norms other than moral ones (for example, social and political norms). The decent person is advised not to choose moral norms on utilitarian grounds, but she or he is not advised against one or another social and political norm or rule on such grounds.

Maxim 3 is also a further concretization of the categorical–universal orientative maxim *in so far as it excludes the instrumentalization of morals itself*. The instrumentalization of morals would permit the instrumentalization of others as well as ourselves *on moral grounds* – and this would be perhaps the grossest violation of the *categorical* maxim.

Maxim 3 forbids the instrumentalization of morals. However, it does not exclude goals and goods from moral considerations. Finally, shared ends and goods are *values*, and *virtues are related to values*. Virtue norms behave in the same way as other moral norms in so far as practising them is *an end-in-itself*. At the same time, one also practises virtues 'in order to' – for example, in order to promote a cause, in order to eliminate injustices, in order to protect our country. Promoting a goal should not become a moral-norm-in-itself. But, in living up to moral norms, one does promote certain ends and causes. An action the moral content of which is an end-in-itself is supposed to bring about valuable results.

Explication of the imperative maxims

Maxim 1   This maxim is one of the explications of the categorical–universal orientative maxim and one of the generalizations of the universal orientative principle ('Have a proper regard for other persons' autonomy'). The term 'equal' (in the compound 'equal recognition') does not stand for 'equal quantity' or for 'to the same extent'. Recognition, as the maxim stipulates, should know neither quantity nor extent. Each and every person should be recognized as a free and rational being, irrespective of whether she or he behaves as free and rational.

The maxim is not the kind of ought-statement that is deduced from an is-statement. It is not because men and women are indeed born free and are indeed 'endowed' with reason that they ought to be recognized as free and rational beings. The decent person has chosen himself or herself under the category of the universal; thus she or he is *free as a moral agent*. The decent person is ready to listen to good advice whenever she or he asks the question 'What is the right thing for me to do?' Thus she or he is also a *rational moral agent*. The decent person enters into relations of *symmetric reciprocity* with all other persons in his or her daily life. Although the decent person also enters into relations of asymmetric reciprocity within certain institutions, she or he ascribes their asymmetric character to *institutional rules*, and not to the 'substance' of the actors performing their functions according to such rules. If one is a free and rational moral agent in the sense outlined above, and if one stands in the relationship of symmetric reciprocity with every other human agent as such, then one *should* recognize others as equally free and rational human beings, or one will manoeuvre oneself into a *contradiction*. This is, furthermore, an *existential contradiction*, for it annuls and voids the existential choice itself. The reason for this is that a person who does not recognize all human persons as free and rational human beings could not possibly have chosen himself or herself under the category of the universal. She or he can still be, and thus is capable of becoming, a 'moral virtuoso' of a kind (the type of person who cultivates moral gestures as a specialized ability) but not a decent (good) person.

Maxim 2   Whereas the first imperative maxim stipulates the recognition of *sameness* (we are all alike as free and rational beings), the second stipulates the recognition of *difference*. Life forms are diverse, persons are unique, needs are different in quality, quantity, relation and modality. A non-contingent person knows only one proper way of life: his or her own. This is why she or he distinguishes between proper and improper, real and unreal, true and false needs. Proper, real and true needs are the ones which have been generated in his or her own way of life; all other needs are by definition false, unreal and improper. Our 'own' needs should be recognized; the needs of 'others' do not necessarily have to be recognized. A contingent person lacks the authority for distinguishing 'true' from 'untrue', 'proper' from 'improper' needs. In the gesture of existential choice, decent persons take over their determinations as their freedom. They choose themselves as 'persons of such and such needs', and on this account they forgo their right to devalue the needs of other persons.

Maxim 2 is the generalization of all of the principles of orientation. Yet it should be noted that many of the orientative principles have been recommended for acceptance with a proviso: unless moral reasons dictate otherwise. There can be different moral reasons which do dictate otherwise, yet one of them follows from the observance of the categorical–universal orientative maxim: a human being should not serve as a mere means for another. If there is a need which cannot be satisfied without using another person as a mere means, this particular need must not be recognized. One cannot, in recognizing all (other) human needs, recognize the need to instrumentalize other persons. This again would involve a contradiction: we would not recognize the needs for *autonomy* of those who do not want to be instrumentalized.

Maxim 2 enjoins the recognition of all needs (with the above proviso). Recognition is threefold. By recognition it is accepted that the needs are real (not imaginary), that they are not improper (immoral) and that they have a claim to satisfaction. However, this maxim does not stipulate the actual satisfaction of all such needs. No one is obliged by the maxim to satisfy all the needs that she or he could satisfy, for his or her own needs have equal status to those of others. If another person wants you to satisfy his or her needs, and you do not wish to comply, then you have the right of denying satisfaction, but not the right of denying recognition. Rebukes, mockery, reprimands or remonstrations are not called for in such a situation. The answer could simply be this: 'I know you need me but I am sorry: I do not need you.' The person who asks for needs to be satisfied is not obliged to support the request by arguments, since all needs should be recognized; it will do simply to state them. However, the one who rejects the request has to give reasons, unless the rejection is motivated by the lack of a need or the existence of another need (for we know by now that we are not obliged to argue on behalf of needs).

To move from the level of everyday life to the public sphere (or to the sphere of institutions) does not modify the patterns described above. For example, every participant in a public debate should recognize the needs of everyone else (with the above proviso). However, it does not follow from this that decent persons participating in such a debate should also make a case for the simultaneous satisfaction of all the needs which claim satisfaction. The time and resources available, a lack of enthusiasm, and so much else, may make this impossible. Thus proportions have to be gauged and priorities determined.

The maxim enjoining the recognition, although not the satisfaction, of all needs also serves as a maxim of *authenticity* and of *truthfulness*. For it is both untruthful and inauthentic to deny the satisfaction of needs on such fraudulent grounds as the 'falsity', the 'incorrectness', the 'imaginary character', the 'immorality' of the needs awaiting satisfaction, in so far as the needs in question satisfy the moral proviso. It is rather with a spontaneous gesture that men and women who do not wish to satisfy each other's needs start to vilify those needs. Authentic persons 'rationalize' as little as they can. They eliminate ideology (strong rhetoric) from their vision of the world so far as they can. And the maxim helps us to remain authentic.

Maxim 3 All persons should be given equal recognition; all needs should be recognized: the first and the second imperative maxims prohibit the use of the 'according to' formula when it comes to gestures of recognition. The third maxim, by contrast, reintroduces this formula. Recognition is not due 'according to' anything. However, respect is, and it is due according to persons' moral merits and virtues.

Not only respect, but also acknowledgement, is due 'according to' something: namely, excellence. 'To each according to his or her excellence' is an idea of justice,[20] and not a first-order moral maxim.

Justice is a virtue of the decent person. To withhold acknowledgement of distinction and excellence is, however, not invariably unjust outright. Neither hatred nor resentment, jealousy or envy would prevent a person who is decent from acknowledging distinction and excellence where she or he sees it. However, a lack of good taste or good judgement in a particular sphere of excellence can belong to the shortcomings of decent persons as much to those of anyone else. But, in order to recognize goodness, no special taste, skill, understanding or professional judgement is needed on the part of the decent person. Every decent person is competent to be a judge in moral matters; every such person is able to distinguish goodness from excellence and *vice versa*.

Modernity was born in hero worship. While the pre-modern hero was the hero of his own ethos, the modern one is a solitary hero who stands outside, beyond or above any kind of ethos. Contingency permits one to choose oneself under the category of difference without choosing oneself simultaneously under the category of the universal. Persons who choose themselves under the category of difference can become great, and they may even have an immense historical significance; yet they remain, at the same time, morally ambiguous or outright dangerous and destructive. Whether the 'hero' is a political figure or an artistic 'genius' does not make much difference from this particular point of view. Given that contingency is our (modern) human condition, an outstanding example of the transformation of contingency into destiny attracts the attention, captures the mind and the emotions. The great freedom of contingency becomes manifest in the 'man of destiny', as Napoleon was called. There are very few 'men of destiny', but there are hero-worshippers aplenty who all see their own dreams come true in the deeds of their hero. To keep the dream alive, many a 'hero' will be manufactured from mediocre human material, and yet hero-worshippers will worship such mediocrities all the same. Since contingency is our common human condition, and since there are two major ways of transforming contingency into destiny, hero-worshippers will attribute *moral merit* to their heroes. They will regard excellence as if it were virtue, and they will mistake greatness of accomplishment for greatness of character. The good person is a person of character; the good person is a great personality. This greatness is real, for it cannot be faked; it is always authentic. The accomplished, the successful, the person who is great at something can also be a decent, good human being. And, if she or he is, that person should be respected according to his or her virtues and merits, but not according to his or her accomplishments, success or creations.

Maxim 3 does not prevent any good person from warmly acknowledging others, but it is concerned with respect and self-respect, not with acknowledgement. We enjoy our abilities at work; we are pleased with our success as well as with the acknowledgement we receive for our talent. But, if our self-respect is based on such acknowledgements, we shall not be decent. And, more often than not, we shall become outright fools.

Maxim 4   This maxim differs slightly in character from all previous ones in so far as it *links* morality to *general conduct*. Maxim 4 'belongs' to the theory of proper conduct rather than to moral philosophy. However, the decent person is not concerned with such speculative niceties. Dignity is the *modern version* of what used to be called 'honour'. Where modern and pre-modern ways of life coexist, we can still mention 'honour and dignity'. 'Honour' was a central category in the so-called 'shame' cultures, where all members of a community were under each other's gaze. If, in such a culture, one did something that one should have avoided, one was put to shame and *lost one's honour*. Conversely, honour could be restored by a long and strenuous effort. Persons who lived up to all the expectations of their own community (or at least seemed to live up to them) kept their honour. There were certain concrete acts which dishonoured the person at once, while certain others did not: they were just mild blemishes by the yardstick of the *code of honour*.

Since the modern person is contingent, she or he does not live according to a particular code of honour.[21] What was once honour has by now become dignity. There is no 'code of dignity' for morals which have become pluralistic; except in institutions, the norms are less like rules than they used to be; moral personalities are increasingly idiosyncratic ('Everyone is good in his or her own way'). Dignity is more deeply rooted in individual conscience than honour ever was; yet it is still not a merely internal affair. One keeps one's dignity in so far as one *deserves* respect and has self-respect. One keeps one's own dignity if one acts in such a way as to deserve the respect of others and of oneself. Sometimes people deserve respect but do not get it. The decent person should respect others according to their virtues and merits (and according to nothing else). If the decent person were completely solitary, she or he would still deserve respect, although the respect in question could not be the respect of others, only self-respect. Self-respect is not complacency, not a form of constant moral indignation, and does not go with self-pity. Self-respect is *strength*; a person of dignity is in no need of complacency, self-pity or moral indignation – all symptoms of moral weakness – if not respected.

Once again: keeping our own dignity has nothing to do with being permanently severe and sanctimonious, with placing ourselves on a self-erected pedestal. Irony and wit, humour and playfulness, self-abandon and self-surrender may easily go with dignity. Certain attitudes and practices, however, do not go with dignity, even if they are not outright immoral. Constant complaining about 'human nature' and one's own fate, narcissistic self-exposure, complacent boastfulness, a penchant for losing one's composure, a preference for shouting matches, consistently faulty judgement of character – in sum, all those things that make one the natural object of ridicule – are detrimental to human dignity.

The three prohibitive and the four imperative maxims discussed above were found by decent persons who tried to solve moral conflicts arising in their lives. I have not invented any of them; I have only reformulated some of them, frequently following in Kant's footsteps in an un-Kantian manner. I do not pretend to have presented the full catalogue of first-order maxims, although I have good reasons to believe that these alone offer reliable guidance to men and women who need to make decisions in hard moral cases.

In addition, one could formulate a great number of *second-order maxims*. Second-order maxims are *meta-norms*, exactly like first-order maxims; they are also *universal* and *general*, although with one restriction. Whereas first-order maxims need not be tested (for they test all other norms), second-order maxims need to be checked by first-order ones. No norm that contradicts first-order maxims should be chosen – this general prohibition includes second-order maxims as well.

Maxims of the second order cannot be listed. I do not accept the Kantian proposal that a meta-norm qualifies as a moral maxim if the non-observance of that norm includes logical contradiction. One can choose as the maxim of one's action 'Help everyone who is in need' and wish that all those who are in need would be helped. But there is absolutely no logical contradiction, nor is there any moral blunder involved, if someone refuses to act under the guidance of that particular maxim, but rather acts under the guidance of the alternative maxim 'Help everyone who deserves help' (for our person wants everyone who deserves help to be helped). There is no contradiction between one person choosing 'maxim a' and wishing that everyone would act according to that, and another choosing 'maxim b' and wishing that everyone would follow that maxim. Both of them can be decent persons. The maxims are different, but so are the forms of life and decent persons themselves.

Indeed, and this is the Kantian aspect of the proposition, no one should act under the guidance of a supreme (meta-) norm unless she or he thinks that it would be good if everyone were guided by it. Such supreme norms verify whole sets of norms. The concrete norms we choose or observe must not contradict the supreme norms (meta-norms, maxims). Decent persons 'find' their supreme (meta-) norms via intellectual intuition.

There is only one limit set to our intellectual intuition. We cannot choose supreme (meta-) norms for our actions (and for the purpose of testing and comparing normative systems) which contradict first-order maxims. This is why the maxims which we arrive at via intellectual intuition are here termed 'maxims of the second order'. For example, we cannot choose 'self-sacrifice' as a universal maxim, nor the celebrated 'turn the other cheek'. These are supererogatory acts. But what is supererogatory cannot, by definition, be generalized or universalized, nor can we wish that it should be. The maxim of 'self-sacrifice' collides with (at least) the second imperative first-order maxim ('Recognize all human needs'). Another well-known maxim, 'My country, right or wrong', would not withstand the test of first-order maxims either.

Thus, finally, I have not abandoned the Kantian criterion of non-contradiction, only shifted it to another level. There is still something to check second-order maxims with. Yet there is nothing to check first-order maxims with. I recommend the acceptance of the first-order maxims with a *gesture*.

Decent persons who have chosen themselves existentially under the category of the universal have to find out how to become what they are: good persons. We have followed them in their search for moral orientation in daily life, personal relations and attachments. We have followed them in their attempts to make sense of norms concerning giving–receiving and reciprocating. We have seen how they find out which kind of virtues are relevant to, precisely, them and their life, and what kind of bad character traits they avoid and how. We have entered with them the institutions of the modern world, and figured out how they can remain decent within such institutions while still remaining decent as whole persons. By that point we had left the daily world behind, only to return to it in a more complex setting. For in the maze of ethical collisions, decent persons need more universal, even meta-, norms, to do the right thing. They need meta-norms which can serve them as universal yardsticks, applicable both within institutions and outside them – in everyday life, in politics, in social conflicts alike. And, by virtue of the fact that they are decent persons, they find the moral guidance that they need – by doing the right thing and by trying, not always successfully, to avoid doing the wrong thing. From now on we shall accompany them in real-life situations, and see how they act, behave and feel when things go smoothly *and* when the chips are down.

3

The Concerned Person, the Good Citizen, the Care of the World

The universal orientative principles guide decent persons in their daily lives. These persons care about human beings. They do no harm to any human being on purpose. They have a proper regard for other persons' vulnerability, autonomy, morality and suffering. Thus they care for those whom they know, those whom they meet, those with whom they live. But can they care for those whom they do not even know? Can they adopt a decent attitude towards superficial acquaintances and strangers? The concrete principles offer very little guidance on this, as most of them work on the assumption that there is a direct link between the decent person's actions and attitudes on the one hand, and another person's well-being, peace of mind, freedom, and so on, on the other. For example, principle 2 (e) in the list in chapter 2 suggests that one should help others achieve greater autonomy. Yet the principle is qualified by a number of sub-principles which are of relevance in face-to-face situations alone. Sub-principle 4 (b) (ii) suggests that one should offer a proper part of one's time, money and energy for the alleviation of remediable suffering. But it does not specify whether those whose suffering one should seek to alleviate are limited to persons one knows, or include also persons whom one does not know.

As I formulated the principles, I can blame no one but myself if they turned out vague, tentative, in some cases too meticulous, in others too unspecific. I have intentionally left them like this, so as not to hinder us in following the track of decent persons from everyday life to the sphere of institutions and on to the point where the formulation of universal maxims becomes a 'must'. Decent persons walk to and fro on this track; so do we who accompany them. In what follows I wish to find out how decent people care in their journeyings for those whom they do not know, how they act if they witness people suffering from social and political ills. The subject we follow and attempt to understand is the decent person as the *concerned person*.

Aristotle distinguished the good man from the good citizen. The good man shines in all virtues, while the good citizen participates in the business of the state; he is a paragon of the constitution of his city. If the constitution of the city is imperfect, the good man will not be the best citizen, while, if the constitution is perfect, the best men will also become the best citizens. There is also a modern version of the ancient story.[1] The good person and the good citizen are not identical; they would not become identical under the most just of all constitutions either. Given the plurality of contemporary ways of life, persons can be good *in their own ways*. However, citizens should share certain virtues, and, in so far as they do, they can become *equally* good citizens. A good person need not be a good citizen, and, conversely, a good citizen need not also be a good person, for she or he need not practise a single additional virtue above and beyond the shared (civic) virtues. There is, however, a certain dimension of modern life which remains unaffected by the modernized and modified version of the Aristotelian story. What I have in mind is awareness of the contingent character of our world and our institutions.

The contingency awareness of a person springs from awareness of having been 'thrown into' a world where no paths through life are pre-set for the newcomer. Contingency implies something more and other than the mere accident of birth. Each birth is accidental in so far as no genetic code predestines a child to be born into a particular world at a particular time. The accident of birth is thus an ontological datum, an empirical human universal. Contingency is an accident and its sublation (*Aufhebung*) at the same time. This accident is twofold, for not only is my being born into such-and-such a world an accident, but my whole being becomes a mere possibility (a bundle of practically unlimited possibilities) and thus indeterminate. Yet it is precisely as a result of the latter aspect that modern men and women become contingent and simultaneously aware of their contingency (the two aspects coincide). As a result, they discover the empirical universality of the accident of birth.[2] Contingency sublates (*aufhebt*) the accident of birth in the following fashion. We are born by accident since we could have been born into any society, under the jurisdiction of any given norm, at any historical time. However, contingency becomes our lot only and exclusively in the modern world. We could not have been born as contingent persons other than in modern times. Contingency awareness is also *historical consciousness*. It is at the same time awareness of historicity and the experience of the historical character of that historicity.[3]

It is almost preposterous to mention the contingent character of our age, world and institutions in such a light-hearted fashion. It is, after all, the modern age which has invented the great narratives of our own (historical) determination and self-determination. We are the ones who have learned that the World Spirit has developed toward its self-fulfilment precisely in our modern age. We have also learned that the forces of production and the relations of production have (progressively) developed throughout history to arrive at the point where all human needs can be satisfied in full, and another stage of development, the real history of humankind, can begin to run its course. However, had not people of modern times experienced the contingency of their world and their institutions, they certainly would not have invented such strong and all-encompassing narratives of our own historical determination. What has happened at the level of macro-narrative has also happened at the level of micro-narrative (macrocosm and microcosm are always interlocked). It was his awareness of our own personal and dual contingency that triggered Freud's version of a strongly deterministic narrative of our psyche, person and personhood. The social sciences, too, have done their best to provide modern men and women with facts and related theories in order to alleviate the anxiety which results from consciousness of contingency. More recently, this tinkering with the contingency of our world and personality has turned shy and apologetic. Like a terrified man running for his life who suddenly turns round to face his assailant, modern men and women now turn round to face their true historical condition after attempting to rid themselves of their contingency awareness. Contingency fills us with anxiety only as long as we fail to meet the challenge and continue tinkering with our contingent existence via narratives of determination. If we have the resolve to regard our world as contingent, we can at least begin to comprehend the world not just as a chain of necessity but also as a bundle of possibilities.

Once the world is regarded as contingent, it becomes pregnant with possibilities, open-ended, bereft of an in-built telos and indeterminate. A contingent world can even be considered one of unlimited possibilities, just as a contingent person is a person of unlimited possibilities. It goes without saying that the term 'unlimited possibilities' does not stand for 'everything is possible', either in the case of the contingent world or in that of the contingent person. Several things are utterly impossible so long as we think in terms of immanence and exclude miracles and redemption. Furthermore, neither an 'anthropological revolution' nor an abundance capable of satisfying all needs seems to be part of our real possibilities. In addition, contingency should not be understood as a 'lack' of determinations. Just as several determinations can exist in a person's life without this life being 'determined', so can determinations exist in social life without the course of the world being fully determined by them. We can do the same thing with determinations in the broader world as we do with our own determinations: we can *choose* them. In choosing ourselves, the prevailing formula reads roughly like this: 'I choose myself as a child born here, at this particular time, into this particular family, with these particular talents. . . . I choose all these determinants, *and, as such*, with all my determinants, I shall become this particular person [or: a decent person].' We can choose certain determinations of our world with the same gesture. This is what we do practically all the time without conceptualizing what we are doing in existentialist terms. We frequently state, 'These are the hard facts of our world; such-and-such features are inherent in its history.' Let us then *choose* the history of our world, all the 'hard facts' and limitations, which are, exactly as they are, vehicles and harbingers of unlimited possibilities. Let us choose them and make this world a better place to live in. This manner of thought does not imply voluntarism, nor does the existential choice. Turning round and facing our contingency is not voluntarism: rather, it reverses determinations and transforms them into our *practical* freedom. Despite some superficial similarities with the Hegelian–Engelsian identification of freedom with the 'recognition of necessity', my thesis has basically nothing in common with this rightly controversial piece of theoretical heritage. The thesis that freedom is identical with the 'recognition of necessity' makes sense only if contingency is either eliminated from human history or conceived of as a mere appearance which serves as a mediator for the actualization of necessity. 'Necessity', which is supposed to be recognized and thus become known, is in fact revealed as the historical telos. Freedom is thus transformed into an act of contemplation (of grasping what has already been destined). Should the contemplative act guide action, action itself becomes either pragmatic or ideological in character.

Just the contrary happens in my model. We choose the determinations of our world, and thus we must be as familiar with them as we can. It is this choice that makes us free to turn towards the present, as well as the future, in order to make something come true which has been hidden as one possibility among many within the conditions of our life and actions. Knowledge is merely one condition of choice (or, rather, one aspect of the choice); yet the choice itself is not completely rational. (My only reason to choose precisely the world in which I live is that I happen to live in precisely this world.) This not completely rational aspect makes the choice predominantly *practical*: I choose the world in which *I live* since I can *act* only in a world in which I *live*. My freedom is my gesture of 'turning round', of accepting the challenge of contingency with the gesture 'I make the best of my contingency, my life, in contributing to the actualization of such-and-such a possibility and not others.' Freedom, then, is pre-eminently practical. It is *praxis*.

I would add, in order to avoid misunderstandings, that the choice of our world is *not* an existential choice. I can choose myself *absolutely*, for there is no other party to my choice, even if another party is constantly present in the 'before' and 'after' of an existential choice. In choosing my own determinations I decide that a person *as I am* will become *what I am*. When I choose my world *as it is*, I commit myself to certain possibilites of that world and reject others. However, for a number of reasons, a choice of this kind cannot be absolute. Knowledge of the world has something in common with self-knowledge: both are knowledge of a kind, and as such approximative, providing insufficient grounds for a choice. However, knowing myself is different from knowing my world; 'approximation' is too vague a category to put such a complex issue into proper perspective. Paying attention to the opinions of our neighbours will not induce us to comprehend certain determinants of our social world. Knowledge, above and beyond our everyday life world, must also be collected, and critical reflection practised. Introspection is no great help in this matter either. In addition, on my own I cannot make my choice good, as I certainly can in an existential choice (in choosing myself).

All this is perfectly obvious and I could further illuminate the assertion that the choice of our (contingent) world is not tantamount to an existential choice despite similarities between them. Similarity stems from the circumstance that the choice of a contingent world is shaped by the existential choice. The person who has chosen himself or herself, transforms his or her contingency into destiny. Choosing ourselves is choosing our determinations, the contingent person being one 'thrown into' a contingent world; thus the choice of a contingent world accompanies the choice of ourselves as contingent persons.

The choice of a contingent world is therefore inherent in the gesture of self-choice. We choose our contingent world because we choose to transform our contingency into our destiny and not because we choose to transform the world. However, it is an entirely different proposition to be ready to choose the world of our contingency *not* as the condition of our own lives, but as that of the lives of others, irrespective of whether or not those others have chosen themselves existentially, whether or not we know them, whether or not we witness their suffering and joy, whether or not they will ever know about us.

Contingent persons who have chosen themselves, and have thus transformed their contingency into their destiny, have already chosen the contingent world as the condition of their existential choice. The existential choice is thus the precondition of the choice of the world as contingent.

The attentive reader may have noticed that in the course of this discussion I have been discussing 'existential choice' in general, and not existential choice under the category of the universal. This is not an accident. The choice of the contingent world goes with each and every existential choice. In choosing themselves under the category of difference, men and women transform their contingency into their destiny and it is in this way that they choose the contingent world, at least indirectly.

A preliminary conclusion of considerable interest for decent persons, my addressees, can be drawn from all this. Decent persons who have chosen themselves under the category of the universal have chosen the contingent world indirectly just like anyone who has made any other kind of existential choice. They can make the choice explicit by choosing the contingent world directly through commitment. In other words, they can choose to make a move which can be and is certainly made also by men and women who have chosen themselves under the category of difference. The latter choice does not make anyone decent; some of those making that choice are unscrupulous, even outright indecent, persons. As a result, decent persons who make the second move, choosing the contingent world directly, must be aware of certain difficulties stemming therefrom. Not only do they have to communicate and interact with unscrupulous and outright indecent people, as is usual in everyday life, but they must also make common cause with them, act together with them, share concerns, joys and sorrows with them. Decent persons must make up their minds concerning such alliances and, irrespective of their decision for or against, they must face the consequences.

Decent persons cannot and will not, of course, intentionally violate universal maxims. Before becoming engaged in an action, entering into an institution, they will reflect upon the principles, norms and rules they are supposed to follow and see whether or not those norms contradict universal maxims. It is exactly because they need those maxims that modern men and women discover and forge them in the first place. Yet the observance of universal maxims does not necessarily prevent decent men and women from acting in concert with indecent and unscrupulous people. For example, one of the universal maxims suggests that a person should not be a member of an institution whose rules in principle entail using other persons as mere means. One is free to join such institutions if one can observe the rules without actually using others as mere means, while remaining keenly aware that one's comrades-in-arms, equally intent on changing the social arrangements, do use others as means. When decent persons make common cause with scoundrels, universal maxims can sometimes remain conspicuously silent.

Contingency awareness is past-, present- and future-oriented. It suggests that everything that has happened could have happened otherwise; that everything that is could be otherwise: and that in the future all sorts of things may happen. The possibilities are practically unlimited. Contingency awareness is also accompanied by an awareness that possibilities can be transformed into destinies. Although everything that is could have happened otherwise, *it is more than mere chance* that it has happened in (roughly) the way it has happened or that everything is (roughly) the way it is. It is more than mere chance, *for there are people who have transformed certain possibilities into realities* while other people have failed to do so. Missed possibilities give rise to new ones, and it is, again, contingent persons who actualize some or other of them. Marx's dictum that men make their own history under pre-given circumstances (where, let me add, those circumstances are nothing but a bundle of possibilities) sums up the modern contingency awareness. That the author of this dictum sought shelter in the concept of a historical telos, a historical agent of necessity and the idea of (necessary) progression, instead of turning round and looking our contingency in the face, is another story. For, once contingency is faced, the conclusion is ready to hand: *there is no 'ruse of reason' but the ruse of our own reason.*

Modern men and women are contingent irrespective of whether they are completely, more or less, or not at all decent. Every time they come across something that they disapprove of, consider unjust or improper, they are confident that this particular thing could be otherwise.[4] They often regard institutions, patterns of distribution and much else as unjust precisely because they hold the firm belief that things could take a different direction. The wrongs and ills of the world are perceived by human beings as contingent occurrences and, in so far as they are explained by them, they are explained as such. We normally regard the concrete sufferings and evils of our world as avoidable in so far as we explain sufferings and evils by social *causes*. This is not necessarily the case when it comes to formulating general world-views or philosophies. However, this is certainly the case at the level of everyday reflection. Even the spreading of diseases is often attributed to social injustice, neglect, insufficient expenditure on health care, or unruly social practices. Modern redemptive para-digms[5] drive contingency awareness to an extreme point by prophesy-ing the reduction, even the abolition, of suffering, injustice and evil of all kinds through human action, on the grounds that they all stem from social causes alone.

One need not be a particularly decent person to be sensitive to the ills of world. Decent persons indeed feel empathy; however, their predominant emotional state of mind is one of concern rather than one of compassion (though it does not exclude the feeling of com-passion). Concern is the readiness to comprehend the nature of those social arrangements and institutions which one suspects of being the source(s) of other persons' undeserved misfortune. It is also the readiness to do something about these 'social causes'. The spectrum of concern can be very wide. One can be concerned about urban conditions, immigration laws, unjust regulations in one's office, the state of education in the village school, famine in a region of Africa, civil-right violations all over the world – and be concerned about several such issues simultaneously. Being concerned includes the readiness 'to do something about it'. This is more than, and should be distinguished from, lamenting a state of affairs and feeling com-passion for those affected, or from forming a proper judgement on the matters of concern. 'Being concerned' implies getting involved and rendering active help to those in need. Since there is a limit to the number of issues that one can be actively concerned about, the decent person has to decide how many and which kinds of issues should engage his or her concern. Here phronesis is the umpire.

At the beginning of this chapter I referred back to the catalogue of orientative moral principles in chapter 2. I remarked that the cata-logue does not specify whether certain principles apply only to everyday life and our dealings with people we know, or whether they should be interpreted within a broader framework. The principles I referred back to are (1) 'Help others achieve greater autonomy' [2 (e)], (2)] 'Moral judgement should be passed irrespective of others' lack of concern or outright hostility, and irrespective of the conse-quences' [3 (c) (iv)]; and (3) 'Offer a proper part of your time, money and energy for the alleviation of remediable suffering' [4 (b) (ii)]. At this stage in the discussion of the decent person as the *concerned* person, it should be assumed that the principles of moral orientation, which are in themselves interpretable both in a narrower and in a broader framework, need to be interpreted here in a broader framework. A concerned person is oriented by these moral principles whenever she or he engages in alleviating suffering, curing social ills and eliminating injustice. The third principle mentioned specifies the kinds of contribution a concerned person can make. This is why it presents us with no further problems. However, the first two first principles are problematic.

It has been pointed out that the choice of a contingent world is inherent in the existential choice as such, and, further, that all those who have chosen themselves can make a second move to choose the contingent world directly. A decent person who has made the second move is a 'concerned person'. However, as already indicated, it is not the privilege of the decent person to be concerned. All people who have chosen to destine themselves to carry out one or another social project can be concerned. In addition, active participation in social or political action of any kind is not restricted to concerned persons: *interested* persons may also participate. Persons are interested in alleviating suffering if they are the ones who suffer, who are the victims of (institutional) injustice. Concerned people can be interested as well, for they challenge injustices committed against themselves to the same extent as they challenge injustices committed against others. However, not all interested people are concerned, and it stands to reason why. Adamant as they may be in their own case, interested persons may remain indifferent towards the grievances of others. It is for guidance in their relation both to other concerned actors and to interested persons that decent persons turn to the two orientative moral principles that we are considering here.

One of those principles says that we should pass moral judgements in all matters of moral relevance irrespective of the lack of concern, or outright hostility, of others. If extended beyond the scope of everyday life, this principle will offer good guidance precisely in those matters which perplex decent persons at this point. Decent persons, as concerned persons, can be concerned about the same thing as those who are not decent or are unabashedly indecent. Since pragmatic reasons often compel decent persons to make common cause with indecent persons[6] – that is, to act together with them – and since the common cause yields a common perception of justice and injustice, decent persons must here accept the result of indecent persons' action as being precisely the result for which they too were striving. Yet no utilitarian morality follows from this consideration. For, as soon as the persons who share a cause with the decent persons behave indecently, and make their base, egoistic, self-righteous motivation explicit, the decent persons, their former allies, will preserve their integrity by passing moral judgements. Moral judgments can be personal or institutional (passed either on the 'hero' or on 'hero worship'); but they are not private: they are made publicly.

In this context, 'private judgement' is tantamount to the judgement someone passes on another person as a whole. I use the notion 'private judgement' for the judgement that our decent person passes (of total or qualified disapproval) face to face. Of course, she or he might make discretionary exceptions under the guidance of phronesis (proper judgement). Moral disapproval should be publicized only if there are *moral* reasons for making it public. Two factors should here be taken into consideration: the *circle of people* in which moral disapproval should be publicized; and the *kinds of behaviour* that merit public moral disapproval. Moral disapproval needs to be publicized in the circle of those whose autonomy of action and judgement may be impeded owing to their ignorance of the moral character of the person in question. Further, the kinds of behaviour that should be publicized in such a case are those indecent attitudes, character traits and actions which have bearing upon the social, institutional or political performance of the person in question. As a result, decent persons who have made common cause with not entirely decent, or outright indecent, people are compelled to *disapprove publicly* of their indecent character traits or actions if, and only if, those character traits and actions have a bearing on their *public performance*. Making one's disapproval public when it has only private ramifications is a sign of either fundamentalism or self-righteousness, while not making one's disapproval public when there is sufficient reason for such action is sign of opportunism or cowardice. This circumstance is implied in the qualification of the orientative principle advising us that moral judgement is necessary even in the face of the lack of concern, or the outright hostility, of others.

I have also indicated that decent persons as concerned persons may make common cause with interested individuals. In this regard, our decent person relies upon the principle that one should help others achieve greater autonomy. Conflicts between those who have chosen themselves under the category of the universal and those who have chosen themselves under the category of difference surface at this point in their strongest form. Unless they have chosen themselves *also* under the category of the universal, those who have chosen themselves under the category of difference believe that they are destined to be great at something and strive to become what they are: great in their chosen field. As self-appointed 'men of destiny', they would not necessarily use others as mere means on purpose (they might have the delusion of acting on their behalf). But they would very rarely ask those whose fate they were shaping whether they were happy to have their fate shaped in that way. 'Men of destiny' are a new, modern breed, who are free from tradition, convention, normative limitation and all external authorities, God included.[7] Equally new are the persons who have chosen themselves under the category of the universal. Since, however, they have chosen themselves under this category, they constantly return to the relationship of symmetric reciprocity with their fellow creatures. Democracy is the only public institution which suits a person of this kind. For it is only within the democratic institutional framework that ties of symmetric reciprocity can be established and reproduced in the public realm.

After this long detour I shall return for the last time to the Aristotelian distinction between the good man and the good citizen, as well as to all streamlined versions of this distinction. The Aristotelian categories need more than merely to be reinterpreted: they need to be supplemented.

We have already learned who a concerned person is and what she or he does. The concerned person cannot be identified with either the 'good person' or the 'good citizen'. The reason for this lack of equivalence is that, while decent persons normally become concerned persons, indecent persons can also be concerned. A concerned person can become a good citizen ('good citizen' by definition implies concern), but a concerned person does not necessarily have to become a good citizen. (And this applies also to countries with a democratic order where the term 'citizen' makes sense.) It is the complex network of the social and the political, the civil society and the state, where all aspects or issues can be combined with all others, that provides the concerned person with room for manoeuvre, irrespective of whether or not she or he is a good person or a good citizen. However, in one respect, and in this respect alone, I associate concerned persons with good citizens rather than with good persons. The virtues and vices most characteristic of concerned persons are similar to civic virtues and vices. Wherever concerned persons also become citizens, their virtues are those of good, and their vices are those of bad, citizens.

II

The attempt to outline a modern moral philosophy, the particular venture I am engaged in, is based on the assumption that a contingent person has the authority to address all other contingent persons because she or he is like them. Modern moral philosophy does not claim the authority to advise non-contingent persons whose destination (social telos) has been pre-set, and who ought to make their choices within this predetermined framework. It limits its scope to contingent persons born without an imputed telos of this kind. Contingency *versus* non-contingency is not a matter of belief – of, for example, whether or not one believes in God; rather it is a matter of consciousness (that of the awareness of 'being destined' *versus* that of being born with open possibilities). A moral philosophy which addresses only the modern (contingent) person cannot claim universal validity, nor can it proudly state to have discovered the eternal and immutable moral law. However, it must make one particular claim: that it has been formulated to address *all* contingent persons so that all contingent persons can turn to such a philosophy when they want to determine what is the right course of action in a given situation. This claim is based on the assumption that a modern moral philosophy follows the life path of the contingent persons who have chosen a decent way of life, and that it sums up their concerns, life experiences and typical decisions. Moral philosophers themselves are persons who have been advised by decent men and women, who have asked what is the right thing for them to do. Thus they are scribes, not authors, people who commit to paper the accumulated moral wisdom and nothing else.

Modern moral philosophy addresses all contingent persons in so far as all of them, particularly the ones who have chosen to be decent, can turn to it in any life situation. So far it has seemed reasonable to abstract from the concrete character of the contingent world into which contingent persons are thrown. It has sufficed to stress that contingent persons relate to their world (implicitly or explicitly) as to a contingent one, provided that they choose themselves existentially. In a somewhat more lax formulation even the latter proviso can be dispensed with. For here too there is a 'more' and a 'less' in everything, and one could confidently state that people who have begun to reflect upon their own situation, and on the situation of their world, will see themselves, and their own world, as 'lightly' contingent. Incidentally, they will make efforts to patch up this contingency through strong deterministic narratives (and this operation is the only accurate rendering of the term 'false consciousness'). There are also degrees of reflection: some people never reflect, some do but let others choose for them, while others (the majority) sometimes reflect and choose for themselves, and sometimes abandon themselves to others.

As soon as the (contingent) social–political arrangement is more than implicitly chosen, in so far as it becomes the decent person's direct concern – that is, at the point where the discussion of the *concerned* person begins – the following question arises: when it comes to the moral issues of socio-political engagement, can we address all contingent persons in all life situations in one breath? One would assume that the general attitude of choosing a contingent world is identical for all good (concerned) contingent persons everywhere in the world. One chooses precisely the world that one dwells in, in so far as one chooses to accept that it is precisely in this world that one becomes decent, that it is precisely this world that one is concerned with, that it is precisely the wrongs, ills, grievances and injustices of this world that should be straightened out, cured, eliminated or abolished. However, while the ontological structure of the choice may be invariable, the moral effort required by the choice is certainly a variable, and, moreover, one which cannot be rendered in quantitative terms.

Modern moral philosophy needs to address all contingent persons. Yet it has arrived at an impasse, for at this point there seems to be a serious incongruence between the ontological structure and the moral effort required by that structure. In a more charitable rendering, several different kinds of moral attitude are *equally* (to the same extent) *congruent* with the common ontological structure (contingent person – contingent world, and both to be chosen). And it is only the decent person in action who can verify or falsify the truth claim of this charitable formulation. If it could be proved that whatever has so far been stated of decent persons in a contingent world qualifies them to do the right thing if public commitment (of any kind) so dictates, we would have corroborated the charitable formulation. For we would have proved that different kinds of moral attitude are equally (to the same extent) congruent with the ontological structure of the modern world. Everyday wisdom and life experience alike speak on behalf of this statement. Put bluntly, a decent person is supposed to face social and political tribulations in a decent way, whatever they are. The person from whom one can expect precisely this is the decent person; and precisely this is what we can expect from the decent person. For the decent person, the moral variable is congruent with the ontological invariable. Only those who have chosen themselves under the category of the universal and have transformed their contingency into their own destiny in becoming what they are (decent persons), and who have explicitly chosen the contingent world as one given into one's care in the single act of choosing oneself, are worthy of our complete confidence. They, and only they, can be credited with the moral intelligence, intuition and phronesis – all the necessary qualifications – to do the right things in civic engagements in all possible (modern) circumstances. Complete *confidence* and *trust* are not devalidated by the fact, often mentioned here, that even decent persons can commit serious moral errors. For trust and confidence are needed in the absence of absolute certitude.

The scribe, the moral philosopher, commits to paper what has been dictated by others. And, when it comes to the morality of public commitment, many equally decent persons will tell different stories. This moral philosopher in her capacity as scribe does not have sufficient space to commit to paper all these stories, nor can she be sure that the addressee will have the patience to read them. So they will be summarized, and illustrated by two models. Both will be abstract (as models normally are) and skimpy. In addition, they will be sketched in the knowledge that, as a rule, people live and act in a sort of mixture of the two models. There is no democracy completely lacking in authoritarian and dictatorial institutions, and versions of modern totalitarianism in which all avenues of democratic action have been completely eliminated prove short-lived (measured, of course, by world-historical standards, not the lifespan of their victims). In what follows, only totalitarianism and liberal democracy will be discussed, because both are typically modern inventions, and it can be said of both that they respond to the contingency of the person. Soviet-type society is completely functional, even more so than the Western social structure, because it does not, generally speaking, provide space and occasion for transfunctional institutions and actions, while Western society does. Liberal democracies are prepared to face contingency, whereas totalitarian societies, having an equal amount of contingency awareness, develop and promote the false consciousness of determination narratives (be they 'historical' or 'biological', i.e. racist, in nature). This contrast is my sufficient reason for choosing the two 'pure' models.

The hero of decency

Hegel dismissed morality (*Moralität*) as mere subjectivity. In his presentation, morality had been a pathbreaker in the development of world history, a force which had failed constantly but had contributed to the emergence of modernity. In the modern world, however, morality (moral subjectivity) becomes again the mere subjective aspect of an all-embracing general ethos, of *Sittlichkeit*. Yet this time *Sittlichkeit* realizes (encompasses) the freedom of all at the level of the objective spirit. This narrative can be of some assistance to decent persons in democratic societies, but its message is entirely misplaced in totalitarian societies. 'Reconciliation with reality', in the sense of reconciliation with the state of the objective spirit, where this includes concentration camps and gas chambers, is precisely what decent persons must not accept. The leading institutions of totalitarian states (societies) embody an extremely rigid and strong kind of ethos, one which *excludes autonomy*. Accepting an ethos of this kind in full is tantamount to resigning one's own moral autonomy and to resigning the existential choice itself (for the choice of ourselves as good persons is at the same time the choice of ourselves as autonomous persons). In consequence, decent persons cannot accept a totalitarian ethos as a *Sittlichkeit* to which they subjectively relate[8] or which they can 'internalize'. Decent persons must, under such conditions, stick to their own subjectivity (morality) and take counsel with their own mind, soul and moral conscience. For the moment they pay attention to the 'advice' of the totalitarian ethos, they are lost and become (morally) non-persons. The earlier statement that the decent person is decent for his or her own sake, applies here as well. This is why the *attitude of sheer morality*, dismissed by Hegel, is *resurrected* as the normative attitude of the decent person in a totalitarian world. If persons in such a predicament ask the question 'What is the right thing for me to do?', the only answer is 'Listen to your own conscience, and to it alone.'

Obviously, such a principle cannot be generalized. Under no other circumstances would modern persons advise one another to listen to their conscience alone, particularly in matters of common or public concern. Rather, they would recommend that one should listen to the opinions of others, take account of traditions, circumstances and much else, and only after having clarified and corrected one's opinions, and come close to the point of making the final decision, to consult one's own conscience. Under totalitarian conditions, however, the principle of 'wide-range consultation' would, in all likelihood, lead to the internalization of false rationalizations, all conducive to serious moral blunders or even to something graver. It is then that one should heed the maxim 'Listen to your own conscience, and to it alone.'

One can only listen to something that tells one something – so what has this celebrated conscience to tell us? This has been a perennial topic of philosophical rumination, and the conclusions reached have invariably been highly ambiguous. Since totalitarianism is a modern phenomenon *par excellence*, an offspring of modern rationalization and instrumental rationality, modernity *in toto* has often been blamed for it. If the charge is correct, then conscience, this sole antidote to the venom of totalitarianism, must have a pre-modern substrate. We have in fact been advised, by the advocates of the 'nihilism narrative', that the substrate of the antidote (conscience) is of religious extraction. It is simply a vestige of our education by a religious tradition, and it is this 'archaic' voice that advises us to resist evil when we meet it face to face. To my mind, the 'nihilism narrative' has overgeneralized a merely historical and particular phenomenon. For there is a certain kind of *entirely modern* (post-traditional) moral conscience that one can rely upon, irrespective of belief or the lack of it, and irrespective of whether one is committed to one particular tradition, faith, culture or philosophy or none at all.

Post-traditional conscience does not appear to us as being entirely void of content. In fact, the whole train of thought in chapter 2 focused on deciphering this particular content. There we followed the path of decent persons who have decided to become what they are and who search out principles, norms and maxims that they can rely on in this pursuit. Thus, if we ask what it is in modern (post-traditional) conscience that men and women in totalitarian societies can listen to and rely on, we know the answer in advance. People in such circumstances who rely upon their conscience alone take the standpoint of morality and pit their subjectivity against the ethos of the totalitarian machine. This morality is the distillation of the acts, the attitudes, the trials and errors, the life experiences of decent persons in the modern world. And there is always a *possible Sittlichkeit* adequate to this morality. More precisely, there is a variety of possible *Sittlichkeiten* adequate to this morality, with one exception: that of totalitarianism. In totalitarianism morality must remain subjective. Modern men and women choose the modern world as a contingent one. They are aware that whatever exists does not exist by necessity, for it could also not exist. Just that which they stand for in full autonomy is beyond contingency, for they are the ones who make it destiny. Hence, the mere subjectivity, the mere morality of resistance, of relying on our conscience alone, is far from being an objectless gesture. For the gesture is related to the *possibility* of an object, to a possibility which stands higher than the totalitarian actuality in so far as it is adequate to the subjectivity of the decent person.

The attitude of mere subjective morality is the right one in totalitarian situations and the wrong one (to a greater or lesser extent) in all other situations (in the modern world). This statement follows from the content of modern moral conscience as elaborated in chapter 2.

A fair view of the decent person's predicament under totalitarian conditions can be gained if one constantly bears in mind that the modern person's conscience contains the principles of moral orientation, the norms of reciprocity, the virtue norms, and the maxims of the first order. In totalitarianism, state and society (provided that the latter has been totalized by the former[9]) have the authority and the prerogative to make claims on persons' whole lives. They will not let you decide for yourself in any matter of importance. They will decide for you in matters of family life and family planning, of taste, culture and religion; dictate your values and virtues and their interpretations, your duties (without allotting corresponding rights), your talents, and almost everything else. How could you live up to the requirements of the most elementary principles of moral orientation, even within the most narrow circle of your family and friends, under constant pressure to abandon precisely those principles (concerning human suffering and vulnerability, and particularly autonomy)? The imperative 'Listen to your own conscience and to it alone' leaves one with almost no space for manoeuvre under such conditions. One should rather stick to the principles of elementary decency whatever the costs. Since decent, good and righteous persons, modern and pre-modern alike, observe moral norms regardless of consequences, the elementary moral principles of orientation must not be bypassed, regardless of consequences. Utilitarian considerations must not be introduced at this point. One has to listen to one's own conscience *alone*, which is what one fails to do every time one begins to amend principles under the influence of utilitarian considerations. Conscience requires one to observe those principles, but it does not require one to refrain from attempts to save one's life or freedom, even one's social position, provided that this can be achieved without infringing those principles. If the principles are not bypassed or violated, their application would allow for self-defence, and sometimes even leave room for utilitarian considerations. Knowledge and self-knowledge belong to the main conditions of the proper application of the orientative principles on each and every count. Although we shall go on to discuss the issue in detail, certain pertinent considerations need to be spelt out now.[10]

It is when one is relying on one's own conscience alone that wilful ignorance and self-deception are most likely to interfere with and distort one's perception of reality. Decent persons relying on their own conscience would not attribute a generative power to it. One does not rely on one's own conscience as the sole authority in moral matters,[11] because the content of conscience must be tested against the objective (intersubjective) moral yardsticks discussed in chapter 2. One can only use those yardsticks properly when one has a fairly correct view of what is going on around one, of the mechanisms of power and one's own place within them. One can marshal a fairly good degree of self-knowledge, yet still remain deceived or turn from one kind of self-deception to another. But having a good insight into the mechanisms of power is something a person cannot achieve without assistance. The decent person who wants to find out what is the right thing to do must therefore solicit all kinds of information concerning power mechanisms to make up for the limitations of his or her own experience. One must, in order to protect oneself from wilful ignorance and self-deception, heed the following advice: '*Gather information about the mechanisms of power from all available sources, separate the facts from their evaluation, and relate your own moral values to those facts.*' However, neither the principle requiring one to rely on one's own conscience alone nor this second one can be generalized.

Under totalitarian conditions, extreme morality is the proper means of protecting elementary decency. This, the most unfortunate of all worlds, needs heroes not for heroic deeds but to undertake the task of remaining decent. As a result, the distinction between the good and the concerned person disappears, not because good persons inevitably become concerned ones, but because goodness itself becomes an attitude of political relevance. The coalescence of three distinct attitudes – those of decency, concern and heroism – makes the category 'supererogation' obsolete. So far, our decent person has just been decent, neither a hero nor a saint, not even a person capable of extreme self-sacrifice. It has at the same time been assumed that there is a parallel and superior kind of goodness with its virtuosi, heroes and saints and supererogation *sensu stricto* (this being exceptional goodness, beyond the level required for decency). But if mere decency demands the sacrifice of profession, freedom, eventually of life itself, then mere decency becomes supererogatory.

In chapter 2, in discussing the fundamental virtues of the (modern) decent person, I briefly mentioned those kinds of vices that all men and women must shun. I further added that both virtues and vices are *character traits*: you cannot be a coward today and courageous tomorrow. Sudden changes of this kind suggest that you have not chosen yourself existentially as a decent person; rather you let others choose for you from time to time. At the beginning of this chapter I pointed out that a decent person will be decent under all possible (modern) circumstances: in other words, well prepared for all political and social eventualities. Those who change morally in response to changes of the political setting prove that they have not chosen themselves under the category of the *universal*. To paraphrase Aristotle, one can resemble a good person without being one. This is one of the reasons why a moral philosophy which concentrates on discussing ethics within the framework of a particular political setting is worthless precisely as a moral philosophy. Change the setting, and your moral philosophy will go down the drain. It would be absurd to work out a brand-new moral philosophy with every coup, revolt or military takeover, as one would have to, following the above recipe, in certain countries. Our constant is the same decent person who is decent amidst all circumstances. All features of the decent person which have been discussed so far, all orientative principles and norms, all the virtues to which decent persons are committed, all the maxims that they use as a crutch are *universal* in so far as they are valid for all modern persons who choose to be decent in everyday life as well as in functional institutions and in the public–political domain.

The *fundamental virtues* of decent persons are therefore the same in all circumstances. However, these virtues are practised in different ways in different circumstances. While the fundamental virtues are universal, certain others are not. Not all decent persons share the latter, but they do all share the former. In addition, the values that they do not all share can be practised in public (political) action or concern. But the distinction between private and public, social and political, individual and collective remains blurred wherever being merely decent needs supererogation and heroism. So far as the values common to all decent persons are concerned, they are not practised in the same ways under totalitarianism as in less threatening, more relaxed circumstances.

This is obviously true of courage. Totalitarianism is the state of the great terror.[12] Modern dictatorships of all hues and colours atomize society and spread general fear. Total control is the monstrous wish of all tyrannies, but it took the modern world to provide wish-fulfilment. Total control is possible under two conditions: one is a situation in which people can be totally controlled; the other is the situation in which the means of total control are available. In a not-yet-atomized, communal and organic society, the first condition cannot be met. Membership of a human group, particularly the family, stands higher than anything else, and genetic closeness is accompanied by trust and fidelity (also in public matters). So long as one can trust the members of one's own community, one cannot be subjected to total control. Controllers need informers in the most private niches of life, and this became possible only with the rise of modern technology. Furthermore, modern technology has provided the instruments of mass-intimidation, mass-execution and mass-indoctrination. Every non-democratic political institution begins to resemble totalitarian ones: those who control the means also control the persons.

Fear, as a human affect,[13] is innate and has a very strong motivational power. That is why, as a rule, it is 'socialized', kept in check, by other affects. In traditional societies it was the threat of *shame*, another affect, that stimulated bravery when it was required by the communal ethos. One controlled fear and behaved bravely rather than face the disapproval or contempt to which one would otherwise be subjected by the 'gaze' of the community. In a totalitarian state, where the communal ties have been dissolved, the shame factor serves the controllers: they are the 'eye' that watches you. One fears the *Führer*, the party, the military dictator while one seeks their approbation. What is the affect that induces one to overcome fear? It is shame all the same, but shame of a kind which merges with conscience: one looks in the mirror of the self and sees a person who ought to be put to shame by the community, which happens to be embodied by the self alone watching the mirror. In addition, there is the disgust we feel for ourselves at moments when we lose our self-esteem and self-approval.

Enormous courage is needed to preserve elementary decency when decency and supererogation have merged. One must be ashamed of, and disgusted by, behaving otherwise; one can remain decent only under the impact of such powerful motivations. Courage is an all-encompassing (non-intellectual) virtue in this setting, for it embraces almost all others. Take, for example, the norms of reciprocity, which one can normally live up to without being courageous. Lending money to someone as an act of reciprocity for former similar services, and visiting the family of one's gregarious neighbours are not matters of courage under normal circumstances. But they become acts of enormous bravery in totalitarian societies if the other is a Jew, a member of an alien class, or the 'enemy of the people'. Another example is the issue of the (restrictive) norms of truthfulness. According to one of the maxims set forth in this book, a person who does not trust any other human person cannot be decent. Moreover, this is a requirement which 'under normal circumstances' requires no particular courage. And yet in a totalitarian society it is a common feeling that no one can be trusted. People withhold trust not because they enjoy the dubious pleasures of incognito or because they are irresistibly repressed psychologically, but simply because they cannot tell who would turn informer under pressure, and therefore a mutual, all-pervasive fear reigns supreme. And yet one must trust at least one person completely and fully, for one cannot be decent without taking this risk. Nor can one remain decent without discussing common concerns of overriding importance at least in a small circle. Finally, one cannot be decent without subscribing to the truth of the proposition 'Decent persons exist.' Those who are decent should be trusted. But who are they? How can they be found? This is where enormous courage is needed. A decent person must take the risk of confiding in persons without first having absolute proof of their decency and reliability. Tragic mistakes are often made in these acts of daring. Yet it is better to risk tragic mistakes, even to make them, than to live completely without trust, confidence or openness of any kind. Without mobilizing an enormous reserve of courage on behalf of trust, a decent person in a totalitarian setting would tend to become self-righteous, bitter and misanthropic – as Kierkegaard put it, 'a man of closing reserve'.

If preserving mere decency requires enormous courage, what kind of courage is needed for acts of active resistance? Active resistance can be personal or collective. In a completely atomized society collective acts of resistance are normally excluded. Under such conditions, active resistance by the single individual is supererogatory beyond the 'normal' level of supererogation.

Active resistance of a single person requires *civic courage* under normal circumstances. Such acts sometimes have serious consequences (for example, loss of job, public humiliation, and the like). This is why they are acts of civic *courage*. Yet in such cases the stake is normally not one's life. However, under totalitarian conditions the active resistance or overt intervention of a single person implies, as a rule, the danger of violent death. Men and women who undertake such acts of courage know full well in advance that they put their lives at risk by their acts. Facing the danger of violent death is equally a *conditio sine qua non* of military valour. But it is normally a *collective* act, while men and women who display civic courage under totalitarian conditions are *lonely fighters*. They are atomized, they fight alone, they die alone, more often than not in total anonymity; even the compelling force of military valour, the threat of losing honour in front of others, is absent from their undertaking. The lonely fighters of active resistance under totalitarian circumstances have a task which is heavier than that of the professional soldier: like him, they run the risk of death, but they have neither the powerful motivation of collective action nor the prospect of reward. It is only when collective acts of resistance are initiated that such civic fighters have, like professional soldiers, a common cause to spur them on. Then they can march together and die together.

Decent persons may forgo active resistance whenever elementary decency is not endangered by refraining from it. They need to exercise good judgement in deciding whether this is the case. Utilitarian considerations can play a role here. For example, one can legitimately ask whether a particular act of bravery would help others, or whether it would be merely a private gesture, an outlet for inner tensions, a gesture of bravado, or the like.

Under totalitarian conditions, *refraining from certain kinds of action* can also sometimes demand enormous courage. Someone who during the Nazi years had stubbornly refused to greet others with a 'Heil Hitler' told me that this refusal needed more courage on her part than her participation in a secret political organization in the concentration camp where she eventually found herself. The more a society, not just the state, is totalized, the more will positive and negative courage overlap; the less totalized it is, the more separate they will become.

Refraining from certain actions is also a matter of *resisting temptation*. Temptations are different in kind and each kind will tempt different people. The following are a few typical traps that decent and indecent persons alike can fall into: the temptation to gain greater influence (in order to use it for good, one could rationalize it); the temptation to achieve a position in which one could support the eventual victims; the catchphrase 'If others did it, it would turn out worse.' The main source of self-delusion can be located in two justificatory arguments, both of which are of utilitarian provenance. The first goes, 'I would co-operate with the Devil himself if human lives could be saved.' The other is 'One can change these institutions only from within. Once I am within the institution, I will contribute to change, while those who remain outside in order to preserve their empty morality will be politically impotent and sterile.' The source of temptation for decent persons is that these are genuinely moral arguments. The dilemma of being, for example, 'God's spy in the SS', to use the phrase coined by Rolf Hochhuth, is serious indeed. The Hungarian Jew Kessler, who fraternized with high-ranking officials of the Gestapo and the SS, in fact saved more Jewish lives in Hungary than any resistance fighter, yet he was called 'the scum of the earth' by Hannah Arendt. Nor can it be denied, as a number of examples bear witness, that people who have decided to transform certain institutions from within sometimes do contribute to the alleviation of sufferings. But it is still safe to say that in the overwhelming majority of cases justificatory arguments remain, and must remain, empty rationalizations.

But it is not on these grounds that I am opposed to the foregoing line of argumentation. The justification is utilitarian in nature. Once utilitarian justification has been accepted as a *substitute* for justification through norms, principles of moral orientation and maxims, one is bound to subscribe to a utilitarian moral philosophy in full. This whole book is written in the conviction that a utilitarian moral philosophy is singularly unfit to provide general guidelines for decent persons who pose the question 'What is the right thing for me to do?' And it is on the basis of my conviction that I state that the safest way to resist temptation is to figure out whether or not participation in an action or institution will allow you to live, think and behave in accordance with the principles, norms and maxims to which you otherwise subscribe. If they do, utilitarian considerations could play a secondary role in your decision. If they don't, you must resist temptation. This moral rigidity is all the more warranted since decent persons too are prone to succumb to moral rationalizations. It is indeed difficult to tell moral reasons from moral rationalizations in the case of utilitarian arguments, notwithstanding sincere efforts to keep them apart. Even if we can never 'play it safe' in moral arguments, some avenues better protect the person from committing fatal mistakes than others do.

Refraining from doing something is, furthermore, tantamount to *resisting threats*. No decent person is compelled (by his or her own decency) to speak completely openly under mortal threat. In such an extremity, the norm of (explicit) sincerity is suspended, as is that of (overt) truthfulness. Yet under no duress must a person who wants to remain decent either denounce others or make an oath, or statement, of allegiance to an institution, power or apparatus whose function is torturing other human beings. If the threat becomes less severe or less imminent, or both, resistance to threats should also become more outspoken. Finally, if resistance to threats becomes again an act of civic courage involving only the normal risks of an act of this kind, all the suspended principles regain their validity. The bottom line is that the moral courage of a person in a totalitarian society (state) cannot be measured by the person's action alone: the number and intensity of related threats and temptations to which that person is exposed must also be taken into account.

Decent persons give the following advice to decent persons under totalitarian conditions: 'Listen to your own conscience and to it alone'; 'gather information from all available sources, separate the facts from their evaluation, and relate your own moral values to these facts.' Enormous courage is needed by people who act according to *both* postulates. Gathering facts about the horrors of a tyrannical regime is in itself an undertaking of extreme courage. If society, and not just the state, is totalitarian, separating facts from their evaluation could put the decent person on a collision course with those who have already been thoroughly indoctrinated and so have stopped thinking with their own minds. Beyond and above civic and military courage, courage of a third type is needed for such acts: *intellectual courage*.

In enumerating intellectual virtues, Aristotle insisted that only one of them, *phronesis*, is a moral requirement in the active way of life. Phronesis has retained its relevance in modern times (as will be demonstrated in chapter 4). However, certain other intellectual virtues have also gained moral relevance, even prominence, during the last few centuries. Since questioning and testing the validity of certain norms and rules of justice is no longer an esoteric theoretical exercise or an exceptional event, but something that through continuous practice has become one of the fundamental *norms* of political and social contestations, it can be *a virtuous undertaking in its own right*. This particular intellectual exercise is nothing but the generalization of an attitude that I have elsewhere termed 'rationality of intellect'. In a liberal-democratic setting, where the practice of 'dynamic justice' (testing and querying the justice and rightness of existing institutions) is taken for granted, one need not be particularly courageous to criticize a state of affairs from the position of 'rationality of intellect'. Moreover, adopting such a position is not even a virtue in itself; rather, the virtue is to exercise rationality of intellect[14] in a proper way. I shall return to this issue shortly. By contrast, in a totalitarian society (and state), where people are compelled to accept the dominant institutions, and where the very attitude of rationality of intellect is outlawed, the readiness to use one's reason to adopt this attitude becomes a virtue in its own right. It is this readiness that I term *intellectual courage*.

Intellectual courage includes the resolve to *find out 'what is really going on'*. This is a difficult task when censorship and indoctrination block the avenues of information flow, where people are kept in the dark about basic facts, where statistics are regularly tampered with, and where doubt, even curiosity, is denounced as a sign of disloyalty, perhaps even of criminal intentions. Many people of good will, among them sophisticated, even brilliant, persons, commit fatal mistakes owing to a lack of intellectual courage. For sophistication and brilliance are qualities of excellence, but intellectual courage is a *virtue*. This foremost intellectual virtue runs counter to rational calculation; those committed to it are often regarded as eccentrics, as people who have lost their common sense. And this not by accident. It is modernity that brings about the consciousness of contingency. Existing institutions could also not exist. Rationality of intellect becomes a habitual manner of thought precisely as a result of contingency awareness. While this is a general feature of modernity, modern totalitarianism practises contingency awareness with a Manichean touch. On the one hand, all institutions of the Other should be mercilessly criticized; they should not exist although they do. On the other, 'our' institutions should be protected, acclaimed, eulogized, because they are by definition good; they are also threatened by the evil Other. The Manichean use of contingency awareness is highly irrational. Small wonder, then, that the reaction to it, intellectual courage in revolt, often has an equally strong flavour of irrationality. It will be certainly regarded as irrational by those who take the attitude of 'rationality of reason'. The point of departure for independent thinking in a totalitarian society (state) is the abandonment of 'means–end' calculations while becoming impervious to the arguments of the Manichean creed.[15] Decent persons must be aware of the limits of rationality in an irrational world. In order to remain decent, one has sometimes to do things which defy common sense. But decent persons will not find pleasure in defying common sense. Their ideal remains the state of symmetric reciprocity, the more the merrier. And decent persons will refrain from defying common sense in proportion to the growth of symmetric reciprocity in the world around them.

The good citizen

Modern men and women are citizens of a liberal-democratic state; they *have become* its citizens. Men of limited means, particularly working-class men, as well as all women, fought for their citizenship, which, through their own efforts, they finally achieved. Their newly gained contingency awareness was their most powerful motivation. They knew that the world not only should, but also could, be different from what it was, and that the change could only come about through their efforts. This is how liberal-democratic states, with men and women as their citizens, were first established. Liberties (as rights) provide the framework for socio-political contestation. Where liberties (as rights) are guaranteed, by written or unwritten constitutions, dynamic justice is taken for granted. In other words, the just character of all existing institutions and social arrangements can be continually queried and tested. If undertaken from the position of 'the rationality of intellect', radical interrogation of existing institutions does not necessarily defy common sense.

Men and women, as citizens of a liberal-democratic state, are either concerned or non-concerned persons. The latter can be termed 'passive citizens'. A good citizen is a concerned person, although not all concerned persons are good citizens. *A good citizen is concerned with matters of justice and injustice in the state* (his or her 'city'), and participates in acts which aim to remedy injustice.

A good citizen interprets his or her rights as responsibilities.

In the ancient city states (with imperial Rome as an exception) citizenship was not a right but a status and a privilege. The citizen was part of a political body (as Aristotle put it, the state was the sum total of its citizens). However, as early as the dawn of modern times, the representative thinkers noted that the model no longer worked.

Their major and generally known argument concludes that the size of modern states makes direct governance either outright impossible or at least not particularly viable. Contingency may be added to the list of factors which have made the ancient city state obsolete. These city states, including the democracies, were far from liberal. Modern liberalism is not merely the self-justification of capitalism (understood as a self-regulating market), nor is it merely an expression of possessive individualism, although it allows for both of these interpretations. Modern liberalism equally gives voice to contingency awareness, and this has become the typical life experience of the modern individual. We no longer see ourselves as having been born with a 'status' which defines our responsibilities in the cradle. Rather we believe that we are able to determine our life path by choice, impulse and design. This had been fairly obvious even before historical examples proved how resolutely we were prepared to defend our contingency, or our 'right to contingency' (after all, we were 'born free'), every time political obligations were foisted upon us instead of being chosen by us. The circumstance that citizenship can be passive in modern liberal-democratic states, that we can choose not to participate as well as to participate in political life, that rights can remain barren, not used and not interpreted as responsibilities – all of this is a negative tribute paid to our contingency. Of course, one can hope that, under certain conditions, the majority of today's passive citizens would become active. Yet we should not even want to hope that everyone would become active, as this hope of uniformity itself contradicts contingency. Mere citizenship in modern liberal-democratic states carries no obligation or responsibility in itself (military service for male citizens, where there is still conscription, is the major exception). As a result, the responsibilities of citizenship have to be chosen, 'adopted with resolve'. It is only the good citizen who interprets his or her rights as responsibilities.

A good citizen is concerned with matters of justice and injustice.

A person who is *not* concerned with matters of justice and injustice *cannot* be a good citizen, although she or he can be a decent person. Decent persons are frequently concerned about the lot of the victims of unjust arrangements without forming opinions on the arrangements themselves. Under no circumstances could Dostoevsky's Sonia (in *Crime and Punishment*) and Myshkin (in *The Idiot*) qualify as good citizens, yet both of them are beyond doubt good and concerned persons. There is also a certain kind of goodness which is 'no longer', rather than 'not yet', interested in matters of justice and injustice. Persons who demonstrate this kind of goodness affectionately care for those justly convicted, the criminal, the undeserving. Personal goodness of this kind can become completely irreconcilable with being a good citizen, for the latter should stand for justice (although not perforce with the rigour of 'and may the world perish', but often with sinking heart).

Men and women can become good citizens if they are concerned with matters of justice and injustice alone.

A good citizen need not necessarily be a decent person. Performing all acts required by 'good citizenship' is perfectly possible without abiding by the general principles of moral orientation in matters of daily life. It frequently happens that men and women who do not pay the slightest attention to the joys and sorrows of their neighbours, who do not care for another human being, still perform their duties of citizenship punctiliously. To be engaged in matters of justice and injustice and to care for others as human beings require different attitudes. Good citizenship is not related to the existential choice. A citizen understands rights as responsibilities, but may or may not undertake these responsibilities. This is how good citizenship, too, is a matter of choice. Thus one chooses to become a good citizen *but one does not choose oneself as a good citizen. To be or to become a good citizen is not a destiny.* A person can choose himself or herself as a political actor existentially under the category of difference (this is what 'politics as vocation' means in the broadest sense of the term), and can simultaneously choose to become a good citizen, but the second choice does not follow from the first. A person can also choose himself or herself existentially under the category of the universal and undertake to become a good citizen as though this commitment actually followed from the original choice, even if it does not. Finally, a person can choose to become a good citizen without having chosen himself or herself existentially at all. Many good citizens remain contingent *qua* persons. They may interpret their civil rights as responsibilities and care for matters of justice and injustice merely because others around them do so or because they realize that it is in their interest to do so. The distinction between concerned and interested persons, as well as the blurring of the distinction between them owing to interaction and constant dialogue, has already been mentioned. It has also been noted that one who has become a good citizen out of interest motives may remain such, out of habit, when those motives no longer apply.

The attitude required of the good citizen and the attitude required of the good person were already seen to be slightly different when the distinction itself was drawn, and this was the reason for drawing it in the first place. Aristotle, who discovered the problem, attributed the discrepancy to the imperfection of constitutions and institutions. In modern times, the problem has further and different implications: the discrepancy can no longer be attributed solely to the imperfection of constitutions and institutions, because it may simply be that we no longer wish the virtues of the good citizen and those of the good person to coincide completely. I shall briefly address the present situation from two aspects.

To repeat, the good citizen is concerned with matters of justice and injustice. This should be a general concern of all good citizens and this alone makes a citizen good. Since there are two kinds of justice, there are likewise two kinds of injustice. First, just norms can be applied in an unjust manner (inconsistently, not continuously, or to the member of a cluster to which the particular rules do not apply). Second, the norms and rules themselves can be regarded as unjust. A good citizen seeks to remedy injustices of both kinds.

If right norms are unjustly applied, particular individuals or groups of persons are hurt. A good citizen embraces the case of these individuals or groups not out of concern for the particular individual or group but out of concern for the particular issue. The good citizen, not necessarily guided by the general principles of moral orientation, may or may not care for those involved *qua* persons, but she or he certainly cares for 'other human persons'. The operative principles then read as follows: these people are victims of injustice; no one should be a victim of injustice; injustices should be remedied; justice should be done. Not even personal acquaintance with the victims is required; knowing about their case will suffice.

Involvement in the contestations of justice as dynamic justice abstracts, however, considerably from the particular fate of individuals. The extent of abstraction depends on the locus and the manner of contestation. Each time the rules and norms of a certain institution are contested and it is claimed that these rules are unjust and should be replaced by alternative, just sets of rules, there is a particular group of people, the contenders, who carry out the contestation or are the referents of such a contestation.[16] The locus of contestation can be the public sphere or social-political institutions, while the manner can be of a very wide range of types, including publication, speech, action and collective action. In contestations of justice one can mobilize one's own life experiences as well as gather accumulated knowledge concerning the matter in question. One can participate in a contestation as an individual or as a member of various groups: either groups whose needs are at stake or groups whose objectives lead them to elaborate alternative proposals for more just institutions. In some of these actions, being concerned with matters of justice and injustice may be completely divorced from any concern for particular human beings. Designing institutions and toying with alternative patterns which are supposed to be more just, discussing alternative proposals in committee meetings, and submitting proposals and humbly accepting the results, even when adverse – all this can be done without having any contact, beyond and above the requirements of civility, with those who would be directly affected by the proposals (and civility, by the way, may or may not be a requirement in a particular culture).

Given the complexity of modern society, the size of the modern state and the diversity of socio-political institutions, it would be ludicrous to blame the 'imperfection' of constitutions and institutions for the circumstance that the virtues of good persons and those of good citizens do not coincide. I have argued in detail in *Beyond Justice* why, in the perception of modern (contingent) persons, a perfectly just society is both unattractive and undesirable.

There is yet another reason. In chapter 2 I set about the task of constructing a modern moral philosophy by tracing the path of contingent persons who have chosen to be decent. I chose this particular course because I had come to the conclusion that the two main routes followed by earlier attempts to create such a philosophy were wrong, and in fact were nothing but alternative versions of the same theoretical enterprise, directing us to draw authority for our moral proposals from our membership of a group, be it small, broad (the state) or universal (the phantasmagoric cluster 'humankind'). This approach remains, in my view, under the spell of the premodern. In the modern world, I argued in chapter 1, an ethics based on 'group authority' is either particularistic or merely formalistic. Thus I decided to start from the contingent person who chooses himself or herself under the category of the universal. The choice is universal in so far as it can be undertaken by each and every contingent person, by all such persons. Yet it does not make the persons who make the choice 'universal', because it leaves all of them in their concreteness and singularity, self-abandoned to their own destinies. In this new approach, the general principles of moral orientation (including the sub-principles), the norms concerning giving–receiving–reciprocating, and the virtue norms (including the restrictive ones concerning truthfulness) *are by no means formal*, and they offer concrete guidance. Not even the universal maxims are completely devoid of content. The content conveyed by all these principles, norms and maxims is at the same time *general*. They are general and not abstract, for abstraction is rightly associated with formality. They need not be concretized but they do need to be specified. General norms remain the same when specified. Yet they can be specified in a variety of ways, and each and every specification of general norms has an affinity with a particular form of life. Good persons are good in their own distinct ways.

When I juxtapose 'general' and 'specified', instead of juxtaposing 'abstract' and 'concrete', I do not pursue experiments with a neo-Platonic scenario. No general guidelines, maxims and norms are 'out there' which should be specified in concrete forms of life; the latter involve far more than just morals. Decent persons are decent whatever they do; but what they do is not 'decency' but rather something else. While doing everything others normally do in their life world, decent persons figure out whether or not doing particular things has a moral connotation. If the answer is affirmative, they abandon themselves to the guidance of norms, maxims and virtue norms. However, these principles will be specified in the actions of decent persons according to the concrete ways of life (*Sittlichkeiten*) in which they participate.

If a 'perfect' constitution could be designed, would, under modern conditions, the virtues of the good citizen and those of the good person coincide? The great variety of different kinds of good persons follows from the similarly great variety of (modern) ways of life; each of them carries different yardsticks of measurement. The most we should expect is mutual tolerance for the difference. A modern person who is considered decent by a given standard of *Sittlichkeit* should indeed be regarded as decent provided that this particular standard qualifies as a specification of the general norms, principles and maxims put forward by the selfsame decent person.

In subscribing to certain yardsticks of decency, we are inclined to measure ourselves by them. Assume that a woman, a good person, living under a 'perfect constitution' takes upon herself certain civic responsibilites (as is implied by the term 'perfect constitution'). As a fully good person, she would apply same yardsticks in her public and political life as within the confines of her day-to-day form of life. At the same time others, coming from different forms of life, wish to remain true to their own standards. Let me illustrate the problem with reference to a banal issue. If three persons decide to do something about an injustice that has befallen their neighbour, the first could offer money, the second try to console the victim, and the third write a pamphlet on the issue. The problem arises at the point when one of them demands that the other two should copy his or her method of dealing with injustice or begins to criticize their approach. This simple example gives a fair illustration of the modern condition. It suggests that the attitude of the good person and that of the good citizen should be kept apart even under the best of constitutions. For this is the only way of achieving both of two objects: first, public co-operation between persons who participate in different ways of life; and second, a situation in which decent persons can remain decent according to their own standards, as well as be good citizens, without imposing their particular standards on others.

To sum up: good citizens are concerned with matters of justice and injustice, and with these matters alone. Good persons are concerned in addition, and in their own different ways, with a variety of other issues. The value that a good citizen shares with others is justice. Regardless of all other personal values, good citizens must share the conviction that justice is, while not *the* supreme good, certainly the supreme *public* good. Action based on such an asssumption is poss- ible in so far as the expectation holds that others also act on the basis of this assumption. More cannot be required from citizens. Citizens pass judgements on others as citizens, regardless of the fact that persons, as a rule, pass judgements on others as persons. The good citizen would not collapse these two different kinds of judgement into one. For, in the pursuit of the supreme public good, it is the public act, and not the (assumed) private motivation, that counts – nothing else.

My preliminary 'definition' of a good citizen read as follows: 'A good citizen is concerned with matters of justice and injustice in the state (his or her "city"), and participates in acts which aim to remedy injustice.' Some aspects of this statement call for further explanation.

A good citizen is concerned with matters of justice and injustice *in his or her own state ('city')*, and takes responsibility for its *laws and institutions*.

In so far as one takes responsibility for what happens in one's closer environment, one is a concerned person but not a good citizen. Furthermore, while citizens are concerned with matters of justice and injustice, someone who is concerned with a particular matter of justice and injustice is not by the same token a good citizen. To be (to become) a good citizen is a *political commitment*. Even if the issues addressed by citizens are social in nature, in so far as they are addressed by citizens they become politicized. This is so because the matters of social justice are raised as issues for legislation.

There are two major ways of politicizing social issues, and the second follows on from the first. The first step is to alert the public to an issue, and the second is to participate in the process of legislation. The politicization of social justice is by no means tantamount to giving priority to the so-called 'social question', as Hannah Arendt once believed. Both steps in the politicization of social justice can be undertaken by good citizens *only under the condition of political freedom.* In politicizing social issues, the priority of the political (of liberties and liberal-democratic rights) is reconfirmed rather than negated.

Good citizens are concerned with matters of justice and injustice *in their own state* because they feel responsible for everything that happens in their state and because they want their state to have the best (the most just) of constitutions, laws and social arrangements. Good citizens want to take pride in their state; they are resolved to do everything to facilitate this, and it is in this sense only that good citizens are *nationalists.* As members of a particular body politic, they are responsible for, and take pride in, this particular state and not another. It is sufficient if their concern is confined to their own state. More than that cannot be required unless the state in question has responsibility for matters of justice and injustice in other states. What is termed 'enlarged conscience' is by no means expected from good citizens. They need not be 'anti-ethnocentric'; nor do they have to demand that their state take responsibility for all the past and present calamities of the world. But they need to be brave in order to demand that their state take responsibility for all injustices which it has committed.

A good citizen is thus a kind of *homo politicus,* if not necessarily a politician (it goes without saying that politicians may or may not be good citizens). Good citizenship may be a pastime (for those who love politicking) as well as a matter of duty (for those who prefer seclusion and private enjoyments). But one can hardly be a good citizen without a certain continuity. The preliminary definition of the good citizen included participation in acts which aim to remedy injustice. It is perfectly clear that, if someone participates in such actions once in every five years, then, however well she or he performs on such occasions, that person cannot be considered a good citizen. The obverse of this statement is that the busybody who wants to be 'in' and 'well informed' about matters of public concern but is totally lacking in dedication, prudence and commitment cannot be considered a good citizen either.

The above distinction is particularly important because of the recent wide acceptance of the odd proposition that forming a right opinion on matters of public concern is the crucial (and perhaps the only) criterion of moral decency. I have already made the point that having the 'right opinion' on a public issue makes no one a decent (good) person. I would now add that forming a 'correct' or 'right' opinion concerning matters of justice and injustice does not make anyone a good citizen either. A person having 'incorrect' opinions on such matters can still be a brave and good citizen, while others, having what is deemed the 'right' opinion, can totally fail as citizens. This is particularly true in the case of theorists and the professionals of speculative thought. No university lecture or café small talk requires civic virtues or, for that matter, virtues of any kind (under the conditions of liberal democracy). One cannot be a good citizen without acting like one. Being a good citizen makes heavy claims upon the actor's time, money, energy and interests. In one's capacity as a good citizen, one has to sit in boring meetings, listen to silly speeches, act in the public space when one would prefer to stay at home, and write long documents which cannot be published to promote an academic career. One has also to be prepared to face disappointments and even to start everything afresh. Without doubt, there are also the hours of celebration: those of the victory of justice. Yet, on the whole, being a good citizen seems to be an unrewarding exercise. None the less, it has its own rewards, even in the absence of the kind of 'status' which accompanied good citizenship in ancient times. This is so first and foremost because certain needs generated by our contingent existence can only be satisfied by being a good citizen. For, if everything in the socio-political sphere could be otherwise, then, when things do indeed change, and for the better, citizens appear as the chosen ones who engineered the change. In a manner of speaking, 'the philosophy of praxis' is the natural attitude of modern men and women. Since we can transform our contingency into our destiny, we can act in the conviction that we can similarly transform the contingency of our socio-political arrangements into a kind of destiny, and invest our energies in creating a destiny (in the sense of 'destination', not of 'telos').

To rehash an important commonplace, everyone is equally able to become a decent person but not with equal ease. Among other things, there are social factors which make fully living up to the standards set by decent persons particularly difficult. Immense inequalities of wealth, opportunity, education and power certainly belong among such factors. Greater social justice improves the *conditions* for making an existential choice (of decency) and fully living up to it. In so far as one creates, or contributes to the creation of, a moral environment which eases the burden of existential choice for others, and in so far as this activity is extended to regions beyond the pale of merely personal relations, one can promote the conditions for decency in a wider framework. Moral decency cannot be extended to the public domain in full, but a one-track extension is possible and viable.

The single track of 'being a good citizen' is not a mere addendum to personal decency; it is its extension. Beyond decency, there are other aspects of the good life, such as developing our best abilities or establishing deep personal attachments. It is precisely these 'goods' of life which hold us back from practising good citizenship. In this respect, the decent person is no exception. Since decent persons can decide against exercising good citizenship, this 'one-track extension of decency', preferring instead to develop their best abilities or to cultivate deep personal attachments, the injunction '*Be a good citizen!*', addressed by one contingent person to other contingent persons who have chosen themselves under the category of the universal, is no empty sermon.

One *should be* a good citizen.

If one's passionate interest in exercising one's own mental or physical abilities or cultivating deep personal relationships is so overwhelming that doing something else becomes a burden, one can still follow the second-best path by being truthful to others and sincere to oneself. The person would then say 'I know that it is better to be a citizen than a mere private person; those who have taken the burden of citizenship on their shoulders, regardless of how they feel about it, have all my respect. I know that I have made a commitment (one recommended by a maxim of the first order) to feel respect for men and women according to their goodness (and not their excellence). In paying my respect to the good citizens, I have already stated that I regard good citizenship as a kind of decency and not as a kind of excellence. Although I fall short of their degree of decency, I still remain a fully decent person, and I expect to be respected *for what I am* and not to be despised for what I am not.' This is the honest way of forgoing the exercise of good citizenship while remaining authentic and decent at the same time.

Whenever one forgoes the exercise of good citizenship on the grounds of ethical considerations ('Politics is dirty. I do not want to soil my hands') or of the futility of the venture ('Nothing can be achieved anyway'), one becomes *inauthentic*. Even a one-track extension of decency cannot be denounced in the name of decency. One need not accept an office, if one believes that holding an office inevitably compromises one's morality, to act as a good citizen. As for the argument of the 'futility of the venture', it is self-defeating: if no one becomes a good citizen, there is certainly no hope, but there is no venture either. The very term 'venture' includes at least the possibility of change. This argument is a cover-up for the egoism of the free-lance, for bare indifference or misanthropy. Combined with purificatory self-justification, it becomes an exercise in a combination of self-aggrandizement and self-pity. The worst way of shunning public duties is to claim 'perfect knowledge' about the just social and moral order, in writing or talking from the rostrum, while denouncing others, particularly good citizens who try to bring about positive change, for the mediocrity of their efforts. The only way to remain decent without also becoming a good citizen is the royal road of truthfulness, sincerity and authenticity.

We already know that good citizens are concerned with matters of justice and injustice and that they wish that everyone would be concerned with these fundamental issues as well as with the remedies for injustice. They wish, too, that everyone would participate in the debate over the justness of institutions and laws – in short, that everyone would become a good citizen. But at this point the good citizen faces two dilemmas. What happens if people remain unconcerned about matters of justice and injustice, or are concerned but do not voice their concern? And what happens if people have such widely divergent ideas of justice and injustice that they could not agree to change anything, even if the opportunity were there?

Without a doubt, people *may* remain unconcerned about matters of justice and injustice in modern society. Good citizens may even face an impenetrable wall of total indifference. In this atmosphere, acting on behalf of justice demands a great deal of civic courage. Courage, which in chapter 2 I called half of all the virtues, is emphatically present in a good citizen, who sometimes takes responsibility amidst almost total indifference, sneers or even contempt. On this count, public life is no different from everyday life: here too those who fall short will sneer at those who do not. In this atmosphere, the injunction has a special emphasis: *Be courageous!*

In discussing the 'concerned person', I also referred to the 'interested person'. People of the latter sort participate in socio-political actions because they have an interest in realizing certain objectives. Interested persons are not necessarily concerned, and it is even less likely that they will become good citizens. But they make their grievances, demands, objectives and needs explicit; they are also active in so far as they work for the achievement of their goals. Good citizens lend – or, in a deontic formulation, should lend – support to interested persons where they believe that the latter's cause (objective) is just. This will inevitably be a partial commitment, for being a good citizen is not a full-time occupation, but the inherent norm of 'taking responsibility'[17] – active participation – should be accepted on certain occasions on behalf of interested persons.

Sometimes good citizens realize that certain groups (foreigners, ethnically 'alien' enclaves, the under-educated, the extremely poor, the handicapped, and the like) are adversely and unjustly affected by norms, laws or institutions, and that they have neither the means nor the opportunity to translate their grievances into public issues. They are natural targets of unjust practices: they are not aware of their rights, or, if aliens, they do not even have rights; they cannot make comparisons with other groups (or similar groups in another environment); and they are easy prey for power-seekers, exploiters, bureaucrats and criminals. It is almost a natural duty of good citizens to act on behalf of such groups and help them translate their grievances into public issues. But at this point the problem of autonomy arises. Good citizens act as representatives in so far as they take responsibility for their own citizenship; however they cannot be the proper representatives of the groups in question if they have never been empowered to act for them. Good citizens may therefore manoeuvre themselves into a situation of asymmetric reciprocity for the sake of justice. Should they insist on the norms of absolute symmetric reciprocity and walk away from such blatant cases of injustice, or should they rather act as representatives, substitutes for those who have never empowered them to act as such – this is the question. The principle of autonomy ('Have a proper regard for other persons' autonomy') can serve as a reliable guide in this delicate situation: the good citizen should *advise* the victims concerning their rights and possible ways of airing their grievances, and *encourage* them to be (literally) their own advocates. Good citizens who follow this course are then qualified to become committed to the case, in so far as nobody with a better claim offers. But they are not entitled to regard themselves as the proper representatives of the victims. This would be a misconstruction of their mission.

A readiness to participate in actions initiated by interested people, in so far as justice is at stake, and commitment to the just cause (without pretending to be the proper representative) of those who cannot voice their own grievances are *acts of solidarity*. This kind of readiness becomes the *character trait* of good citizens: *the virtue of solidarity*. The relevant injunction would be 'Show solidarity with the victims of injustice!'

However the good citizen is aware that solidarity with a group of which one is member is not obligatory on the basis of membership alone, regardless of the rightness of the cause. Solidarity must be based on justice, not on membership. Furthermore, the good citizen will not confuse solidarity with emotional attachment: solidarity is rather a matter of participation and commitment. Solidarity includes loyalty to the state, and the courageous defence of it, so long as the cause is just. Though the virtues of courage (including military valour) and solidarity are distinct, they are, as a rule, practised in concert.

Good citizens are guided by the idea (the model) of the consensus of free (responsible) citizens. They insist on the model, although they know that the idea is counterfactual. And it is at this point that the good citizen faces the second, and more serious, difficulty. One can change a state of affairs autonomously, together with other autonomous beings, on the basis of an autonomous agreement. An agreement of this kind is one reached by the free decision of all those concerned. An institution is completely just in so far as everyone concerned with it freely agrees that it is just. The practical idea of consensus is perfect, because it embraces 'all those concerned'. But if in fact an overwhelming majority of those concerned agree, rationally and autonomously, that certain institutions should be replaced by functionally equivalent but more just ones, and if, therefore, more just, even though not completely just, institutions are created, the good citizen will still be overjoyed. His 'republican arithmetic' suggests to him that 'more' is more than less.

The good citizen is thus committed to reaching agreement with others – not only with other good citizens but with the majority of those concerned with a particular institution, law or norm. It is this, rather than any private inclination, that is the good citizen's most powerful motive for sitting on committees, punctiliously participating in meetings where matters of justice are at stake, and being indefatigable in mobilizing public opinion. The good citizen is never too tired to explain issues, if need be, all over again. She or he is also a good listener – to grievances as well as to the different views and opinions. Put philosophically, *the good citizen is ready for rational argumentation in a practical discourse.*

This is *not* meant as the 'characterology' of the good citizen, for *citizen virtues are those of attitude, not necessarily those of character.* This distinction is underscored by the circumstance that certain 'virtues of attitude' (for example, being a good listener) do not preclude the expression of various peculiarities of temperament (for instance, a degree of irritability) or differences of taste.

Readiness for rational argumentation in practical discourse is the main intellectual virtue of the good citizen.[18]

I have termed the two main attitudes of practical reason (rational action and argumentation) 'rationality of reason' and 'rationality of intellect'. As noted earlier, it is in modern times that 'rationality of intellect' has first become generalized. Modern men and women constantly devalidate existing (valid) norms (moral norms, virtue norms, socio-political norms and rules) which contain the aspect of 'right and wrong' and can thus be rejected as unjust. Devalidating statements may be made from the standpoint of 'rationality of intellect', and those who make them may find themselves engaged in a conflict with the repositories of 'rationality of reason', who, in turn, take the existing order of things for granted as something 'natural' and thus good and right. In order to *make* rejections of an existing reality rational, men and women have to refer, or to be able to refer, to *valid* (abstract or universal) norms and pinpoint the contradiction between them and the reality they reject.[19]

In our (extreme) model of a totalitarian state or society, rationality of intellect appeared as *intellectual courage*. It was added that, owing to the irrationality of the regime, the intellectual courage required in order to challenge it need not be linked with rational procedures. Where naked force and violence are the rule, rational argumentation cannot be the norm and decent persons should not even listen to certain opinions. In our (equally extreme) model of liberal democracy, intellectual courage should still hold its place, for the honest and inquisitive mind detects problems at points where others do not even dare to perceive them. But, as mentioned, it is the readiness for rational argumentation in practical discourse that becomes the main intellectual virtue in this political setting. When everyone is free to argue, and nothing but cowardice, indifference or ignorance can hold one back from argumentation, a sudden chance to extend the relevance of the golden rule of justice to dynamic justice emerges. The positive formulation of the golden rule of justice runs, 'I do unto you what I expect you to do unto me.'[20] This formula is translated into the language of dynamic justice if one adds 'What I do unto you and what I expect you to do unto me, should be decided by you and me.' But decisions about setting up institutions are never the result of spontaneous impulse; they are always the outcome of discussions. The intellectual virtue of the good citizen appears most pregnantly in these discussions.

The good citizen's cause is the cause of justice. This is the *only* cause good citizens share; on almost all other issues they diverge. They are particularly different in so far as the forms of life they cultivate, professions they pursue, means they have, offices they hold, and pleasures they enjoy are concerned. While they co-operate, they also clash with one another. Yet they are bound, in so far as they wish to be good citizens, to make attempts to bridge the differences, to be *tolerant* toward each other. Behind this seemingly liberal virtue there is a strict and demanding postulate. Good citizens must recognize all forms of life, and all of them equally, as well as the needs of all human groups.

Radical tolerance is thus a citizen virtue *par excellence*. The good citizen acts on the assumption that all needs, virtues, values and positions, as presented and represented by good citizens, have an equal right, and should therefore have an equal opportunity, to be presented in the public arena and share in the contestation of justice. Tolerance is, of course, not acceptance. Nor would radical tolerance lead to *total relativism*. Anyone who is actively concerned with matters of justice and injustice would challenge and contest such needs, claims, interests, values and value interpretations as undermine the very existence of the good citizen and erode 'rationality of intellect', autonomy and symmetric reciprocity. This is particularly true if the good citizens are also decent persons and, as such, under the obligation of the universal maxim which forbids the use of other persons as mere means. The maxim also forbids joining any institution that in principle allows the use of other persons as mere means. However, the rejection of total relativism, which implies the non-recognition of such needs as in principle entail the use of others as mere means, does *not* imply the *actual exclusion* of the advocates of socio-political instrumentalization from the public realm. While needs that clearly entail the instrumentalization of others should not be excluded from representation in the public arena, they can be excluded from participation in a rational discourse. The good citizen, a person otherwise bound by definition to listen to diverging opinions, is bound not to pay attention to overt claims on behalf of domination and instrumentalization.

Are there any criteria for excluding such needs, as well as their representation, from argumentation (rational discourse)? If so, who has defined and set such criteria? These questions turn out to be mere rhetoric, as the answer has actually preceded the question. Since freedom is the formal precondition of the very existence of a good citizen, and since without freedom of contestation dynamic justice would not exist at all, one is certainly justified in disregarding the opinion of those who do not accept freedom in the sense of 'equal freedom for all' (in our state) as *the* supreme value to which the arguments should have recourse. Similarly, since dynamic justice translates social questions (matters of social justice and injustice) into political issues, good citizens, who are particularly concerned with matters of justice, can certainly disregard the opinions of all those for whom social injustices do not matter.

Radical tolerance is a 'linking value', on two counts. On the one hand, it links theoretical reason and phronesis with the intellectual virtue of readiness for practical discourse, and, on the other, it links intellectual virtues with the care of the world. At this point, however, we have already left the good citizen behind. This last 'citizen virtue' is not merely the citizen's virtue.

III

The elder Zossima in Dostoevsky's *The Brothers Karamazov* re-marked that every human being is responsible for every other human being; they are merely not aware of it. If they were, there would at once be paradise on earth. For his part, Zossima *knows* about universal responsibility; he is aware of something that others are not aware of, and without this something paradise on earth is not a reality. Heidegger sets forth the concept 'shepherd of Being'. The philosophical metaphor can be interpreted in a manner very similar to Zossima's dictum. The shepherd is responsible for the flock; he is in charge. Men and women are in charge of Being. Since Being is the Being of beings, one lives up to the responsibilities of a shepherd in so far as one cares about all beings, human beings above all, but also beings other than human, organic and inorganic alike. In a deon-tological formulation: men and women should care for Being, they should care for the world which has been left to their charge.

Zossima, who sought to find his destiny in the monastery, is the paradigm of the contingent person. His formula is thoroughly mod-ern, as is Heidegger's. So too is the idea of 'taking care of the world' a modern one.

In the wake of Kant, I am going to term the attitude of 'taking care of the world' one of *enlarged consciousness* or *enlarged conscience*. I have only borrowed the term from Kant; the attitude described by the term is basically un-Kantian and the similarities with Kant's position are merely superficial. Enlarged consciousness of this kind springs from *knowledge* of a kind which is not, and cannot be, empirically grounded or proved true. That every person is responsible for every other person and that we are the shepherds of Being are propositions of a metaphysical character (in the Kantian, not in the Hegelian or Heideggerian sense). The statements appeal to us, and we can feel that they are true in a deeper sense. But this only holds if we add to our agreement with them the qualification 'in a deeper sense' and if we indeed feel that they are true. In short, these are gnostic statements and our knowledge is mystical. In this particular case, mystical does not stand for 'intuitive' pure and simple, even if mystical insight is also a kind of intuition. 'Mystical' here means an intuition of general relevance (which is not an experience), an intuition which can be spelt out and, once it has been, appeals also to others. Such and similar mystical statements are pieces of wisdom which appeal not to our pragmatic common sense or to our sense of beauty or to our inquisi-tiveness, but to our *conscience*. For it is about matters of responsi-bility that they advise us.

From the beginning modern humanism has been rooted in generalized metaphysical statements such as 'All people are born free and endowed with reason and conscience.' Humanism has manifested itself, and still does, in the emergence of 'enlarged conscience'. In discussing 'humankind', we do not simply mean 'the sum total of persons we share the globe with'. We also 'feel' that the 'mana of humankind' resides in every single human being. Hence the impulse, made explicit by Schiller and Beethoven, to 'embrace millions'. To associate modern humanism with Cartesian epistemology or mere subjectivism or technological reasoning is misconceived. Modern humanism has rather a mystical streak. In making statements about 'humankind', in saying 'I am a human being', the speakers are *elated*. At least in thought and feeling, they indeed embrace and feel that celebrated 'mana of humankind' dwelling in themselves as in other human beings.

The mystical experience of enlarged consciousness (or enlarged conscience) is one of *responsibility*. If responsibility is not involved, the experience is aesthetic rather than ethical. Embracing millions is not a simple gesture of 'hugging'; its yield is not sensual pleasure. But it has a meaning: 'You all are like me, although you are also all different; let us be like brothers and sisters!' The testimonies of both Dostoevsky and Heidegger in favour of this mystical experience are of great significance given that both were sworn enemies of the Enlightenment and almost everything that it stood for ('humanism' in particular). But, since the statement 'I am a human person' is, willy-nilly, an expression of the experience of contingency (it means, 'I stand here naked, stripped of all social telos, an undefined bundle of unlimited possibilities'), and since, further, the (naked) human person is the singular whose corresponding universal cannot be other than 'all human persons', or 'humankind', the basic message of modern humanism is intrinsically linked to our contingency. Not even its sworn enemies can circumvent or eliminate it in so far as they face the modern condition candidly.

What kind of action and behaviour follow from the enlarged consciousness of responsibility? Why, and especially how, would Zossima's (Dostoevsky's) 'paradise on earth' come to pass were we indeed aware that we are responsible for everyone else? No paradise is in evidence as a result of our existing knowledge that we are responsible for the members of our family, our friends, and the like. But suppose that one could take responsibility for another only if one had an 'enlarged consciousness'. In this case, 'taking responsibility' would always have been confined to the select few having a mystical knowledge of their responsibility for other human beings. What is their secret? They cannot translate their responsibility for all others into the language of practice, but they can at least be good to those whom they come across. What is the secret of this goodness? The answer again must be hazy: those having an enlarged consciousness *know*, and this must be assumed, how to be (become) good. It is their mystical genius that provides the know-how. Clearly, one gets very little real ethical guidance from the wisdom of an enlarged consciousness.

Heidegger's 'shepherd of Being' fares no better than Zossima. The consciousness becomes here even more enlarged; in fact, it assumes gigantic proportions, for it is no less than Being itself that we carry responsibility for. Being was given into our care (by whom?), but Heidegger grants us not so much as a hint about how we should care for Being, about the kinds of action involved in the *proper* care for Being. The ethical yield is thus even less than in the case of Zossima's dictum.

It is not proposed that we show now return to traditional humanism, with its resolve to 'embrace millions'. When the chips were down, traditional humanism proved an erring and erroneous guide. However it would be misconceived to infer from the above that I deem 'enlarged consciousness' morally sterile and irrelevant. That 'enlarged consciousness' (the mystical experience of the expansion of our consciousness) *alone* does not offer much moral guidance seems to be true enough. But *it can prepare the ground for something else or, rather, 'circumscribe' something else or be linked with something else, and in this way participate in moral guidance*, whatever the latter may be.

Since the enlarged consciousness is one of the manifestations of the modern historical consciousness and, as such, constantly present as a possibility of consciousness also in everyday life, taking this attitude *can trigger the existential choice of ourselves*, under both the category of the universal and that of difference. Although nothing can determine an existential choice, the conditions under which such a choice is made can be more or less favourable. The state of the enlarged consciousness is a highly favourable condition for such a choice. The 'knowledge', and corresponding elation of 'knowing', that everyone is responsible for everyone else, or that the 'mana of humankind' dwells in each of us, or even that we are the shepherds, the caretakers, of Being does not carry any distinct moral message. Yet each of these distinct types of 'knowledge', as well as the accompanying feeling of elation, can prepare us to be receptive to such a message.

So far I have discussed the ethical commitments of decent persons and good citizens. I have also briefly mentioned the concerned person, the hero of decency. The reason for not mentioning the 'enlarged consciousness' earlier is that it has been practical goodness, goodness as manifested in action, that has been under scrutiny. Morals are first and foremost manifested in action. The radius of a single (decent) individual's action is rather narrow, while that of a good citizen, although broader, still does not extend beyond the borders of his or her state (except in special circumstances). If we link the term 'radius of action' with the state of the 'enlarged consciousness', we must have in mind actions (of ethical provenance) which *directly aim* at acting 'on behalf of humankind'. Since 'humankind' is a fictitious entity in that it does not exist as a definable cluster, 'acting on behalf of humankind' is sheer nonsense.[21] At the same time, the decency of modern contingent persons will be seriously flawed if they confine their attention exclusively to subjects or objects within the reach of their radius of action. In fact, as a rule, *moral interest* reaches far beyond this horizon. I would add, the more we know about the miseries of the world, the more moral interest *should* reach beyond this horizon. In a manner of speaking, enlarged consciousness surrounds all our actions – in particular, actions with a strong moral content.

In this capacity, enlarged consciousness can also be seen with a degree of suspicion, because it may provide the cheapest substitute for action (for example, tears over the suffering of those beyond our horizon without the slightest sacrifice to help them). It may even be used as a cover-up by people lacking in decency or as a medium of sentimental self-deception. And yet the way in which the 'enlarged consciousness' surrounds, so to speak, our normal life activities as decent persons is far from being morally worthless. To measure our own life against the backdrop of the fate of others teaches us well-advised modesty. Also, certain issues of certain human groups can be brought 'within reach' through our well-intended actions, even though the life of 'every human being', that of 'humankind', in-variably remains beyond our reach. One cannot help all, yet one can help a few; one cannot always help, but one can help sometimes. This puts the issue into proper perspective: if it were not for the 'enlarged consciousness' and 'enlarged conscience', we would *never* say, when the fate of someone beyond our horizon is at issue, 'I am a human being, and as such, I am duty-bound to do my best for other persons.'

I have briefly analysed the attempts of decent persons to bridge the gap between active goodness within their own radius of action and their impotence in the face of the accumulated sufferings of 'human-kind', a cluster which is beyond their reach and, as such, is for them fictitious. Men and women of supererogatory goodness, however, listen to another call. 'Go and share their fate' – this is the battle cry of supererogatory goodness. And they follow this call. They go and suffer *with* those who suffer most; they die *with* them. They are impervious to the national or cultural differences, religion, gender or ideology of those they suffer *with*. The important point about them is that they do not suffer 'for' – that is, in order to achieve a goal, or to contribute to a cause, including the 'cause of humankind'. They are the only authentic carriers of the 'mana of humankind'.

Our constant protagonists, the good citizens, would, in so far as they are aware of the surrounding 'enlarged consciousness', mobilize their civic virtues in actions aiming at rectifying injustices in other states, regardless of the actual responsibility of their own state for the plight of others. They may go and directly share this plight, but more often than not they will remain within their own radius of action and continue to act as good citizens. It is not the space of their action but the space of their commitment that will be enlarged. This is why, at this point, intellectual courage becomes a major virtue: one needs to know to what one is becoming committed before confirming the commitment. Intellectual virtues are also needed to ensure the employment of proper hermeneutics, in order to avoid paternalism. In reaching beyond one's 'natural' – that is, familiar – environment, one should confine one's recommendations to the *conditions of justice* alone, and read the alien 'text' well enough to avoid substantive recommendations which could offend the subject/object of one's commitment.

The problem with the wisdom of the elder Zossima is not merely that it teaches us a sense of responsibility which, in itself, provides no proper moral guidance concerning its ways and paths. The genuine, and historically realized, problem appears when attempts are made to distil *political* blueprints from it. All such attempts so far have concluded in a criminal and terrorizing misuse of 'global' responsibility. Let therefore the albatross descend to earth. Having been edified by Dostoevsky's mystical vision, decent persons must resume posing their prosaic questions: 'What should I do?', 'What is the right thing for me to do?' Decent persons may well be dreamers, mystics, poets. They may take their soul on joyous journeys or drag it through an experience of apocalypse; they may also pray for redemption. But, when it comes to *political involvement*, they will look around and repeat their sober questions. As practical, moral agents, they are immune to the temptations of paradise on earth, of this-worldly redemption. After all, they are just contingent persons who have destined themselves to be decent; this is their life. In choosing themselves, they have (implicitly) chosen the world in which they live: a world of contingency. They act as if everything that exists could also be otherwise; they reach out to *destine* a contingent world for the better. They reach out *to transform the modern world, our contingent world, into our common destiny.*

4

How to Live an Honest Life

I

Morals are the individual's practical relationship to the norms and rules of proper conduct. It is a much-discussed issue of philosophy to what degree proper, right, good, true thinking about matters of 'right' and 'wrong' contributes to the goodness of one's actions or one's way of life in general. Yet hardly any modern thinker would share the extreme rationalist creed ascribed to Socrates that right action follows from right thinking, even though some still insist that wrong actions ensue from the wrong way of thinking. But I would not have proposed to follow the ways of the good person in pondering orientative and fundamental norms, as well as universal maxims, had I not shared the conviction that one has to know how to act in the right way in order to act in the right way. Decent persons have to discern which signposts should be followed in order to go in the right direction, to act in a right way and to remain what they are, decent persons. Yet 'signposts', observance of right norms, are no guarantees of always doing the right thing. Furthermore, along this road there can be two or more signposts at the same junction. It is the traveller's task to discern which of them to follow.

Exploring the moral problems as they appear to decent persons, and to them alone, is far from a theoretical innovation: this is precisely the traditional fashion of doing moral philosophy. As a rule, moral philosophies scrutinize the *normative* attitude, behaviour, character traits and action patterns. They are not interested in numbers (of those complying with the norms). They discuss what they term 'human nature' in order to establish the possibility of normative action and normative attitudes, on the one hand, and to ponder, if briefly, the typical motivations and reasons which prevent men and women from living up to moral norms, on the other. However, the major interest of moral philosophies cannot be located in the dissection of 'human nature'. The first written records of our history comment on the 'wickedness' of human beings, and, whether in despair, indignation, irony or malice, the same comment has been repeated ever since in each and every culture. This is the language of moralists, not that of moral philosophers. The difference is that moralists take moral norms and ideals for granted (this is the vantage point from which their judgements on 'human wickedness' are passed), while moral philosophers explore precisely the normative domain. Moralists engage in narratives about the actual, non-normative attitudes of the 'human beast', whereas moral philosophers rarely indulge in exhortations. The popular formulation of this contrast states that moralists describe human beings as they are and moral philosophers as they should be. The popular formula, often repeated by representative moralists (for example, Mandeville), is, however, misleading, for the panorama is more complex. Some moralists censure human beings with glowing passion or subjective indignation; others dissect the entertainingly wicked ways of our race with a kind of detached objectivity. Some moral philosophers do contrast Ought to Is, while others make efforts to deduce the moral norms from the human condition. However, regardless of whether moral philosophers address the issue from one aspect or another, they never mistake the norm for the average. They instead make the modest proposal that the 'average' should not be identified with 'reality'. For normativity is real to the same extent as average is; moreover, the actual behaviour of the 'average' cannot be understood at all without having first explored the character of normativity. Moralists too are aware of this connection. As La Rochefoucauld put it, hypocrisy is the tribute paid by evil to virtue.

The distinction between moral philosophy and the moralists' approach is a *distinction of genres* in connection with which *no hierarchy can be established*. When with moralists, one finds oneself in the best, and, at the same time, oldest of company: in that of fallen gods, seers, prophets, wise men, poets, enthusiasts, martyrs and lawgivers – on the whole, a colourful lot. One must, however, reluctantly add that our own age does not favour traditional moralists. For moralists, as mentioned, take moral norms and ideas for granted; it is on this basis that their statements about 'human wickedness' ring a bell in our ears. But in a world of normative pluralism and increasing relativism, statements on 'human wickedness', at least statements without reference to the negative limits of human performance, such as Auschwitz or the GULAG, fail to ring a bell at all. The major appeal of moralism, that of *de te fabula narratur*, is clearly absent from our age. Moralists are confined to the stage, as the great example of Bertolt Brecht testifies. This trend was foreseen by Kierkegaard, who contended that 'in the present age' neither moral nor religious truth can be communicated *directly*; they must don the guise of narratives of 'indirect communication'.

The same person as adopts the position of moral philosophy can also adopt the position of moralism, though not, unless it is a dialogue, in the same work. Among others, Aristotle remarked quite nonchalantly in the *Rhetoric* that 'most men are bad rather than good', and that 'as a rule, men do wrong whenever they can'. However, he made no similar remarks in his *Ethics*, where the task was to discuss the normative aspects of morals. The main tradition of moral philosophy has been resting on Aristotle's *Ethics*; this book itself is no exception. It takes as its centrepoint the normative subject, the unity of Is and Ought.

As a person, the modern moral philosopher, this writer included, shares with his or her fellow creatures the commonplace observation that human beings are generally neither good nor wicked but, rather, sometimes act decently and sometimes wickedly; that the path dividing decency from wickedness is bewilderingly narrow; that in moral matters, as in everything else, luck, good or bad, plays an enormous role; and that certain concrete decisions can prove morally momentous without the person knowing about it at the time of the decision. Such and similar commonplace observations are the raw materials for moralists; what they do with them depends on the character of their moralism. However, the moral philosopher, even if she or he is potentially a moralist, cannot adopt the position typical of the moralist: that of the observer of one's fellow creatures. The moral philosopher speaks as a member of *a* community, as a member of the human race or, as I have been doing, as a 'contingent person like others'. *Moral philosophy is a speech act in a practical discourse.* Moral philosophers draw the raw material of commonplace observations, which is actual life, from the process of actual discourse.

Yet actual life eludes philosophical categorization and generalization in its infinitude, concreteness and variety. At most, moral philosophy can arrive at the stage of designing ideal types or heuristically presenting valuable examples of a Chinese emperor or an American pharmacist. But ideal types or rigid and heuristically presented single cases are artificial and mostly haphazard, particularly in modern times, when the common ethos is gone.

This is one of the reasons why discourse ethics shies away from exploring actual life situations. It is why the philosophers of discourse ethics must admit to an inability to elucidate their own problems, as they face them in real-life situations with their own philosophy. Discourse ethics does not answer the question 'What is the right thing for me to do?' It answers only the question of how valid norms (of justice) should be established. Yet I cannot engage in a moral discourse at all unless I also raise the question 'What is the right thing for me to do?' If moral philosophy, this peculiar speech act, refuses to elucidate the moral problems proper of the author of the speech act, then we are no longer dealing with moral philosophy proper; practical discourse will revert back to theoretical discourse.

In presenting the good (decent) person as the normative subject of my ethics, I make the presentation of this normative subject *to myself as a person as much as to anyone else as a person*. I share with my fellow creatures all commonplace observations concerning the behaviour of 'people in real-life situations'. I also know that good persons exist. It is only natural that I want to find out how they cope with real-life situations; how they walk the tightrope dividing decency from evil; how they can overcome tough luck; what they will do when they discover that they have made some momentous decisions in ignorance.

I have not ignored 'real-life situations'. My starting point, contingency, has been rooted in real-life situations; I have accompanied the decent person on his or her life's way, from the everyday context via a commitment to institutions through to commitment to matters of justice and the 'cause of the human race'. But I have focused on one aspect while abstracting from others. So far, in my eagerness to keep in focus the very norms (and virtues) which have been reached by the decent person in the quest for his or her own path, I have failed to elucidate the conflicts, the painful decisions and the moral mistakes. The first three chapters share the same objective as discourse ethics: the establishment of valid norms. But, whereas discourse ethics limits itself to laying down a *procedure* for establishing valid norms, I have, in the company of the 'decent person', made explicit *what these norms actually are*. This was only possible because I followed the path of decent persons and did not abstract from actual life situations more than was necessary to achieve my objective. Now, in the possession of these norms, I may return to the already familiar terrain of life situations to explore them from a different angle: that of conflicts, painful decisions and moral mistakes.

For simplicity's sake, let us assume that decent persons have indeed arrived at the discovery of the moral norms presented in the previous chapters. Later we shall glance at decent persons in their moral predicament.

An apparent paradox presents itself at this stage. I have conceded that 'real life' eludes philosophical categorization in its infinitude, concreteness and variety. At the same time, I have been insisting that a moral philosophy which fails to address actual life situations remains an exercise in theoretical, not practical, discourse. But how can one discuss decisions and actions without presenting heuristically representative, but otherwise abstruse, cases or without drawing up an abstract and empty typology? As we have accompanied the decent person on his or her life's course, including the decisions, actions, and moral problems which are actual life situations, not just speculative eventualities, a theoretically promising solution has offered itself. At the same time, two additional difficulties have emerged. First, while every decision and action is singular, philosophy is not concerned with singular cases. Second, unlike technical manipulations and theoretical–cognitive operations, actions and decisions of moral provenance are unrepeatable. Both difficulties, however, as well as the general methodological dilemma, can be overcome through the following approach. In discussing single decisions and actions in concrete life situations, I will not use them as 'exemplifications', but instead will discuss any and every decent person in action and decision. Nor will I formulate an infinite number of alternative action patterns in order to ascribe them to one or another type of institution in the process of creating 'ideal types'. I will, rather, focus on *how* decent persons remain what they are: decent. My question will be *how* decent persons handle divergent and concrete situations; *how* they make up their minds to do one thing rather than another; *how* they cope with conflicts and face trivial as well as momentous matters. In brief, I shall discuss *the modus operandi of the virtue of phronesis*, good moral judgement, in modern times. I am justified in proceeding in this manner because in the modern world there is at least one, though crucial, homogenizing factor in the 'class of decent persons': in so far as they have made the existential choice under the sign of the universal, they are all decent alike. One can presuppose that all of them want to find out *how* to do the right thing.

In general terms it can be stated that, as soon as decent people know what the right norms are, the goodness of their decisions and actions will only depend on phronesis, good moral judgement. Aristotle, who first identified phronesis as the intellectual virtue operative in moral decisions, also exemplified the way it works. Contingent men and women who have chosen themselves as decent persons have, by definition, also chosen to act and decide decently in concrete life situations. In other words, the choice of phronesis is inherent in the existential choice of goodness. But there are differences between the *modus operandi* of the phronesis of contingent men and women in a contingent world and its *modus operandi* in the world Aristotle described. This difference must be accounted for. Reading the acts and decisions of decent persons is tantamount to reading about the operation of phronesis in the modern world. The best way of conducting such a discourse is to raise, and eventually to answer, the question concerning the fulfilment of the virtue norm phronesis in our modern age. Since phronesis, like every virtue, is also a character trait, our question can be formulated as follows: 'How can modern men and women develop, under the primacy of the ethical, the *habit* of employing theoretical reason in the service of practical decisions?' I now turn to this question.

II

Since morals do not constitute a sphere, there are no 'moral actions'.[1] Men and women do different things but they do not 'do morals'. Yet actions are approved, disapproved or considered indifferent from the moral as well as from any other point of view. We approve or disapprove an action, or declare it morally indifferent, in so far as we appraise this action with the standards of a moral value orientation of 'good and evil'. As a rule, the same action can also be appraised by the standards of other categories of value orientation, such as 'useful–harmful', 'successful–unsuccessful', 'beautiful–ugly' and 'pleasant–unpleasant'. An action which is thought to enhance one or several (substantive) goods is considered good. *In the case of a happy action, moral good and substantive good coincide.* It belongs to our human condition that all men and women prefer 'happy actions'.

Before embarking on an action or a series of actions, one normally makes projections, which may include as well as exclude the moral point of view. Decent persons invariably include it in their deliberations – that is, they are interested in the moral quality of their intended action or series of actions. And, if they come to the conclusion that their intended action is not morally indifferent, that it stands in a moral relation (in a relation to moral norms), they will give priority to the moral point of view against all other points of view. They will project only an act which can be performed without violating moral values and norms. Since sincerity and truthfulness are fundamental virtues of decent persons, as discussed in chapter 2, their deliberation and decision will also be sincere. 'Sincerity' here means, above all, freedom from rationalization which deludes ourselves and misleads others.

This is how a decent person makes an authentic moral decision prior to action when time is not of the essence. Certain actions, however, allow for only short deliberations. This is where the *habit* of appraising actions from the moral point of view becomes crucial. Habit develops *intuition* which operates like lightning: it illuminates the dark corners of projected action; moral decision and action can almost be simultaneous. Intuition guides the decent person almost automatically in familiar circumstances; a longer process of deliberation is required in unfamiliar or morally crucial circumstances. It is a matter of the good moral judgement to develop a 'feel' for the time element. If time is not at our disposal, we make decisions purely out of intuition and with a clear awareness of the risk.

This is the most simple and most usual scenario for 'taking a moral risk'. No conflicts between norms are as yet involved. The person is not thrown into a 'borderline situation'. There is no ambiguity at the start: had the person had sufficient time for deliberation, she or he could have arrived at a perfectly right decision to his or her moral satisfaction. And, needless to say, if the action taken under pressure of time proves retrospectively to have been morally at fault, *the decent person does not loose his or her decency as a result of the misconceived action.* For awareness of the moral risk also implies a readiness to revoke one's action retrospectively in the case of moral failure. To say 'I am sorry' is a simple but magnificent human invention to cope with moral mishaps. It stands for 'I did not mean it' or 'I did not intend it' or 'I did not mean it to happen *that way.*' The intention to cause harm to another person is bad in terms of moral standards (unless it is done for moral reasons). As a result, the declaration of non-intention transforms an act of negative moral content into an act of indifference *without changing the act itself.* The ability of a ceremonial statement such as 'I am sorry', 'Forgive me' or 'I forgive you'[2] to change reality is of crucial significance, because it proves that *the perception of something too is reality.*

Decent persons do not like taking moral risks; as a rule, they prefer certainty to ambiguity. This is also true in modern times. Given the rapid changes in *mores* and the increasing heterogeneity of situations, the 'crutch' of universal norms is frequently needed and intuition becomes less and less reliable. This is why modern men and women prefer to have plenty of time to make momentous decisions. Modern drama reflects well the over-reflectiveness of modern persons, particularly when they really intend to find the morally best course of action. Time at one's disposal is, of course, no guarantee of the right decision, and, if a person is more clever than truthful, it can make things worse. A sophisticated actor will conjure up the kind of rationalization that she or he would not have been able to find if pressed to act on first impulse. Although it is preferable to avoid a moral risk rather than take it, one must develop a 'feel' for those occasions when one simply must take it. Since phronesis, like all other virtues, is acquired, not inborn, mistakes are inevitable while the 'feel' is being developed.

If our decision involves other persons (or just one), and the resulting action would either benefit or harm them in various ways, the time at our disposal is most properly spent in discussing the issue and our decision with all of those concerned. A preliminary dialogue may prepare the ground for a decision on behalf of what I have termed a 'happy action'. And, even if the 'happy action' does not eventuate, a dialogue of this kind has several ethical merits. One can test one's own authenticity and gauge the possible consequences of the action, as well as gain an idea of one's own ability to assess them. Furthermore, entering into such a discussion is in itself an act of observing norms: in so doing, one shows respect for other persons' autonomy. But conducting a dialogue with those concerned does not make the decision dependent on their judgement. *There are no collective decisions in morals: each decides on his or her own*, even if the action that originates from several (similar or identical) decisions is collective. The other party's position should be accepted in one case alone: if one becomes convinced of its *ethical superiority*. The possibility of having at the end of the dialogue two options, *equal in moral decency*, will be discussed later.

It is wise to spend some of the time available for decision discussing the problem (the choice) with a 'third party' or with impartial judges of the matter. In bygone times there was always a friend, 'the natural counsellor', to offer advice; nowadays, the lamentable loneliness of people, particularly in big cities, is in part caused by the disappearance of such friends. 'Professional counsellors' fill their place. They are sometimes preferred even by people who have a friend whose advice could be sought. For it is rightly assumed that, unlike the friend's, the professional counsellor's insight is completely independent and thus applicable to all situations. It is equally rightly assumed that a friend, in full awareness of the moral complexity of certain situations, may be reluctant to give unequivocal advice and take a strong moral stance, or, perhaps, incapable of overcoming the spirit of relativism. Aristotle's matter-of-fact statement that real (true) friendship is based on sharing a virtuous life and goodness is painfully out of tune with our time. But is it not true today, just as it was true 2000 years ago, that a decent person is the friend of another decent person? It is best, even today, for a decent person to have others of the same kind for friends; yet she or he can no longer expect them to be ready with advice in the same way as friends were in former times. The major reason for this is the increased complexity of our life situations: *one cannot offer advice before having full knowledge of a situation.* The competence of the 'natural counsellor' in modern times is limited by this complexity. However, the limitation disappears as soon as the act in progress threatens to violate universal norms. In such cases, the friend will act in the old-fashioned way and will tell the other, 'You should not do that!'

For all of this, discussion with the 'third party', the impartial judge, the friendly but objective counsellor, becomes extremely difficult even if the person in question has the time for a full discussion. The norms of justice (socio-political norms) are a strong point of discourse ethics. Such norms can best be established by discourse, and in the case of their application it is relatively easy to offer advice. But, when it comes to moral decisions other than those concerning justice, modern persons prefer to conduct a dialogue in their own soul rather than entrust the burden of decision to those who in the end may only say, 'Do what you deem best.'

Given that intuition, the famous 'good moral sense', can often fail us and that we are rarely able to turn for good advice to men and women whose judgement we trust, it seems as if moral risk is much greater today than in pre-modern times. But this is not a realistic assessment, since certain other conditions of the moral choice have conspicuously shifted in the opposite direction. First, the number of substantive goods to be morally evaluated, whether positively or negatively, is smaller than it was under either the Greek or Christian ethos. And, if a substantive goal, a means to the goal and an activity are considered adiaphoric, a decision related to them is no longer a moral decision. As a result, decisions may carry risks other than the moral one without the moral one. Second, the decrease in the density of moral norms and the increase in the formalization of the norms and rules of justice further diminish the danger of taking a moral risk. Finally, the time element also helps reduce the dangers inherent in a momentous risk.

The first two of these factors (the expansion of the territory of adiaphoric substantive goods and the formalization of matters related to justice) decrease the number of the decisions which could imply high moral risks. But what I have called the 'time element' is a quantity of a different kind which affects the quality of our lives. Modern, contingent persons make mistakes that people in a traditional environment would not make, but they live long enough to make up for them. In proportion to the increase in our contingency, our life expectancy also grows. However, this is expectancy *in sensu stricto*: men and women expect not to die before having explored all chances to become what they are. Those thrown into a traditional world could become what they were within a very short lifespan. They learned from their own, one and only, environment how to act decently and how to develop good moral judgement (phronesis). By contrast, modern men and women need to live a long time, experiencing a range of different environments and coming to know a variety of institutions, ideologies, people, and much else. In this complex process, mistakes can be made; yet there is time to make and rectify many such mistakes. A decent life is not an unbroken continuum of decent actions; it is the continuity of many discontinuities, changes, choices good and bad, failures and successes – a continuity in which, ultimately, decency gains the upper hand. Whatever decent persons do is impregnated with decency, their moral failures included. Decency is not a terrain that decent persons conquer: it is what they are. But modern decent persons do need time in order to be able to live up to their existential choice. And we have this time, unless our life is cut short by violence. Borderline situations, to be discussed later, are termed 'borderline' precisely because they are outside this pattern.

III

It makes good sense to discuss the 'application' of the norms and rules of *justice*. These are *clusteral norms* – that is, they constitute social clusters and so apply to each and every member of a cluster. In *Beyond Justice*, I make a distinction between *static* and *dynamic* justice. In the case of static justice, we accept the norms and rules as just. In order to be just ourselves, we have to apply the norms and rules consistently and continuously to each member of the cluster to which they apply. In the case of dynamic justice, we question and test the rules and norms themselves. In contesting the justice of existing norms and rules and in making a case for replacing them, we must have recourse to certain values other than justice (for it is a tautology to say that something is unjust because it is unjust). Strictly speaking, one can only talk of the 'application' of norms and rules in the case of static justice. Yet in *Beyond Justice* I strongly support the recommendation of Habermas that new (alternative) norms and rules should be accepted by everyone concerned in a rational discourse. Such a discourse has norms and rules of its own which need to be applied. In the case of rule application, there can be no doubt concerning *how* to apply them, for the 'how' is inherent in 'what', 'when' and 'to whom'.

In the case of norm application, the situation is more complex. It has to be decided which norm applies to a particular situation, how to apply it, and so on. Yet it is still appropriate to talk of 'application'.

It is when it comes to actions which have moral implications *other than those related to justice and injustice* that it becomes difficult to talk of the 'application' of norms and rules. There is nothing odd in saying that the referee 'applied' the rules correctly (justly) in granting a penalty or that the teacher applied the rules correctly (justly) in grading essays. However, it is decidedly odd to say that our friend applied the norm of truthfulness and this is why she told the truth instead of a lie, or that in a quarrel someone applied the norm 'Do not kill' and so did not kill the man he was quarrelling with. Moral norms proper are *transclusteral*; they do not constitute social or political clusters in our modern world. One 'lives up to' rather than 'applies' them – and even the idea of 'living up to' them can be misleading. Moral norms can become 'second nature' to men and women; some of them do become 'second nature' to decent men and women. But norms and rules of justice never become 'second nature'; only *the habit of applying them does*. If the norms and rules of justice themselves were to become 'second nature', men and women would lose their ability to enter into a discourse in which the validity of those norms and rules is tested (defended or rejected).

Whatever a person does leaves its mark on the lives of others. One cannot escape from the human condition, the condition of togetherness, and, in fact, no one really does wish to escape from it. Kant coined the expression *ungesellige Geselligkeit* (unsociable sociability) to describe the paradoxical character of this condition. Men and women do everything in order to be recognized by their neighbours: nothing matters but this recognition. People commit crimes against their fellow creatures, ruthlessly compete with them, arouse their jealousy, envy and hatred just so that those same fellow creatures will accord them the highest possible recognition. By contrast, decent persons choose the path of *gesellige Geselligkeit* (sociable sociability). They struggle 'against' (other persons or groups) only if matters of justice so require; otherwise, they only struggle 'for' (themselves and others). Being 'sociable' in the Kantian sense of the term makes us less vulnerable to non-recognition by others. Although he used different terms, Aristotle was aware that virtuous persons have a stronger ego than others – not because they are less pleased with recognition, but because they are not prepared to pay for it with their morality.

At the same time, decent persons develop a special sensitivity for others' ego weakness, a sensitivity of the greatest import in modern times. For even the performance of a completely adiaphoric action could wound persons with weak egos. Lukács points out in *The Theory of the Novel* that *tact* has become a main ethical quality of the 'problematic individual' (or, in my terminology, the contingent person). Tact is a remarkable virtue because it is *not* a virtue *norm*. An act is rebuked as tactless not because of what it is but because of how it is executed. Nor can tact be termed a subcase of phronesis. A sense of tact is a talent, whereas phronesis is not. Yet tact is similar to phronesis: to use Wittgenstein's term, they have a 'family resemblance'. But tact is not identical with good judgement: it is good, but it is not judgement. We all are familiar with the *ceremonies* and *mannerisms* of self-presentation and self-protection, of which Goffman has provided such a comprehensive and witty portrayal. Ceremonies and mannerisms of this kind also have something to do with tact. Like tact, they too gain momentum in modern times within the stream of Elias's celebrated 'civilizing process'. And yet tact and protective ceremonies are not identical. For example, the ceremonies of 'saving face' are impersonal: we pretend not to notice the person when we notice the *faux pas*. The person whose self we thus protect becomes an impersonal X. Tact, too, is face-saving, but it is elastic, adjusting to persons and situations, and perceptive in the way it does this; this is how it is experienced by the other party as well.

One can notice something if one pays attention. Although unfailing tact is a gift, paying attention to others is not. 'Sociably sociable' persons pay attention to people in the company of whom, for whom, with whom they act and about whom they decide. They do their best to protect the ego of their fellow actors. Finally, 'acting tactfully' also has an aesthetic dimension. Tact can lend a unique form to a trifling act, for acting tactfully is also acting beautifully, elegantly, in a noble manner. Yet, as in all junctures of the aesthetic and the ethical, here too the primacy of the ethical must be maintained.[3]

As mentioned, decent persons assess possible and probable actions from the moral point of view. If the prospective action seems to be adiaphoric, the decision is made from a non-moral point of view. But it must first be tested whether the action is indeed adiaphoric or, rather, has moral connotations, and, if so, what they are. How can a test like this be performed?

Two action patterns, slightly different from each other, need to be discussed here separately. In the first case, one wants to discern whether an action which is about to be undertaken is *morally permissible*. In the second case, one intends to do something which is *good, noble and valuable*, and searches for the best ways to do it. In both cases, everyone would prefer what I have termed a 'happy action'. In the first case, the definition of the 'happy action' is that the proposed act should be permissible; in the second, that the act should not be unduly costly. Textbooks on morals tend to concentrate on actions that place great demands on the actor, and have little to say about 'happy actions'. The latter, however, are not as infrequent as this may suggest, and at any rate deserve scrutiny to the same extent as 'unhappy actions'.

These two types of action patterns can be described in strict Weberian terms as *goal-oriented* and *value-oriented*, respectively. But it must be stressed in advance that goal-oriented actions are also value-oriented in a broader sense. Since moral good is a value of the highest order, the good person's resolve not to embark on actions of negative moral content is an attitude of prime value orientation even if the act itself is adiaphoric, and, as such, 'goal-oriented' in an orthodox Weberian sense.

In the case of goal-oriented actions, the distinction between *action proper* and *techne* needs to be further scrutinized. Every act of moral relevance is an action, and it is practical, not merely technical–pragmatic, in character. Furthermore, there are certain acts which constitute a technical procedure and which become actions (praxis) without ceasing to be technical acts, by virtue of the fact that they *should not be performed* (for example, certain kinds of vivisection).

The decent person poised to embark on an action seems to be too rigid a model, far removed from the reality of everyday action. After all, we are constantly acting in one way or another, and there are no absolute zero points in the chain of our actions. In spite of this, the model makes sense. It may well be true that one rarely chooses *a* goal or *a* framework or *a* person separately, that our choices overlap or are interconnected and that they cannot be separated except artificially. Yet there are certain momentous decisions in each and every person's life which narrow down the framework for subsequent choices or create derivative situations following from the initial one. These are the points at which the 'new course of action' originates, when we are 'poised to embark on an action' in the sense that, while we know that the given moment is but one link in the chain, *we date our new course of action from that moment.*

Let us assume, then, that our person 'poised to embark on an action' is decent. Let us further assume that that person has been standing in a network of human relationships – that is, 'such and such a person' with 'such and such a past'. Yet we can hardly 'assume' in advance that, at a given moment, that person would find himself or herself in such and such a situation or would stand before such and such a decision. Situation is not a mere given, as we open up situations for ourselves, nor, for the same reason, is it a 'something' we 'stand before'. But we can assume that the person in question has already decided to do something which is morally permissible. This will be the model of a goal-oriented action, for, in the case of a value-oriented action, the person first has to check whether the intended action is indeed the most valuable, or the morally optimal, one. One normally decides to pursue a substantive goal, a 'this' or a 'that', or certain interconnected goals ('this goal' together with 'that or those'). Interconnected goals can be simultaneous or consecutive, hierarchically ordered or not. They can be practically anything: a thing, a position, a person, a framework for future actions, an institution, or whatever. But no substantive goal can be an ultimate end, because it is not goal-oriented actions, but regulative ideas, that aim at ultimate ends. However, the goals must be considered 'goods' by the actor, otherwise they would not be his or her goals.

Goals are pursued amidst certain *constraints*; *potentials* need to be mobilized in order to achieve and effect them; and the goals themselves are embedded in certain *frameworks*. Yet the framework in which the goal is embedded is external to the actor at the time of the decision. The actor's decision aims precisely at getting into the framework.

In the case of a goal-oriented action, both the power and the character of constraints and potentials are of crucial importance from a pragmatic point of view, yet, unless they are of relevance for the foreseeable moral consequences of the action, they are of no importance whatsoever from the moral point of view. Making this distinction with ease is the sign of good moral judgement (phronesis). The reverse also holds: good moral judgement is developed by making this distinction frequently and correctly.

The decent person must check the permissibility of both goal and means. The infamous thesis that the ends justify the means has very little bearing on this process of checking. So long as the decent person only wants to discover whether a particular goal is permitted, not whether it is the 'ultimate end', the whole question of 'what justifies what' will not even be raised.

As is well known, goals are always related to substantive values (other than ultimate ends), and 'actions towards goals' may be, but are not necessarily, related to (positive or negative) substantive values other than their goal(s). Yet neither goals nor actions 'embody' substantive values as such. Rather, so-called 'pure substantive values' are related to concrete actions and goals. In actual fact, it is not 'health' that we aim at, but at being cured of a certain disease, protecting ourselves from epidemics, keeping ourselves fit, and so on. So far as actions are concerned, we may take pills, submit to operations, do exercises, undertake medical research, quarantine others, penalize those who offend standards of hygiene, and much else. One can hardly find an action (or goal) which stands in no relation to at least one 'pure substantive value'. This is one of the reasons why an action or goal cannot become morally permitted merely by virtue of being related to a pure substantive value, and a decent person is fully aware of this. Using distilled 'pure values' as justifying devices is a precarious business needing a very good moral judgement, for, while pure values cannot be entirely neglected in the process of justification, neither can they become its sole criterion. The extent to which we can proceed, the point at which we have stop if we wish to remain decent, is again a matter of phronesis.

IV

I have indicated that constraints and potentials, as well as the framework in which the goal is embedded, must be considered from a pragmatic point of view. I have added that, from the moral point of view, both constraints and potentials can be neglected unless they are of relevance for the foreseeable *moral* consequences of the action. But one must reflect upon the framework both from the pragmatic and from the moral point of view. The goal is always embedded in at least one framework, but usually in several. The framework in which goals and actions are invariably embedded is *the life of the actor*. The multiplicity of frameworks relates to the lives of others. In traditional societies and ways of life the distinction between the two kinds of framework can be neglected, for two interconnected reasons. First, as a member of a collectively shared ethical world, one can be virtually certain that what is permitted for one is also permitted for others. Hence there will be almost automatic consensus on which actions may be regarded as adiaphoric. Second, where actions are customary, they are also permitted by virtue of being customary. Modern everyday life is also replete with goals and activities which are 'taken for granted', and thus permitted, so long as the actor endorses the customs. Sometimes it is simply a sign of *moral hysteria* when people question trifles. Phronesis discerns the 'middle ground' between moral hysteria, on the one hand, and moral cynicism, for which every goal and action is a trifle, on the other.

The proviso that customary actions are permitted so long we endorse the customs needs to be further investigated. Ethical customs are *concrete norms*.[4] There are concrete ethical norms also in modern times, but their character and density have become variable. This circumstance indicates the plurality of ethics and ways of life. Modern contingent persons set such goals and perform such actions as either are directed toward men and women who do not share the actors' ethical customs, or at least exert an influence on the lives of such people. What I have termed 'framework' is the customs, the moral convictions, the forms of life, and the institutions amidst which those affected by our goals and actions live; goal and action are embedded therein. In a pluralistic universe, goal and action can be embedded in a variety of frameworks. Thus the question about the permissibility of actions and goals has to be reformulated in the following manner. 'Is it permissible *for me* to pursue this particular goal?' 'Is it permissible to pursue it with this *concrete* Other?' 'Is it permissible to pursue a goal which is embedded in the framework of such others as do not share my concrete moral norms?'

What is at issue here is not whether decent persons can deliberately do indecent things but the need for each decent person to be decent in his or her own ways. After the existential choice, one develops a way of life which is a singular form or kind of decency. It includes concrete commitments to persons, institutions, particular ideas and movements; it also includes commitment to certain *interpretations* of values and virtues, to a profession (or professions), certain kinds of activities, the development of certain talents, and much else. To become decent *in another way* was, of course, open to this contingent person, this bundle of possibilities. Yet, once certain possibilities have become actualities, they exclude or limit the realization of other possibilities. To become and be 'such and such a (decent) person', a true individual, is not merely a matter of personality qualities: it is also a matter of values and obligations, promises and commitments. To be true to oneself is not the maxim of honesty: dishonest persons can be completely true to themselves and cynical rascals even cherish living up to their own true selves. But for persons who have chosen honesty and have become 'such and such an honest person', the maxim 'Be (remain) true to yourself' will carry a particularly great weight. The first conclusion that follows from this is that a goal that is permissible, and the pursuit of which is permissible, in a general sense will be impermissible for concrete honest persons who would be untrue to their own individuality were they to pursue it. In discussing a man's duty towards himself,[5] Kant had self-perfection in mind: developing our abilities and propensities, perfecting ourselves, is our main duty toward ourselves. Although I believe that developing our best endowments into talents is one of the conditions of the good life, I do not believe that self-perfection should be considered a duty. To be decent is one of the conditions of the good life; developing our best endowments into talents is another; and being able to establish steady and close emotional personal attachments is a third. Yet one can be decent without developing one's best endowments into talents, since one can be decent in different ways. Remaining true to oneself has the *appearance* of being a duty, in the sense that the person 'owes' it to himself or herself. Imagine any situation in which a decent person begins to pursue a goal that, while not impermissible in itself, is completely out of keeping with the concrete quality of his or her decency. That person has *no duty proper* to keep intact his or her image of 'such and such a decent person'. But there is certainly a semblance of a duty implied here, for in a vague fashion we associate goodness with knowledge and self-knowledge.

In pursuing a goal which does not fit well into the framework of his or her usual way of life a decent person normally *gives reasons* for so doing. The reasons given are typically of two kinds, subjective and objective. The subjective reason has recourse to the notion of a new *initiative*. The decent person takes initiatives in order to change his or her own life. The objective reason has recourse to the *frameworks* in which the goal is embedded (in addition to the actor's own way of life). True enough, people very rarely give thoughtful consideration to the particular frameworks in which their goals may be 'deflected', so making them untrue to themselves. I shall return to this issue, and the conflicts ensuing therefrom, at a later stage of my analysis.

Nowadays, even people in the same household can subscribe to different concrete norms. Upbringing, personal choice, affiliation with different institutions, the generation gap and much else contribute to such diversity. It is not the diversity of *interests*, but that of *normative expectations* that is under discussion here. Interests can be diverse, or on a collision course with one another, even if normative claims are shared. Needless to say, the difference in normative expectations can also find expression in the conflict of interests. Decent persons need to scrutinize goals which are, in their moral universe, perfectly adiaphoric in order to find out whether the pursuit of such goals will be acceptable, from the moral point of view, for other members of the same household or community. To pursue atheist propaganda is adiaphoric in itself, but it is not necessarily so for a young atheist who pursues this goal in the home of his deeply religious parents.

Certain moral theories suggest that goals pursued for one's own sake are always morally inferior to those pursued for the sake of others. These theories were devised in ages where ethical life was still homogeneous; and they have survived their times of conception without serious revisions. In our modern life, such simple recipes do not offer proper guidance. True, a person who does everything for his or her own sake alone cannot be decent. But it does not follow from this assertion that each single goal pursued for other persons' sake is morally superior to goals pursued for one's own sake. George Bernard Shaw's deep *aperçu* that we should not do unto others what we expect others to do unto us, since others might have a completely different taste, applies here. Put bluntly, the goal is always a 'good' for the person who does something for his or her own sake; in this case, the respect for the autonomy of the beneficiary is inherent in the act. In doing something for the sake of others, however, one may or may not respect the autonomy of the supposed beneficiary, who may desire something completely different.

Assume that a decent person wants to do something for his or her own sake and that the act is in itself adiaphoric. In trying to fathom the 'framework for others' in which the action is embedded, she or he has to consider both the life interests and the values of the persons *directly* concerned in the decision. No norm of decency demands more than that; going beyond this requirement would be moral hysteria. In fact, when people do go farther, they normally are guilty of verbal excesses that rightly invite the accusation of hypocrisy. Of course, it might happen that, in the pursuit of goals in themselves adiaphoric, the interests or value systems of other persons are involuntarily hurt. But only transculturally good persons – that is, saints or perfect beings – can attempt to take all these eventualities into consideration before embarking on a goal-oriented action. For the (normally) decent person this would be a sign of moral hysteria, which she or he tries to avoid. To demand that others behave towards one as transculturally good persons would therefore be to apply double standards, the avoidance of which is a norm of decency in every culture. Not double standards, but rather the standard itself, should be discussed here briefly.

In the modern world of the functional division of labour, the increasing abstraction (and universalization[6]) of norms, the plurality of ways of life and the individualization of ethical lifestyles, the standards of expectation and (moral) judgement have become more general, sometimes even vague and elastic. This has the following consequence for the case under consideration. In so far as my goal is adiaphoric, and in so far as I pursue it for my own sake and have taken into consideration how my action may be expected to affect people directly involved, I have done my duty as a decent person and I can proceed. But, if another person does the same, I have no right to moral disapproval, even if that person's goal collides with my interests or hurts the feelings which I have invested in personal values and concrete norms. In a word, the value of *liberalism* is of crucial significance for the life practice of honest persons. Liberalism is more than mere toleration. Toleration is a prime value in action, approval and disapproval where ethical pluralism or pluralism of lifestyles is still new and has not set firm roots. Liberalism is an attitude based on the conviction that we have no reason, authority or right to disapprove of others simply because of their preference for other goals or values.

It goes without saying that liberalism must not be extended to actions which are morally wrong and thus, in terms of the well-known criteria, impermissible in themselves. Since decent persons will never set themselves a goal which, *qua* goal, is morally evil, or the pursuit of which requires the violation of norms, they will not be liberal if actions of these kinds committed by others are to be judged. Transculturally good persons may extend the goodness of their heart to murderers and other persons of violence or ruthless ambition. Decent persons can only go as far as forgiving an act of aggression committed against them, even when decency does not require forgiveness. However, it is highly questionable whether the decent person has the authority to forgive a crime committed against a third party. For, in the final analysis, we are all contingent persons; we do not wield the authority of judgement by virtue of belonging to a particular community (for example, a nation), nor are we empowered by any transcendental authority to take the cause of justice, the right to solve and bind, in our own hands.

In pursuing goals (goods) not for their own sake but for the sake of others, decent persons will again make efforts to discern whether the pursuit of a particular goal is permissible. The goal being a good, the person pursuing it will assume that the outcome will be useful, pleasant and satisfying for the beneficiary. Where one is the intended beneficiary of one's own action, one can err only on one count: by misjudging the assumed benefits to be gained from the goal if achieved. In acting for other persons' sake, the possibility of erring on that count is increased. Furthermore, in acting for others, we might prevent those others from acting for their own sake, from pursuing their own goals or from maintaining their own values in their own ways. The standard answer of mild egoists – 'I mind my own business; you mind yours' – eliminates the problem without facing it. One cannot help pursuing a goal for the sake of someone else even if one pursues it for one's own sake; and, further, decency does require one to act on behalf of others also.

Although we are still discussing goal-, and not value-, oriented actions, values too play a certain role given that goals are goods. One does not do justice to the complexity of real-life situations by contrasting interest-regulated and value-regulated actions as if they were mutually exclusive. A father may ponder the ways of rescuing his son from taking a course which he regards as detrimental for the son. All his contemplated remedies may be morally permissible, yet the whole action may turn out to be deeply problematic, depending on the context. A host of highly morally relevant issues are related to such situations. For example, should a blood transfusion be imposed on a patient who has conscientious objections to it on religious grounds? In itself, there is neither moral credit nor moral debit in blood transfusion, which is part of the doctor's daily routine. The issue here is neither the consequences in general nor the (good or bad) motivations but rather the consideration of the framework in which the goal is embedded (other persons' goals, convictions and values). What makes the issue complex and controversial is that, even if one's action for others' sake produces no direct ill consequences, we may still do for others something that they do not want to be done for them. And sometimes our action, because it is at cross-purposes with the beliefs and value preferences of others, results in outright hostility. No general principles can be applied here to help decent persons who pursue adiaphoric goals for the sake of others to bypass the danger zone that lies ahead of them. For the imposition of values is here indirect–implicit, and the correct assessment when an apparently technical and value-neutral situation ceases to be value-neutral is extremely difficult.[7]

The most general recommendation that can be given to decent persons who intend to avoid moral blunders of this kind is *to follow the guideline of the orientative principle concerning autonomy*. Before embarking on goal-oriented and adiaphoric actions for other people's sake, one first has to find out whether the goal and the pursuit of the goal diminish or increase other persons' autonomy. One need not necessarily resign immediately the pursuit of such goals as tend to diminish the autonomy of others. We may give those others additional information about the goal and enter into discussion with them, and finally they may accept the goal and its implications. However, enlightenment has its limits, even if it is mutual. And, if we find that people refuse to approve our pursuit of goals for their sake, even if we are convinced of its beneficial character, we cannot proceed further. Life-saving is the one exception to this. (And even preventing others from committing suicide has a problematic aspect, as so many advocates of the right to suicide have contended.)

The orientative principle concerning autonomy offers but general guidance. The *sphere* in which the goal is pursued is crucial. In a family or among very close friends, the orientative principle concerning autonomy is, at least in modern times, the constitutive principle of daily life. This is why it would look odd if we were to scrutinize every single step from the aspect of whether or not it decreases the other's autonomy. And yet in an authoritarian family it is precisely this indifference for the autonomy principle that creates the atmosphere of subjection.

The more remote the framework in which our goals are embedded, the more we need to check our goals by the standards of the orientative principle concerning autonomy. In this context, phronesis will not suffice; nor can we rely on available information. When our goal, or the goal of the institution of which we are members, may influence the lives of others or the survival of institutional structures, ethical consequentialism enters the picture. To collect all available information and knowledge before embarking on a project of this kind is a moral must. The pursuit of goals must also be preceded by practical discourse. But practical discourse with whom? – this is the question. Can we conduct a practical discourse with everyone (including those wielding power who would benefit if one particular goal were pursued rather than another) even to the detriment of the persons for whose sake we initiate the action? Can we conduct practical discourse with those who have not mastered the language of the discourse (in a literal and a metaphorical sense), whose typical reaction to life's calamities is either blind submission or equally blind rebellion? Do we have authority to make strong recommendations concerning the economic objectives and practices of others, even if we provide them with the financial means to implement those recommendations? If not, *whose* autonomy do we respect? Discourse is the optimal answer to the problems of autonomy, but the optimal solution may not be within our reach. In this predicament, the best that we can do is to conduct a limited discourse, and we learn to use autonomy in the process of using it.

Goal-oriented actions are therefore normally adiaphoric, and, as such, permitted. Yet permitted actions can also become problematic. In so far as we pursue goals for our own sake, we can blunder morally by becoming untrue to ourselves. In so far as we pursue goals (design projects) for others' sake, we may gravely blunder by disregarding the autonomy of others. Since the line of demarcation between the permitted and unpermitted is here blurred, the general orientative principle of autonomy needs to be consulted frequently.

V

I now turn to value-oriented actions. In promoting one of his or her values, a decent person is not intent on fathoming whether or not the action is permitted, but on determining whether it is *positively good, virtuous, meritorious*. Though goal-oriented actions are performed within the framework of value preferences, and value orientation does not exclude, but rather includes, goal-oriented actions, the difference between the two cases is more than one of emphasis: it is also one of *attitude* (the actor's). Ultimate values can be extracted from goal-oriented actions, but it is alien to the attitude of goal-oriented actors to have such ultimates in mind. As a rule, they do not pursue a particular goal in order to realize an ultimate value or to get closer to 'ultimate ends'. But this is precisely the attitude of actors in value-oriented action. Certain concrete goals can be shared by both value-oriented and goal-oriented actors, although their respective attitudes are different.

Modern men and women perceive a very strong connection between having 'noble ideas' and becoming decent persons. In addition, they associate 'noble ideas' with noble goals. Moral merit increases with the pursuit of noble goals and decreases in proportion to the laxity of the pursuit. The young Hegel traced this image back to ancient Greece, but without much justification. For the ancient Greeks, and particularly for their idealized type as presented by Plato and Aristotle, the republic (*politeia*) was indeed an 'end'. Yet the goodness of the citizen was not regarded as a derivative of, or a means to, this end. Citizens should become virtuous first, for it is only virtuous activity which supports the *good* state as the condition of the citizen's happiness. Lukács was right when he insisted the Hegel's view of the morals of the ancients had been inspired by the French Revolution.[8] It was indeed during the French Revolution that self-abandonment to an idea (the idea of the republic, the Supreme Being and much else) became the chief manifestation of moral merit and goodness. The more a person had vested his or her life and labours in the pursuit of an *end* which was supposed *to embody the idea*, the better a human being she or he was supposed to become. I have termed this idea *abstract enthusiasm*.[9] The era of widespread cynicism subsequent to the French Revolution and the Napoleonic period did not lead to the extinction of abstract enthusiasm. Rather the opposite: abstract enthusiasm contributed to the emergence of the age of cynicism, which in turn gave rise to new waves of abstract enthusiasm. For all kinds of political practices can be related to lofty ideas. Ever since abstract enthusiasm was invented and first practised, no major political force has missed the opportunity to mobilize it. Abstract enthusiasm became particularly vested in the lofty idea of 'the nation' or 'our nation' on the battlefields of Europe. Finally, the abstract enthusiasm of 'the liberation of humankind' promoted wittingly–unwittingly the emergence of a totalitarian regime.

Kant, in referring to enthusiasm as the promise of a moral progression of the human race, had the enthusiasm not of the actors, but of the *spectators*, in mind. So long as the spectator remains in solidarity with the lofty ideas of the actor, he remains an autonomous being. Strong feelings vested in the idea of liberty do not transform men and women into mere instruments. Their personality remains an end-in-itself together with self-abandon. Enthusiasm vested in a spectacle, even in the majestic spectacle of the fight for freedom, remains an aesthetic feeling, the respect for the sublime. But 'liberation' is not a mere spectacle for the actors precisely because they are actors and not spectators. The question is whether we can possibly vest our feelings in ideas as actors without relinquishing our autonomy.

A committed person is not a mere spectator. One cannot be committed without being actively committed to *something*: a goal or the objective of a people or a group, provided that the goal or objective is related to the supreme ideas, particularly the idea of freedom. In being committed to something, a decent person uses himself or herself also as a means for the goal (the 'something') that she or he wants to achieve together with others. Enthusiasm is vested in the ideas, and thus also the goals or objectives which embody those lofty ideas. But decent persons will use themselves as means without self-instrumentalization: they never resign their *autonomous moral self*. No enthusiasm vested in ideas can induce the decent persons to close their minds to moral maxims. They will not fall back to the attitude of the spectator, for they do not mistake commitment for the source of aesthetic pleasure once it has become practical. When persons abandon themselves to ideas and causes without resigning their moral autonomy, we witness the attitude of *concrete enthusiasm*.[10]

Since concrete enthusiasm is based on the preservation of moral autonomy, decent persons as men and women of concrete enthusiasm can, under the pressure of a moral appeal, but not sheer force, also make moral sacrifices (cheat in order to save lives). But they will never paralyse their own moral alertness or renounce the moral authority of conscience. A decent person can accept that a valuable end, a cause, an idea, her country, religion, party or something else, stands higher than himself or herself, a single person. Yet such a person would never accept that anything could overrule his or her moral conscience, and moral maxims as a higher instance of moral appeal. If any particular end or cause would require an infringement of the norms of the highest moral court of appeal, decent persons would rather abandon the pursuit of that end or cause. Certain ends can be pursued by abstract, but not by concrete, enthusiasts; and there are others which can be pursued by both, but in ways which are different for each.

Although decent persons never resign their *moral* autonomy in value-oriented actions, they may be inclined to decrease their non-moral autonomy in the service of a goal. Self-abandonment to a cause, the pursuit of a goal, decreases the non-moral autonomy of persons; this is conveyed by the expression 'being at the service of a goal'. Sometimes even a part of the good life – for example, the development of endowments into talents – may be willingly sacrificed. In so-called 'borderline cases', to which I shall return, decent persons may voluntarily curtail their life chances or even give up life. It is once again a matter of phronesis to discern which circumstances could warrant such ultimate sacrifices.

Even if decent persons can curtail their own non-moral autonomy in the pursuit of a goal, they would never commit themselves to a cause that could be expected to curtail *the non-moral autonomy of other people* or diminish their personal freedom. If there are exceptions to this rule, they should be in accordance with the principles of justice and just laws. Further, decent persons would be reluctant to pursue (evaluated) actions if certain participants in the action were acting under external constraints, acting unwillingly or motivated by fear of punishment of any kind. Finally, they would simply reject an evaluated act if reaching the end depended on the participation of persons subjected to external constraints.

There is a variety of reasons why abstract and concrete enthusiasts may sometimes find themselves promoting the same cause. One reason is that the *idea* of abstract enthusiasm is equally abstract, and the content eventually given to this abstraction could contradict the abstraction itself. Another reason is that, while abstract enthusiasts never use the abstract value as a regulative idea, but rather identify it with a concrete objective, concrete enthusiasts can use the same abstract idea as regulative and make a temporary alliance with abstract enthusiasts while their respective interpretations remain widely divergent. Repressive regimes, too, could bring together the two different types until the great moment of liberation, which is also that of parting ways. This is another way of stating that people can be committed to the same values but to different causes, or committed to the same causes while interpreting them in different ways.

The spell of abstract enthusiasm induces the belief that, the more universal the goal, the more elevated its moral content. But actors of concrete enthusiasm get rather suspicious if a cause becomes too universalistic. For values and principles, not goals, should be universal. After all, it was in the name of 'the liberation of humankind' and 'the abolition of the exploitation of man by man' that millions perished in concentration camps. A concrete enthusiast is a *concrete* enthusiast precisely because he checks the concrete goals and the concrete aspects of his causes with the universal principles of justice. Abstract enthusiasts do not need to check anything: the 'idea' itself is the highest authority in their universe. Having interpreted their meanings, concrete enthusiasts would find no blemish in universals such as 'the liberation of humankind' and 'the abolition of the exploitation of man by man'; yet they would not pursue them as goals because, as such, they are empty and can be filled either with rubbish or with explosives. Concrete enthusiasts can even subscribe to far more substantive quasi-universals such as 'socialism' and 'the cause of the Third World'. The content of these ideas is not quite empty; it is even particularistic, which is why they are termed 'quasi-universals'. The concrete content (or substance) of such quasi-universals has first to be tested by universal principles, and this is the decent person's first task in subscribing to them. These and similar quasi-universals serve the decent person as regulative ideals and *not* as goals.

There is only a single substantive idea which is not a quasi-, rather a real, universal and which can serve as a goal for every decent person to pursue. This is the idea and the goal of *democracy as the institution of self-determination*. Since decent persons *will* justice, their value-oriented actions are related, both objectively and subjectively, to the *maxim of dynamic justice*. It runs as follows: 'What I do to you and what I expect you to do to me, should be decided by you and me.' The maxim is the shorthand formulation of everyone's right and opportunity to participate in the process of formulating and authorizing norms, rules, laws, or any other regulations which are binding for them. The value-oriented acts of decent persons are *objectively* related to this maxim, for, whenever such persons test the value content of their idea, cause or concrete goal through the universal principles of freedom and life, they objectively, in the same act, promote the realization of the substantive goal of 'democracy'. Their value-oriented actions are also *subjectively* related to this maxim, in so far as they have a proper regard for the (relative) autonomy of others and jealously guard their own autonomy. Finally, decent persons live up to the maxim of democracy in each 'here' and 'now' in several ways.

They enter into value discussion[11] with others, particularly with those who are affected by the success or failure of the evaluated goal or cause. They listen to arguments and are ready to accept the ones which seem to be justified, but only those. They are sensitive to resistance, rational or irrational, for they feel respect for the needs, and not just the opinions, of others.

Given that democracy is the only substantive end without further specification, goals which, if achieved, tend to curtail democracy are opposed by decent persons, even if the majority favours them. But, while a decent person is morally authorized to reject the pursuit of a goal (a cause) embraced by the majority (herein the social space for civil disobedience), she or he is not morally authorized to make active efforts to impose his or her goal on a resistant majority – not even with a firm conviction of the correctness of the goal. Enlightenment requires that one give reasons in support of a cause (an evaluated goal). When in the minority, the best a convinced decent person can do is to enter into the often enormously slow process of enlightenment, and make the pursuit of his or her goal dependent on its success.

If there are two or more concrete goals, none of which contradicts universal values and all of which have substantive free support, the best course of action is then decided on pragmatic grounds. It goes without saying that pragmatic considerations also play a role on the previous level, for concrete goals sometimes gain support owing to their promise of greater or more rapid success. But it is only on the present level that pragmatic considerations remain as the only legitimate ones that can determine what happens.

Value-oriented actions can be happy or unhappy to the same extent as goal-oriented ones. Happiest are the actions which lead to great moments of liberation; it is in them that value, need and consensus are crowned by success. By contrast, the most unhappy value-oriented actions are the ones which result in value conflicts of the first order. I now turn to them.

VI

All moral considerations, decisions, choices and actions discussed so far have belonged in situations in which decent persons can, and actually do, use their good judgement. Both in embarking on a goal-oriented action and in making efforts to fathom whether an in-itself adiaphoric action is permitted in a particular case, and also in efforts to actualize a value which is also a goal and in pondering whether a concrete set of actions is in harmony or at variance with the value, theoretical reason is at the service of practical reason. This is why there has been so much mention of phronesis. At the beginning of this chapter, I voiced my misgivings about talking of the application of norms and rules in relation to moral choices and considerations as they occur in real-life situations. My suggestion was that we should rather find an answer to the following question: 'How can modern men and women develop, under the primacy of the ethical, the *habit* of employing theoretical reason in the service of practical decision?'

Since Aristotle, it has been a commonplace in philosophy that we develop the moral habit of doing something by doing it repeatedly. The procedure of testing otherwise adiaphoric goals on moral grounds in particular (concrete) situations, and the procedure of testing the value content (the normative content) of acts which supposedly bring us closer to evaluated (normative) goals seem to be complicated on paper but are perfectly simple in real-life situations. If one is aware that this should be done and one does it all the time, it actually becomes a habit to the extent that one does it almost instinctively. 'Fine-tuning' to the situation, the other aspect of phronesis, also becomes spontaneous. In so far as they are decent, modern men and women do not activate their phronesis less frequently than their ancestors did.

Certain authors deny the relevance of phronesis for modern actors. They do so because they confuse two quite distinct aspects of a concrete action with moral content. Yet, it is not phronesis – that is, putting our theoretical reason at the service of our practical decisions, fine-tuning our action to concrete situations – that has become impossible, or at least of limited relevance, in modern times, as the sworn enemies of neo-Aristotelianism insist.[12] Rather the very process of gaining theoretical insight has become a strenuous and often formidable task. The crutch of the universal maxims is quite reliable provided that the actors are well-informed in all matters relevant for the decision, big or small. It is at this point that *practical reason itself requires that facts and values be temporarily decoupled*. A complete decoupling of facts and values is certainly impossible. The *temporary* decoupling is a mental exercise of a different kind from phronesis, but one which, like phronesis, can become a habit. While phronesis, a cognitive virtue, has nothing to do with decoupling values and facts temporarily, habit in both cases means the habit of 'readiness' and the habit of proper execution. Further, both in the case of temporarily decoupling facts and values and in that of putting information at the service of practical decision (a precondition of phronesis), one also develops the habit of not acting habitually – that is, by mere routine. In a sense, we train ourselves to have a fine sense of novelty, of the uniqueness of a problem, a situation or a case; for, without changing (modifying) our own preconceptions and routines, we cannot live up to the uniqueness which grasping the moral meaning of a case both demands and permits.

An answer has been repeatedly promised here to the decent person's question 'What is the right thing for me to do?' And we cannot answer the question except by exploring the ways in which decent persons themselves explore situations to find out what is the right thing for them to do. We all have moral arguments at our disposal to justify us in what we want to do; but the decent persons among us want to do something only if it is morally justified. This is why decent persons are more likely to get entangled in authentic moral conflicts than others are. Moral conflict occurs when a person in a situation of choice wants to give preference to the morally justified action (instead of justifying a preselected action), and two or more courses of action, mutually exclusive pragmatically, are morally equally justified. If one of these conditions is missing, there can still be a conflict, but not a moral one. Conflicts between moral commitment and adiaphoric actions are not moral conflicts, for the moral weight is only on one side. And when two courses of action of equal moral weight do not exclude one another, then, even if it is strenuous to undertake them simultaneously, there is no moral conflict.

It is easier to recognize and explain the absence of moral conflicts than to give a general idea of moral conflicts themselves. First and foremost, how can one measure 'moral weight'? How can one know that two moral considerations are equally weighty or that one is weightier than the other, and which that is? In a world with a dense traditional ethos one generally knows which are the most weighty duties, obligations, norms and values, whenever one happens to be in a situation of 'either/or'. The tragic heroes of such a world (Orestes, Antigone) normally chose immediately, with passion and without hesitation, putting their own absolute resolve on the scale of balance. The growing instability of an ethos also afflicts the heroes and heroines of tragedies: Agamemnon in Euripides' *Iphigeneia* ruminates no less than Shakespeare's Hamlet on the questions of right and wrong. Wherever the ethos changes, the relative weight of certain courses of action also changes. And where different kinds of ethos coexist, in a state of co-operation, compromise or conflict, the moral weight of certain courses of action is bound to be relativized.

Decent persons do not address moral philosophy for elegant theoretical solutions or for the elimination of logical contradictions, but instead seek advice in their quest for an answer to the question of what is the right thing to do in moral conflicts. Moral conflicts proper are unlike borderline situations. The latter are rare, and average persons *en masse* are exposed to them only in exceptionally demanding social–historical circumstances.

Kant exemplified moral conflicts while denying their existence. We should not, he argued, lie to the would-be murderer about the whereabouts of the person he is pursuing, for the universal stricture on lying can in no circumstances be suspended. Should the prospective victim have taken refuge in our own house, we should tell the pursuer the truth, and nothing but the truth: that his quarry is hiding under our own roof. There is no moral conflict, since there is no choice between lying and telling the truth.

In a world of traditional ethos, a conflict of this type is settled by answering the question 'Who is who?' If the person seeking refuge with us is 'one of us', there is no moral conflict whatsoever. In such a case, lying to a would-be murderer is rather meritorious. If the person seeking refuge is not 'one of us', whether or not there is moral conflict depends on the weight attributed in the particular culture to the virtue of granting sanctuary. Where humanitarian values (those of *humanitas*) are highly rated, as in our modern world, people will opt for lying if this is the moral price they have to pay for saving a life. Given the weight of humanitarian values, they will again discern no moral conflict. However, some (equally) modern persons will agree with Kant that the stricture on lying does not allow for exceptions. But they will add that the norm of defending innocent lives does not allow for exceptions either. Guilt is here pitted against guilt (if you infringe either of these norms); and – the other way round – observing one norm is pitted against observing another. For those who have this kind of moral perception, *moral conflict proper* will emerge in such a situation. From this point onward, we should no longer be concerned with the Kantian answer, which considers rescuing an innocent life a goal and the lie an unpermitted means to the goal. We are going to be concerned only with the merit of the problem.

We are, then, confronted with a 'situation' which presents a moral conflict for some, but none for others. There are two possible courses of action, both meritorious; but to shun both of them is morally wrong or, at least, problematic. The two courses cannot be undertaken simultaneously: this is an 'either/or' situation. For a start, two preliminary questions must be raised. First: are there specific situations which are prone to trigger moral conflicts in the minds of decent persons? Should all situations which trigger conflicts in the minds of some decent persons also trigger moral conflicts in the minds of all of them? And second: how should decent persons cope with moral conflicts? Is there a general moral norm here to follow? If there is not, why; if there is, which is it?

I first propose to distinguish between *hard* and *weak* moral conflicts. If both (alternative and mutually exclusive) courses of action are directly subject to maxims of the first or second order, we are in a situation of hard conflict. Put simply, the conflict is 'hard' if both norms are perceived as unconditionally binding, and their violation, therefore, is unconditionally unpermitted ('Everyone should act thus'/'No one should act thus'), but the person involved must violate one of the norms to live up to the other. The conflict is 'weak' if the two courses of action are not directly, but only indirectly, subject to maxims of the first order, because the two norms are only conditionally binding, and their violation is only conditionally unpermitted ('for such-and-such people in such-and-such a situation'). One must not be an accessary to murder and must not lie. If one becomes an accessary to murder through telling the truth (this is the Kantian example), one faces a hard moral conflict. In the choice between being a conscientious objector and being drafted, one faces a weak moral conflict. For in this case one can *indirectly* refer to maxims ('No one should act against his or her convictions'); but one cannot refer to norms *directly* (one cannot say, 'No one should consent to being drafted' or 'Everyone should become a conscientious objector').

A weak moral conflict can be subjectively as painful as a hard one, yet the distinction remains valid and important. Those entangled in a hard moral conflict claim that *everyone* should understand, interpret and judge their situation as *one of moral conflict*, and that their moral conflict should be regarded as *objective* – that is, in principle such for everyone. By contrast, those in a weak moral conflict cannot – at least, should not – raise such claims. More specifically, they can claim that their own moral conflict should be viewed as authentic by everyone, that their acts should be interpreted and judged as ones situated within a moral conflict; but they cannot claim general recognition for them.

At this point we are widely exposed to the pitfall of moral mistakes. For it is a moral mistake, and not a minor one, to claim to be facing a hard moral conflict when it is really a weak one. Moral intolerance, fanaticism and self-righteousness result from such repeated misjudgement of moral conflicts. By contrast, one stretches tolerance too far in failing to claim universality for one's hard moral conflicts. Self-righteousness, combined with contempt for others, misanthropy and the like, may motivate such judgemental relativism. Aristotle's advice to heed the 'middle measure' (*mesotes*) in all our doing is particularly well-taken at this point.

In a hard moral conflict, both norms are universal (directly universalizable), as is the conflict itself. (Otherwise it would be impossible to claim that everyone should recognize one's own moral conflict as objective – that is, valid for everyone.) And yet, whatever decision or choice we make, whatever course of action we undertake, we cannot and should not claim universality (universal validity) for it. I term this circumstance *the dilemma of morals*.

All attempts to universalize concrete choices, courses of action and decisions are ethically wrong or at least problematic. Also, all theories which invent sophisticated devices to enable us to make properly universalizable decisions fall short of philosophical rigour.

What has been termed the 'dilemma of morals' follows from the discrepancy between the generality of norms (maxims) and the concreteness–uniqueness of single actions. Our attention is not for the first time focused on this discrepancy: the whole discussion of phronesis has addressed exactly this issue. The proposition that phronesis should make the final decision in the choice of action, and that such a decision should always be fine-tuned to the particular–unique situation in which the action is going to take place, implies the proposition that concrete actions with moral content can never claim universal validity. What is good in one case and for a particular person is not morally good for another case and another person; what should be preferred in one particular time and place should not be preferred at another time and place. Good judgement is our best guide here; and good judgement has a penchant for 'singularizing', not 'universalizing'.

Why introduce the 'dilemma of morals' at this relatively late stage of the discussion? Why is it so crucial to stress that, even if our maxims are universalized, our actions cannot claim universal validity? We quite frequently make a morally motivated choice between a variety of actions. Yet it happens far less frequently that we subject our actions to universal maxims or that we bring the norms of our actions to the form of a universal maxim. We do all this after having exhausted other, far more normal and spontaneous procedures, at a juncture where our otherwise reliable guides fail us and when we are badly in need of a 'universal crutch'. In philosophical speculations we can, if indirectly, subject all actions of a positive moral content to one or another universal maxim. Actors always find a universal moral maxim which can be indirectly related to their action or with which they can justify their action retrospectively, even if they have chosen the course of action prospectively without ever consciously relating it to a universal maxim.

The 'dilemma of morals' is omnipresent, even if we do not perceive it as a dilemma. And our perception is right because the dilemma is latent. We aver that 'Everyone should be grateful' but in reality we do not mind if our concrete acts of gratitude do not qualify for universalization. It is only philosophers that work out formulas with strenuous efforts to 'generalize' singular action choices. Ordinary actors would retort that no two persons are ever in a completely identical situation, that no two actions are completely alike, or that the ethos of the recipient can be different from that of the actor. The dilemma is for the philosopher, not for the actor who has a trust in his or her phronesis and moral rectitude. But, in the case of a moral conflict, phronesis is impotent. And this is when the dilemma of morals, omnipresent but latent, comes to the surface, taking dramatic forms in situations of moral conflict, especially in hard ones. Since in hard moral conflicts both (mutually exclusive) courses of action are directly related/subjected to a universal maxim, it is precisely here that the conflict between the universalizability of maxims and the non-universalizability of actions takes the most dramatic form. In the case of a choice between two universals, where obeying one of them calls for the violation of the other, good judgement is out of place. For what the actor has to do is good and evil (bad) simultaneously. 'Fine-tuning' of the good also implies the 'fine-tuning' of evil; and yet, one cannot do the bad in the right way. In brief, this is no situation for 'fine-tuning' at all: this is, rather, an 'either/or' situation. You either do 'this' or you do 'that'. And you cannot wish that *everyone should act likewise, for, if someone did the exact opposite of what you have done, you could not possibly wish that she or he should make such a universalizing claim.*

This is precisely why the dilemma of morals takes the form of a drama – though not always, and not necessarily, that of a tragedy. For the circumstance that two (or more) options for a morally relevant course of action are *equally weighty* does not inform us about the *actual weight* of the moral aspects. Moral conflicts, 'either/or' situations between courses of action of equal moral weight, can come about where neither (or none) of the courses carries a heavy moral weight. I have already mentioned that in weak moral conflicts the weight of the moral import of the anticipated actions also depends on the individual's perception and sensibility. A conflict can be termed tragic only if the respective moral weights of mutually exclusive actions are not only equal, but also heavy, and if they are perceived as such not only by the actor but also by the spectator.

However, the spectator may recognize the conflict as weighty for the actor, yet not as a 'hard' conflict (one of universal character). If this were otherwise, we could hardly understand many ancient tragedies as the poetic renderings of tragic life experiences.

Assume that there are two (and no more) alternatives in a given 'either/or' situation. This is not simply a working hypothesis: most moral conflicts are of this kind. In such a situation, one course can always be taken, frequently a second, and sometimes a third or even a fourth. The one course which can always be taken is to choose either A or B. A further, second course which can frequently be chosen is to transform the situation of moral conflict into a *borderline situation*. This happens if someone refuses to choose and so gives up his or her life (by suicide or by provoking execution). If the respective moral weights of the alternative courses A and B are heavy but not excessive, suicide will be regarded by others either as a too-easy escape or as an act of hysteria. If, on the contrary, the respective moral weights are indeed extremely heavy, the transformation of the moral choice into a borderline situation will be generally regarded as one of the most, perhaps the most, honest. The actor may thus even perform a *representative* action: she or he wants to prove that the respective moral weights of options A and B were heavier than generally believed.

A third option sometimes at the disposal of the person entangled in a situation of moral conflict is to *postpone* the choice. This can happen for various reasons and with various motivations. One can have faith in fate, destiny, chance or providence and hope that something will happen, that some external power will come to the rescue, that the situation will change, and that one can avoid making such a choice after all. One can also rationally expect a beneficial change in the foreseeable future and decide to wait for such a happy eventuality. One can also wait for others to make a decision for one, although this is not the course of our decent person, a morally autonomous being. Whatever the motivations, the postponement of choice can either decrease or increase the dangerous implications of the moral conflict itself. If something really intervenes, and the moral conflict is eliminated, the dangerous implications are gone. If nothing intervenes, the moral conflict may be rendered more weighty and the eventual transgression worse by the postponement. Incidentally, at the end both norms A and B may be violated, not just one of them. Honest persons know from experience that, if no rational expectations back up the postponement of choice, it is better to transform the situation into a borderline situation, in so far as one absolutely refuses to choose, or else make up one's mind fast and do either A or B.

The fourth, and final, alternative in a moral conflict is *escape*. It can take different forms. If a moral conflict pertains to a particular position, especially to a power position (holding an office or being in command), one can resign the position and thus escape from the situation. One can also physically escape. However, for a decent person, this option is only acceptable if no one else is *under constraint* to take the place thus evacuated.

The representative transformation of moral conflicts into borderline situations is exceptional, heroic and paradigmatic. But moral conflicts *tout court* are far from exceptional: they are a frequent, often painful, experience of every decent person. It is by no means paradoxical to state that decent persons face moral conflicts more frequently than indecent persons do, for they are sensitive to moral issues and they neither overrationalize nor irrationalize certain options in order to defuse moral tensions. Nor do they overemphasize the moral import or content of an option, as they are not morally hysterical. They are moral realists, not moral idealists. Similarly, a moral philosophy which has chosen as its method that of accompanying decent persons in their real-life courses *rejects moralizing*. In the modern world, in the world of pluralism, heterogeneity, and contingency, every good person is good in his or her own way. The moral realist has high standards but elastic ones. By contrast, the standards of moralists are rigid, for they do not make allowances for uniqueness and heterogeneity. This is why they easily turn into cynics.

In the choice between A and B, phronesis is suspended, and it is by definition absent whenever the situation of moral conflict is transformed into a borderline situation. Yet, if the concrete character of moral conflict leaves open the options of either postponing the decision or escaping from the situation of conflict, phronesis is restored to its rights, although not completely and not entirely on its own. The following (and similar) questions cannot be answered without exploring the concrete situation. 'How long can this particular decision be postponed?' 'When do we reach the point beyond which postponement can only cause a greater harm?' 'Do I not use, if indirectly, other persons as means by putting constraints on them to take a position evacuated by me if I escape from the situation by resigning my post?' Asking and answering such questions is a judgemental process and an eminently moral one. It cannot be a habit, for the situation to be evaluated does not belong to any pattern. But, since here a concrete situation needs to be elucidated and the prospective action needs to be fine-tuned, phronesis, as the very habit of fine-tuning and judging the concrete concretely, is badly needed.

If decent persons ask other decent persons what they should do in a situation of moral conflict, the addressees will answer as follows in all sincerity: 'If you are absolutely certain that this is a situation of moral conflict, and if you are equally certain that there are no honest ways of postponement or escape, then I can give you *no moral advice*. From the moral point of view, both of your remaining options are equally good and bad. But are you really sure that there is a moral conflict involved here? If you are, how weighty, in your appraisal, is the conflict? Is it a weak one or a hard one? Are you positively certain that there is no possibility of postponement or escape? Have you considered how far you can escape? Have you thought over the moral risks of an eventual postponement?' Thus, decent persons can advise each other on a host of issues, as can moral philosophy in offering certain ideas concerning the general conditions under which people answer the question 'What is the right thing for me to do?'

But decent persons must remain silent when it comes to the funda- mental decisions. In an unquestionable, unpostponable and inescap- able moral conflict between the respective courses of action A and B, there are no *moral grounds* on which to advise another person either to choose A or to choose B. (I shall shortly return to the possibility that we still might make suggestions on grounds other than moral.) Moral philosophy too must shed at this point its normative skin and be purely descriptive. In choosing either A or B in a moral conflict, both choices certainly remain *morally irrational* in so far as there are no better moral reasons for choosing A over B and *vice versa*. Persons, especially those aware of the seriousness of the con- flict, are unlike Buridan's ass. They make their choice and they make it by upsetting the balance of the situation of moral conflict. They simply put the weight of their own body and soul into one of the scales. In deciding to act in a certain way and in beginning to act in that way, they make the chosen option weightier. In so far as they are honest, persons cannot do otherwise. In taking upon themselves the guilt of violating one of the norms, they must commit themselves to the service of the other norm in the deepest, most complete and perfect way. Vacillation would mean not performing either act in a normative way.

The actor who observes norm B as well as she or he can but violates norm A is still guilty of violating a valid norm. But only if she or he does not vacillate, if she or he is committed in full to at least one norm, can the merit become weightier than the guilt. Shakespeare's Juliet chooses love, Racine's Berenice (political) obligation: both of them make the commitment to the full. Which is the better choice? Since no advice can be given, pondering 'better' and 'worse' is also irrelevant. *One makes one of the alternatives better by choosing it, and worsens the other by not choosing it*, and this is the way decent people act.

Despite putting their soul and body into one of the scales of the balance, despite making the chosen path morally weightier than the abandoned one, decent persons will not forget that they have indeed violated a norm. But for a decent person in a modern world where psychology is in the focus of interest and explicit guilt-feeling may create a halo of attraction, being aware of guilt will be no trigger for cultivating guilt-feeling. Just the contrary. Decent persons will work towards overcoming guilt-feeling without ever blotting the violation of a norm out of their memory. Characters and transgressions are of course different; therefore the extent and ways of self-forgiveness also vary from person to person. Above all, this is a psychological and not a moral issue, with one proviso: in so far as the person is decent, both the extreme of moral hysteria and that of becoming totally oblivious to the violation will be avoided.

It is at this point that we have to return to Kant and his denial of the existence of moral conflicts. To recall, Kant's model case was as follows. A would-be murderer is pursuing somebody who has taken refuge in my house. If the pursuer asks me where the other is, I must answer truthfully. One should not perceive a moral conflict here as there is none: the only moral solution is telling the truth. Kant does his eloquent best to prove an ethically hopeless case, for hopeless it is in terms of everyone's normal good common sense. And yet Kant had his own reasons and they were not minor ones. For he knew full well what formidable dangers threaten human actors the very moment they begin to appraise a moral conflict in terms of means and goals. Telling the truth is not a goal (it is an end-in-itself); but rescuing a person's life is indeed a goal. If, then, I perceive my situation as one of moral conflict, and if I choose to lie in order to save a human life, then I use a lie (the violation of a norm) as a means to achieve a goal (rescuing a human life). And, if this is permitted once, it should be permitted in each and every case. And, if it is continually permitted, immorality will have no bounds, for there is absolutely no such goal as could not be evaluated positively by at least some persons. And once everything can be positively evaluated, everything will also be permitted. Every transgression could then be justified as the means which is supposed to lead to the realization of a valuable goal.

This problem can be addressed from various angles.

Non-decent persons often resort to moral rationalization. While they violate norms in order to achieve their goals, they make frantic efforts to justify their acts in moral language. Such non-decent persons, who are neither wicked nor evil, respect decent people and will try to justify themselves precisely to these; or, alternatively, they will try to justify themselves in order to avoid punishment and shame. In addition, precisely because they are neither wicked nor evil, they will try to justify themselves also before themselves to avoid pangs of conscience, to be able to maintain self-love. So far as the attempts of non-decent persons at rationalization and self-justification go, it makes no difference whether the decent ones are strictly Kantian or anti-Kantian. Nor do philosophical differences matter for the decent ones, who would never try to justify immoral acts by moral means.

The danger of using the violation of a norm as a means to achieve an evaluated goal is no greater in a situation of moral conflict than in any other. Ways of avoiding this danger have already been discussed, and include the following: the actor should never renounce his or her moral autonomy in making decisions; concrete enthusiasm should replace abstract enthusiasm; the value-laden goals themselves must be checked and tested by universal principles or maxims; if they are on a collision course, the goals should be either abandoned or their substance changed or reinterpreted. In actual fact, abstract enthusiasm only pretends to recognize moral conflicts. When Hebbel's Judith utters the famous words 'If God placed sin between me and my deed, who am I to resist Him?', there is in the heroine's perception neither conflict nor choice. Metaphors of this family suggest that, for abstract enthusiasts, the 'supreme' goal always takes precedence over any moral norms that 'stand in the way' of their realization.

The dilemma of morals stands in sharp relief in the situation of moral conflict. Even if both options for action can be directly related to universal maxims (that is, the maxims of actions can be directly universalized on both poles), the action and the choice of action can never claim universal, or even general, validity. Assume that a decent person tells a lie in order to rescue an innocent person who is a prospective victim (i.e. uses a lie as a means to achieve a 'goal'). Both spectators and actor can say that the actor did the right thing, and yet the actor has no claim for universality: she or he cannot possibly demand that everyone should act likewise. Even less could Judith claim that every woman of a downtrodden nation should go to bed with the tyrant and murder him in order to rescue her nation. In Kant's incomparably more plausible example, we would rather opt for telling a lie, yet we cannot suggest that Kant's advice was indecent; that, had he acted in the spirit of his own philosophy, the result would have been a dishonest act. What we are indeed entitled to say is that, while each and every moral conflict is unique, generalization (universalization) is irrelevant for what is unique.

As soon as the decent person is fully aware of the indirect advantages of the dilemma of morals, the fear of accepting a moral conflict is dissipated. Every choice in a moral conflict is unique. Even if one uses the violation of a particular norm in order to observe another, *nothing generalizable follows from it.* Such an act cannot serve as a model, it is far from paradigmatic, it does not call for imitation and it does not contribute to our knowledge, although it does contribute to our wisdom. For wisdom teaches that sometimes we have to make up our mind in moral matters without having a crutch to rely upon and without offering a crutch to anyone else.

So far I have assumed that Kant was right in suspecting the emergence of a 'means–goals' relationship whenever persons conceive of their situation as one of moral conflict. But I would now add that this assumption is unfounded. In various moral conflicts, I can opt for norm A while violating norm B, but I can choose to opt for norm A *without* making the violation of norm B *the means* for observing norm A, and *vice versa.* In fact there is only a limited number of moral conflicts which can be reasonably understood in terms of means–goals.

Let us now turn back to one of the initial situations. A decent person is asked to give advice by another, equally decent person who wants to know whether she (or he) should choose A rather than B, or *vice versa*, after all possibilities of postponement or escape have been exhausted. We by now know that the addressee cannot, even should not, give moral advice: he (or she) is simply not in the situation to advise the other *on moral grounds* to do either A or B. This stricture follows from the dilemma of morals (the non-generalizability of the choice of action). The only advice that can be given is a warning to beware of the dilemma of morals and to resign the *false pretence* of establishing a paradigm, an example to be followed, right at the beginning. The burden of choice is with the actor, but so is the moral satisfaction whenever the chosen act is done swiftly, elegantly, perfectly.

Finally, one can give advice without false pretences on non-moral (pragmatic) grounds. Thus one can tell the actor that, although both courses A and B are equally good, and to violate norm A is as impermissible as to violate norm B, doing A rather than B promises success, whereas doing B rather than A will almost certainly be a disaster. Consequentialism can play a certain role here as a 'second thought'. Needless to say, if the choice is so set that one can opt for the right thing with certain problematic or even bad pragmatic consequences, or for the wrong thing with certain salutary consequences, the decent person will not hesitate over which to choose.

But, in fact, several different right things, and even more permitted things, can be done in almost every conflict situation. Therefore pragmatic consequences are certainly taken into consideration whenever the moral quality of the act remains unchanged.[13] This is precisely the case in a moral conflict proper. If one choice is no better than another and the person making the choice would act without rational moral considerations – in a manner of speaking, on the spur of the moment – one can advise this person to take into consideration the foreseeable non-moral consequences of the action (for example, gaining or losing power, property, position, opportunity or fame) from a personal or a collective aspect.

If a choice made on non-moral grounds comes off, it may be a compliment to the actor's pragmatic smartness, but it cannot be ascribed to the actor as a *moral merit*. If the choice proves pragmatically unsuccessful, it can be attributed to the pragmatic shortsightedness of the actor, but it cannot be ascribed to him or her as a *moral debit*. The blame placed on him or her for the lack of success should not take the form of a moral reprimand or moral indignation – with a single exception. In this case, the actor whose faulty pragmatic judgement has had devastating pragmatic consequences volunteered for the position which generated the moral conflict (or could have escaped the moral conflict with more pragmatic prudence, but decided against it). The difference between responsibility in retrospect and prospective responsibility, as discussed in my *General Ethics*, assumes crucial importance at this point. A person who voluntarily takes up responsibilities, alias obligations, has a certain amount of moral responsibility for his or her non-moral abilities, in so far as such abilities become decisive for carrying out an action or for failing to do so.

VII

Twentieth-century European philosophy developed a predilection for dwelling on borderline situations, particularly in moral philosophy. To the best of my knowledge, the term 'borderline' was first used in this context by Jaspers, but the phenomenon had earlier become the focus of attention and has remained central in a circle broader than the existentialist schools of philosophy *stricto sensu*. Differences in ontology, metaphysics, epistemology, even politics, mattered little when it came to describing, discussing and elucidating the allegedly paradigmatic *ethical* situation. For Sartre much as for Lukács, for Merleau-Ponty much as for Carl Schmitt, the typical ethical situation was tantamount to the borderline situation. Moral discourse meant discourse about friend and foe, ultimate causes and ideas, war, murder, torture, execution and concentration camps, the choice between everything and nothing, between life and death – that is, between the good life and the good death, on the one hand, and lifeless life and meaningless death, on the other. The hero and the human scum, the saint and the devil, became the protagonists of the moral discourse.

It was Dostoevsky, rather than Kierkegaard, the founding father of existentialist thinking, who channelled moral discourse in this direction. But the history of this trend is of no relevance here, nor is the social backdrop against which the new vision grew and was quickly disseminated. However, it deserves to be mentioned that far more thinkers subscribed to the paradigm of the 'borderline situation' than we normally assume. When Wittgenstein suggests that morals are the most important issue, and that this is precisely why we should remain silent about them, for we cannot even talk about them, he mystifies morals to an even greater extent than the vintage existentialists. The furious rejection of everyday life with its 'reified' and 'fetishized' thinking, the yearning for redemption so typical of radicals from Adorno to Marcuse, denies the moral relevance of everyday life as radically as existentialist authors proper do with their predilection for 'absolutes'. For a long while, American pragmatic philosophers remained the sole cultivators of the venerable tradition of scrutinizing morals within an everyday setting, both private and public. Such a solid enterprise may seem pedestrian against the blazing fireworks of the metaphysics of tragedy. In fact, sometimes it not only seems, but also becomes, pedestrian, drab and narrow-minded.

The present moral philosophy aims neither to synthetize traditions nor to bypass them. Its objective is to accompany decent persons on their life's way. Decent persons live an everyday life like everyone else: thus they have to be decent within this framework. Decent persons also live and act within institutions, so they have to remain decent here also. In a similar fashion, decent persons are committed to causes, they are good citizens, and they preserve their decency amidst oppression as well as under extreme political and existential pressure. If a moral philosophy intends to offer a general framework for answering the question 'What is the right thing for me to do?', it also has to include borderline situations. Yet not for a moment would I create the (false) impression that it is exclusively in borderline situations that one finds out whether or not a person is really decent. The person who is decent everywhere and every day needs no confirmation of his or her decency by the borderline situation; this person is simply decent everywhere and every day. Moreover, these days there is less knowledge about whether or not one will have to face the borderline situation, and who will have to face it. In pre-modern civilizations, living the borderline situation was a social privilege (of patricians, noblemen, and the like). The monster offspring of modernity, totalitarianism, has 'democratized' the situation: now potentially everyone can be exposed to trials and tribulations which require stamina on an unprecedented scale. Yet the same age as made us all, equally, prospective or potential protagonists in borderline situations has simultaneously dismantled the strict codes of 'borderline behaviour'. The choice between the loss of honour and death was not a purely moral choice for patricians or noblemen. Very often even the rascals among them chose honour, sometimes with a matter-of-fact gesture. The strong code, never a binding pattern for members of a lower class, is gone or almost gone. The quasi-instinct of honour has now been replaced by the resolve for honesty (decency), which is a far more private impulse, even if it is supposed to motivate men and women to act paradigmatically beyond the solidarity of the group.

In Galsworthy's *The Forsyte Saga* a story is told about an Englishman who had converted to Islam at gunpoint in the Arabian desert. The protagonists of the novel, patricians and old-class gentry, unanimously treat this person as 'morally dead', because an Englishman should not act the coward in front of the colonized. This judgement is still the 'voice of honour'. The problem for decency when the dilemma of abandoning one's conviction or giving up one's life is raised is not – and this applies to *any* man or woman – one of bringing dishonour on one's nation, but one of whether it is permitted *for the person in question* to act in such-and-such a way. Decent persons do not need concrete norms to determine their conduct. As autonomous actors, they want to decide for themselves what is the right thing for them to do. In so far as they seek advice, moral philosophy can offer a general guideline, one founded on the life experiences, choices and ideas of decent persons themselves.

The observation of moral life in the modern world teaches us a particular lesson of considerable interest. It frequently happens that persons who act heroically in borderline situations, who are ready for the ultimate sacrifice, behave in a morally indifferent manner in everyday life; sometimes they even become rascals or cynics once their trials and tribulations are over. On the other hand, it happens equally frequently that persons who are perfectly decent in everyday life fail miserably in borderline situations: loyal sons betray their parents, gentle persons degenerate into murderers, honest businessman rob their neighbours, when the chips are down. It is therefore important to emphasize that persons who have chosen themselves existentially under the category of the universal have made an all-round choice of decency. It goes without saying that they can cope with one situation better than with another. But, since they are supposed to cope with both types, and they intend to, they have to study how other decent persons behave in borderline situations in order to be able to mobilize their forces if ever they find themselves in such circumstances.

A borderline situation is one in which, by definition, *one's life is at stake*. The 'borderline' is precisely *the divide between life and death*. The 'life' at stake can be one's *physical* life, but it can also be one's *life as a human being*, one's *good life* or the *meaning of one's life*. 'One's life' can also stand for the life of the community one belongs to and identifies with, for the lives of one's nearest and dearest, for the lives of those whose lives are dearer than one's own. But the borderline situation does not exist for those who are exposed to the danger of physical death *without* the choice which would result in the loss of the meaning of life.

In the borderline situation, there is still an element of autonomy. If we put our life at stake willingly, our autonomy is wide; if it is the result of external pressure, our autonomy is narrowed. This is why natural death does not fit readily into the category of the borderline situation: it is an uncontrollable situation. We can indeed do something about the *timing* of our natural death (and 'timing' is an element of autonomy); furthermore, 'moral resolve' and stamina may play a role in 'conquering death' (in the sense of postponing it). In addition, there is a close analogy between borderline situations and those of natural death from a *psychological* point of view, which *may* (or may not) be connected with morals. To face the unfaceable bravely, resolutely, with humour, without hysteria and futile protest is dignified. And dignity is a moral category, even a moral virtue. But this attitude does not necessarily derive from dignity: it may also derive from strength of character, and the devil often has a strong character. The moral (as well as sensual) appeal of borderline situations may easily be explained if we keep in mind that it can be perceived as a metaphor of natural death.[14] This is why people sometimes feel empathy for those who do not deserve moral sympathy (for example, in watching a movie about the execution of a vicious murderer).

Fatal accidents have nothing to do with borderline situations even when the victim has put his or her life at stake voluntarily (which is the stuntman's normal risk), for the borderline situation is a *moral* peak experience. However, what is 'stuntmanship' in one particular culture can be a matter of utmost moral weight in another (the samurai's challenging of fate is stuntmanship for us, heroism in his own culture). In our modern culture, decent persons do not put their lives at risk in order to 'prove a point'. For their self-esteem does not depend on the approval of others, even if they take the judgement of others seriously.

Borderline situations occur in two basic scenarios. First, persons may be thrown into such a situation by a physical or moral accident, in which case there is absolutely nothing in their character, moral make-up and biography which would make their relation to the borderline situation one of necessity, and there is also not necessarily anything which would make them fit for such a test. Alternatively, persons may throw themselves into the borderline situation. Regardless of their own understanding of the borderline situation as one resulting from their own character or as one having nothing to do with their previous commitments, there is always something in the character, the (personal or collective) moral biography and the moral make-up of such persons that conditions, although never determines, their fitness for the situation into which they throw themselves.

The second scenario is the subject matter of drama, particularly of tragedy. The halo of greatness surrounds men and women whose lives are a continual preparation for the final showdown. Greatness is far from a non-entity in ethics, for the representative deeds of supererogation are shining examples and they provide powerful images for decent men and women, sublime models to emulate. Yet the ethical distinction measured on *the scale of greatness is a matter of moral aesthetics, and not that of moral philosophy proper*. Moral philosophy answers the question of how to become a decent person, not that of how to become a moral hero or a saint. This is one of the reasons why in what follows I do not emphasize the difference between the two scenarios. I do believe that men and women who act as honestly as they can in testing situations which they neither sought nor were prepared for are just as deserving of our moral esteem and admiration as are heroes and heroines who have stood firmly by their chosen faith, destiny, idea, chosen course of life, and have thrown themselves into a borderline situation. One could even argue the other way round: those unprepared for the borderline situation deserve greater respect. But this preference too would be a *matter of moral taste*, which is beyond the competence of moral philosophy and has to be dealt with in 'moral aesthetics'.

Whatever the scenario, the borderline situation remains the divide between life and death. But if we understand it as the risk of losing not physical but moral life (the 'good life', life which has a meaning), we have to stress that in the borderline situation we may make a choice not only about our own death, but also about the death of others: murder. Murder is of course a sin, a crime and a transgression in every culture and tradition. The borderline situation is a moral situation; murder as such is not the subject matter of a moral tale. Murder can be part of a moral tale on one of two conditions: first, if the act is perpetrated in a moral conflict proper; and, second, if the act of murder has a *retributive* aspect.

There is a moral conflict proper if the sole alternative to letting others (ourselves included) be killed or harmed in our very moral centre is to kill someone else. For nothing short of the loss of life (or of the meaningful life) can balance the act of taking a life and constitute a genuine situation of moral conflict. Murder (in the borderline situation) has a retributive aspect if the victim of the murder is *responsible in his person for the emergence of the borderline situation itself*. There is no tyrannicide without a tyrant. Tyrannicide is the act of deliverance, and, as such, it is rarely perceived as murder. In this respect, we do not differ considerably from our ancestors. However, we do differ from them inasmuch as we narrow down the interpretation of 'acts with a retributive aspect' (to persons personally responsible for the emergence of the borderline situation). This restriction is the attitude of the modern contingent person alone. In pre-modern times, vengeance did not call for too much justification; now we prefer to let law (justice) take its course. And restriction matters. Let us return for a moment to the story of Judith's tyrannicide: she killed Holofernes and delivered her nation. We would inadmissibly distort the traditional narrative if we removed the *tyrant* from the story and replaced him with 'a member (members) of an alien race', or 'a member (members) of an alien class', as so often happens with this moral tale in modernity.

Not every moral conflict is a borderline situation, nor is every borderline situation a moral conflict. People thrown into a borderline situation sometimes lack the opportunity to transgress, to lose their good lives before losing their lives pure and simple; they may also lack the opportunity to vest their concrete enthusiasm in the good life of others, to give their lives meaning before the curtain falls. The lack of moral conflict is not tantamount to the total lack of moral alternatives and morally weighty choices. The way a person behaves in such a situation, the little things she or he does, the few sentences she or he utters, are of enormous moral relevance. These are not actions proper but *gestures*. This is the smallest margin granted to a human being, a being of self-consciousness. If one understands how to use it well, one does the utmost one can, and *ultra posse nemo obligatur*. But what has been described here as the borderline situation without moral conflict can also serve as the typical escape route from moral conflicts. For there is no such situation from which one could not escape at least via *Exit*. And the borderline situation is an escape route in so far as it is an Exit.

We by now know that a decent person cannot give advice to another decent person in the quandary of a moral conflict, although she or he can advise the other to postpone the decision or to seek an escape route. With this, we have arrived at one of the most serious dilemmas inherent in the problem. Although every person can take Exit for an escape route (finally to death) by transforming moral conflict into a borderline situation, the question at every such juncture is whether this is the right thing to do. For moral hysteria should be discouraged, just as much as moral leniency towards ourselves. If one is absolutely convinced that all alternative available courses would inevitably lead to a total loss of self-esteem, moral autonomy and the meaning of life, then, and only then, is it better to opt for the escape route of Exit. Short of such extremity, taking Exit as an escape route is by no means superior to either doing A or doing B. For as long as one lives, things can still be set right. But, in matters of moral nuances, it is anyhow the person's psychology which has the strongest say in the final outcome.

Our Western culture attributes a quasi-metaphysical essence to the moral categories of *innocence* and *guilt*, as if they were 'substances' of men and women, and as if innocence were irretrievably lost by committing a particular wrong deed and we were, as a consequence, 'filled' with the substance termed 'guilt'. Both 'pure innocence' and 'total guilt' are vested with charisma and are at the centre of attraction.

The moral imagination of a decent person of today can have very little to do with the metaphysical substances of 'innocence' and 'guilt' blown out of all proportion. Goethe once walked straight into the trap of those antiquated moral concepts he had so much wanted to avoid, by remarking that only the spectator is innocent: the actor is always guilty. For what does it mean to be 'innocent'? If the term denotes someone who has never committed anything reprehensible, then no one is 'innocent'. 'Innocence' can also be associated with a preconscious state, a state in which one does not know what one does: this is the morale of the biblical story. Since we have eaten from the tree of knowledge, we now know good and evil; thus we are no longer innocent. The story is aesthetically pleasing and wise, but it contributes to the attraction of guilt rather than to that of (boring and unconscious) innocence. Further, innocence can mean that one has no sexual experience. But, whatever our particular sexual *mores*, modern men and women do not define sexual intercourse as guilty *per se*, and even less as a substance termed 'guilt'.

What can then be done with the concept of 'innocence'? First, we obviously have to strip it of its metaphysical and substantive connotations. One is not 'innocent', although one can be 'innocent of something' if one has not done that particular thing. When you plead innocent (not guilty), you do not mean to state that you are 'innocent on all counts', only that you are innocent on that particular count. The same applies to guilt. In committing a moral mistake, which all decent persons do, one does not become 'guilty', but guilty in this and this particular thing. Even in the case of a serious transgression, we use the language of 'being guilty of'. For one does not change substance, does not become a 'guilty person' through being guilty of a particular transgression. Men can be wicked if major vices become their character traits, and they can be evil if they shed all moral regulations by impulse or under the spell of evil maxims. But, while the evil person casts himself or herself out of the human race, the wicked one remains very much part of it.[15] If we all are guilty simply by not remaining completely innocent, what is the difference between decent, non-decent, wicked and evil persons? One could retort to this question that we can be guilty to a greater or lesser degree, the difference being then one of quantity of the 'guilt' substance. However, such a rejoinder would not be adequate, because the difference between decent, non-decent, wicked and evil is *qualitative* in nature.

This interpretation of 'guilt' and 'innocence' is not simply a rendering of the philosopher's private convictions but the actual self-perception of decent men and women of today as contingent beings. They have practically shed their Jewish–Christian heritage in this regard, and have come closer to the ancient Greeks without renouncing the validity of several moral norms rooted in their religious tradition. The decent person can rely upon his or her decent (virtuous) character traits in all possible situations, including borderline situations, and yet, simultaneously, also needs the 'crutch', the guidance of universal norms. It goes without saying that relying upon commandments and norms results from the Jewish–Christian rather than the Greek heritage. It is on these grounds that decent persons can distinguish between forms of transgression, some of which can be set right while others make the resumption of the good life impossible. Since concrete norms which precisely prescribe the particular courses of action are rarely at hand for the modern actor, who, even when they are, can legitimately choose to disregard them, there remains an ineliminably personal, quasi-psychological element in making momentuous decisions. Certain persons will thus take the escape route of Exit from borderline situations, others will not, and no one but the decent person himself or herself has authority to decide whether or not the good life is still within reach after having done a particular deed. There is always an 'upper limit' in such decisions which, if trespassed, would result in absolute moral transgression, and a 'lower limit' below which all acts of transgression can certainly be set right. And it is first and foremost the psychological make-up of the person that proves decisive in the choices taken in the broad field between the upper and lower limit. From the moral point of view, these are equally decent and good choices. To avoid misunderstanding, I would stress that I am discussing here the 'escape route out of borderline situations', and *not* suicide in general.

Let me repeat that not every moral conflict is a borderline situation; nor does every moral conflict offer an escape route. The first statement is self-evident but the second has still to be substantiated. There are certain cases in which escape implies the violation of both norms A and B, and thus it cannot serve as escape from a moral conflict. In some other cases, where the 'escape into Exit' is in fact tantamount to the choice of either A or B (in so far as making one choice renders the other impossible), the choice ceases to be an escape route from the conflict.

Not every borderline situation is one of moral conflict; we transform moral conflicts into borderline situations in taking the escape route of Exit. Moreover, the first scenario of the borderline situation has initially nothing to do with moral conflict. Being thrown into a train with the destination 'Auschwitz' does not contain a grain of moral conflict. The latter may arise within this scenario if there still remains within the situation a choice between two morally momentous courses of action. But this is not a necessary, rather a rare, outcome of such situations. In choosing between the dignified and undignified ways of dying, there is a difference, but *not a moral conflict*.

Moral conflicts mostly occur within the second scenario, where the actors are not thrown into borderline situations, but plunge themselves into them. The most frequent conflicts are those between saving one life and saving many lives; taking a life and saving a life; deliverance and taking a life; saving our own lives and saving the lives of others; saving our own lives and protecting the freedom of others; and the like. However, it has also been pointed out that not every combination within the second scenario is at the same time a moral conflict (see the case of Judith). As a rule, men and women in a borderline situation cannot consult other decent persons but only the one within themselves called 'conscience'.[16] We first consult our conscience as to whether there is a moral conflict proper in the borderline situation. Whenever the competing moral norms (and reasons) are of unequal weight, there is no moral conflict proper, for one *should* at all costs take one's direction from the weightier norms. Since the perception of the moral weight of the norms can be strongly psychologically conditioned, the moment of choice requires reliable self-knowledge in order to take into account (or discount) one's own psychological make-up. In such a situation, there is perhaps a single recipe which will never be replaced by better ones: if the choice is between losing one's own life and doing something against others which is morally equivalent to the loss of life, it is morally safer to lose one's own life. The other, equally time-honoured advice is a warning: never choose to act such that your actions would annul the things dearest to your life – your ideas, causes, the friendships and commitments you have lived for so far. If you so act, you may survive but you will certainly lose the meaning of your life, the good life, and become a non-person. Admittedly, this argument contains reference to consequences. But these consequences are included in the action itself and they are not dependent on external powers; or, at least, their coming true is not dependent on the latter. 'Be true to yourself' is a norm one can rely upon in the moral conflicts of borderline situations as well as in those of everyday life.

I have repeatedly mentioned 'happy actions', as well as the historic moments which provide rich opportunities for 'happy actions'. These are the moments of liberation. There are happy moments also in borderline situations. Happy is the act of the decent man who has chosen to suffer injustice rather than commit it, who has put his life at stake, but whose life will be spared. Even happier is the act of the decent woman in a borderline situation who gets back everything she had before embarking upon her trial, and in addition gains something else: namely, the awareness that she really did what she knew she should. This is the happy instance of *deliverance*.

But at this point an admonition that echoes ancient wisdom is genuinely important: whatever one does in a borderline situation, one should not do it in the hope of deliverance. A person who puts his or her life at stake must assume that it will be taken. It is better to trust the old rationalist insight that hope and fear are equally bad, even dangerous, emotions.

Although fantasies of borderline situations should remain the private domain of poets, there are unfortunately abnormal situations in which people have to indulge in mental exercises about trials that lie in wait for them. In borderline situations, one has to check one's own psychological readiness before 'taking up obligations' or 'taking responsibilities'. As so often in this section, once again the person's psychological make-up appears in sharp relief. Although one's actual behaviour cannot be foreseen in the fantasies of self-preparation, bitter realities could prove easier to bear if one takes counsel with one's forebodings. Psychological 'self-testing', uncertain as it necessarily remains with regard to the future actual trials, can be particularly valuable in helping one determine whether or not one *should create* a borderline situation for oneself. For nothing is more devastating than provoking a test in which one fails, when one could have avoided trials and tribulations and still remained honest.

In discussing the dilemma of morals in section VI, I came to the conclusion that, even if the maxim of our action qualifies for universalization (in Kantian terms, 'universal legislation'), our actions cannot and should not be universalized. Each action is unique, and not even the morally exemplary one can claim universal validity. I have also come to the conclusion that the dilemma of morals attains prime importance in moral conflicts proper, where, faced with competing norms of equal weight, one can act only by violating one of these norms, each of which claims universal validity (indirectly if not directly). Naturally, the same holds true of borderline situations in so far as they are also situations of moral conflict. However, it has to be borne in mind that *awareness* of the dilemma of morals is of crucial ethical significance also in certain borderline situations which are not cases of moral conflict. If one puts one's life at stake in an act of supererogation, one cannot will that everyone should act likewise; this would contradict the supererogatory character of the act. But here not a conceptual, rather a moral, confusion should be avoided. A person who performs a supererogatory act in a borderline situation *must not morally disapprove of those who do not follow his or her path*. A decent person avoids the gestures of self-righteousness. For, if the pitfall of raising universalizing claims is not avoided, moral disapprobation of those who have not been ready for supererogatory actions is inevitable. In such a case, the one who performs the supererogatory acts and makes universalizing claims for them will die bitterly, if she or he dies, and live bitterly, if she or he survives, in self-created solitude. In fact, although supererogatory acts appear in a variety of situations, the temptation to claim universality for them is far greater in borderline situations than in any other.

Borderline situations have a fascination: they are dramatic and spectacular. Since they are situations of *lawlessness*, they offer 'freedom' to men and women to become the law for themselves, for better or worse. They are situations which come and go, for a borderline is not a situation to 'stay': one either masters it and passes beyond it or fails ultimately. They allow for, and require, the concentration of all moral powers. Borderline situations are thus simple; they present the simplest moral equations of human life. They easily lend themselves to metaphorical or paradigmatic use; they can be summed up clearly and succinctly without much equivocation.

These features of borderline situations have contributed to their popularity in twentieth-century ethics. They have surely fascinated people at all times and everywhere. But before the twentieth century they were rarely used as major paradigms for the explication of moral situations. So long as moral philosophers were still moving in a traditional ethos, paradigmatic moral situations were drawn from everyday life or daily political events. In this regard, formal universalism has remained true to the ancient tradition. And it has been able to do this because it has dismissed the substantive elements of morals. It has also *had* to remain true to the tradition, for formal–universalistic ethics is singularly unsuited to discussing borderline situations, let alone presenting them as if they were paradigmatic.

Modern morals have become so complex that they do not offer material for simple paradigmatic stories. Borderline situations bring out both the best and the worst potentials in the moral and psychological make-up of men and women. But so do non-borderline situations. Two components, *the time element and the degree of concentration*, make all the difference. Borderline situations are of short duration; they elicit experience of a heightened kind; they require few but intensive and ultimate gestures. Everyday life is of long duration with a steady flow of experience; it requires gestures of a different kind, none of which is ultimate in itself. Yet the series of gestures in the same everyday situation adds up to the ultimate, for it is through such gestures that men and women become what they are, decent or non-decent. This is why borderline situations can be used as metaphors of life in general, even if they are unlike life – if they are 'utopian', both in a positive and in a negative sense. Yet paradigmatic stories, even if they succeed in illuminating the 'human condition', are not substitutes for moral philosophy. They are the easy exits out of the quandary of a contingent world precisely because they are content with presenting the simple (utopian) moment instead of saying something about the complexity of the non-utopian contemporary reality, about the real-life situations in which men and women must find their way if they want to be decent. Instead of dwelling in the world of powerful images such as death, murder, ultimate sacrifice and ultimate gestures, torture and deliverance, moral philosophers can embark on stories about people who live their lives in full, who have their share of joy and suffering like others, who are neither unusually gifted nor extraordinarily strong-willed, neither the virtuosi of morals nor unique talents. Decent men and women are decent both in ordinary and in extraordinary situations, but it is in ordinary situations that they dwell. Moral philosophy should therefore discuss the ordinary, and in so doing may also have a word to say on the extraordinary, which is, after all, just a simplified and concentrated summary of the ordinary.

VIII

Good persons exist. There are men and women in our world and in our times who are entirely decent. We can and, in fact, we do ponder why one person is good while another is not. Already in childhood we frequently ruminate about such matters. We can also find different answers in different cases in different stages of our lives; yet none of them will prove to be the proper answer. For goodness results, particularly in our modern world, from an existential choice.

How do we know that a person has chosen himself or herself existentially as a good (decent) person? We know it from the *fact* that she or he is good. The fact that a person behaves in a decent way, gives priority to the moral as opposed to all other kinds of considerations, prefers suffering injustice to committing it, does the right thing irrespective of social sanctions is a sure manifestation of the existential choice of goodness. And there is no other manifestation of it. Whether or not decent persons can recall the moment of their existential choice is of no relevance. Each of them will tell a different story in this regard, because recollection is always interpretation. We shall lend credence to all these stories simply because we know that the men and women who tell them are actually good. And, since they are contingent persons like ourselves, we know that their goodness must have resulted from an existential choice.

Kant set forth the idea that, were our institutions perfect, even the race of devils would behave like decent persons. The utopian aspects notwithstanding, the proposition has a certain relevance. Even if our institutions are far from perfect, in certain niches of modern society decent acts are rewarded, and certain crimes are likely to be punished by law. Men and women thus behave *as if* they were decent, although many of them have never chosen themselves as decent persons. And yet it is very unlikely that we will mistake such individuals for good persons. This kind of distinction was a major issue for Kant because in his theory it was here that the rigid line of division between acting out of duty and acting dutifully – that is, between morality and legality – had to be drawn. For the modern decent person, the protagonist of this moral philosophy, the same distinction is a minor issue or a non-issue. Modern decent persons are decent first of all for their own sake, even if they do certain things for other persons' sake. They would therefore be completely at ease in a world where everyone, whether decent or not, behaved decently, because then their decency, the real one, would be a source of sheer delight and happiness. If everyone behaved decently, perhaps we should not know who had chosen decency existentially and who had not. Yet this knowledge would also be completely irrelevant, for it would contain information about another person's *felicity*, and about nothing else.

The existential choice of goodness, like all other kinds of existential choice, has laid the foundation of the main passion of the Self. To act out of the main passion, or in accordance with it, can also be termed self-realization. Knowledge of moral character is of primary importance, for, if we know it well, we can have an idea of what to expect from other persons in a wide variety of circumstances. It is also important to tell the decent person from the one who pretends to be decent. Our expectations will then differ accordingly. Expectations co-determine actions; they belong to the 'situation' in which moral judgements are passed and moral decisions are made. But, under the imaginary circumstances of a just society, knowledge of moral character would have no relevance, given that everyone would consistently and continuously behave as if she or he were decent.

Self-realization is one of the central constituents of the good life in general. The thought experiment with the Kantian model brings this message home quite forcefully. We have come to the conclusion that, if *everyone* behaved decently as a result of the fully just character of our institutions, the existential choice of goodness would add the dimension of essential self-realization to decent actions. However, we do not live in such a world, and no one actually expects that others will act decently in a consistent and continuous fashion. Yet to live a decent life is essential self-realization for all decent people, beyond historical restrictions. This statement is not at all new: in fact, it has been emphasized by all moral philosophies. The equation of virtue and happiness or virtue and freedom, that oldest of all equations in the history of philosophy, needs no further corroboration. The oldest moral paradox – namely, that the self-realization of decency (goodness) frequently bars other kinds of self-realization – follows from this equation. The questions arising from this paradox are as follows. If we are whole persons, why should the actualization of our goodness be at cross-purposes with the actualization of our other wishes, wants and potentials? Why do the good suffer? Or, in another formulation: how can goodness as the sole source of happiness and freedom be also the source of unhappiness and lack of freedom? If the question of 'why' is raised, only religion can provide the answer. If the question of 'how' is raised, it is the responsibility of philosophy to provide the answer.

While the question of 'why' points *upwards* (towards a higher purpose), the question of 'how' points at the world – more precisely, at human institutions. Philosophers almost invariably blame unjust institutions. Their favourite pastime, one of purposes of which is to overcome the moral dilemma, has always been to design the best constitutions and to deduce the patterns of the best, completely just society from certain first principles. This time, unlike in my other books,[17] I shall refrain from indulging in an exercise of this kind. Many contingent and decent persons today believe in the possibility of a completely just society, while others do not have such high hopes but still continue to design patterns fitting for the best societies. Others again are practising sceptics who believe neither in the perfectibility of man nor in that of society, but still share the conviction that human institutions can be changed for the better to become more equitable, more free and more democratic. A moral philosophy which takes up the position of decent persons today has to occupy a position that all decent persons could share. This is why it has to remain neutral on the above controversial issue, whatever the moral philosopher's personal preferences, hopes and commitments may be. Yet there is a strong link between the goodness of contingent persons and the vision of the best possible world, a tie which has nothing to do with belief or disbelief, hope or scepticism, absolutism or relativism. The link I have in mind is inherent in the existential choice of goodness, in the very existence of good persons.

Decency, goodness is a goal in itself; goodness is its own reward: these are the summaries of several thousand years of moral wisdom. In so far as I am going to relativize the truth content of such statements, it shall not be with the purpose of exposing them as platitudes or pious lies. Decency is indeed an end-in-itself, and goodness is indeed, among other things, its own reward. But we also have to pay attention to something else.

A decent person prefers suffering wrong to doing wrong to others, but she or he does not prefer suffering. A decent person does the right thing irrespective of social sanctions, but she or he does not like to be subjected to social sanctions or to subject others to such sanctions. For a decent person, to do the right thing is indeed self-realization, but she or he also desires to realize other aspirations, develop other potentials, and cannot be happy when those aspirations are thwarted as a result of the existential choice of decency. *A decent person accepts and faces the moral dilemma, but experiences pain in so doing and wishes that the severe and heavy pain of a moral kind could be avoided.* This is why decency, decent action and choice, is not completely an end-in-itself, although it is also an end-in-itself, for whoever acts decently acts *towards* the best possible moral world. Decent action is not a means to an end ('the best possible moral world'), but it carries the promise of such a world, for it is the *dunamis*, the potential, which is also the 'movement toward' such a world. The best possible moral world is not a world where everyone is good (for, where there is no bad, there is no good either). It is a world in which people behave *as if* they were decent even if they are not; therefore, it is a world in which goodness, decency proper, can become what it has always been: an end-in-itself and its own reward. The best possible moral world is therefore contained and anticipated in every act of decency which pains the actor, for it is precisely its absence that is being negated by such an act. Further, the condition of the best possible moral world is the best possible socio-political world, where institutions are established as a result of rational consensus among men and women who are tied together by bonds of symmetric reciprocity, where the value of life and the value of freedom do not collide on the practical plane.[18] From our point of view, it is absolutely irrelevant whether the best possible moral world or the best possible socio-political world is pragmatically possible. The only thing that matters is the circumstance that the *promise* of such a world is inherent in the very existence of decent persons; that, as long as decent persons exist, this promise also exists. *Nothing is more real than a decent person.* At the same time, *she or he is also utopian.* Every decent person embodies utopia by the promise that she or he stands for. *The decent person is the ultimate utopian reality.*

As a rule, utopia is associated with the utopia of political institutions. This misunderstanding results from the identification of political philosophy with political institutions. To render this misunderstanding in Hegelian terminology, manifestations of the absolute spirit are discussed as if they were the manifestations of the objective spirit. All futile discussions on the possibility or impossibility of the 'realization of utopias' arise from this misunderstanding. Political utopia is encapsulated in political philosophy, not in political institutions. Political philosophy is *always utopian*, as is philosophy in general, for the simple reason that the language game termed 'philosophy' implies the juxtaposition of an idea (the idea of Truth) to everyday knowledge, action, institutions, and the like. Every 'Ought-

To-Do' and 'Ought-To-Be' is by definition utopian in so far as it is an idea. Yet political philosophy, like philosophy in general, is *also real*. Philosophies exist, and what exists is real. Their utopias are also real, in so far as they exist as philosophical utopias; they are utopian realities.[19] What can it possibly mean to 'realize' something which is real anyway, something which often makes a claim to a reality *higher* than that of everyday or socio-political institutions? The project of 'realizing utopias' is an attempt at *translation*. One is advised to translate the language of philosophy into that of political institutions. This exercise is futile on many counts. To mention only one of them, philosophical constructs are speculative, mental constructs. Practical philosophy is no less a theoretical construct than any other branch of philosophy. Every philosopher is a 'king' of the kingdom of his or her philosophy, for in it the philosopher can change all the political rules, although she or he cannot change, only modify, the philosophical rules. Like the reality of everyday life, but unlike philosophy, political reality is the territory of action and not that of speculation. But utopian realities need not be 'realized' in order to fulfil a practical mission. Their practical mission is to serve as *regulative ideas in and for action*, in everyday life, politics and social interaction. Utopian realities are *normative* in so far as the actors are guided by the images they offer.

The whole realm termed 'absolute spirit' by Hegel and which, not without Hegelian reminiscences, I have termed the sphere of 'objectivation-for-itself' in my theory of everyday life, is utopian throughout. Religion, in so far as it makes it appearance in this sphere, art and literature (with the same proviso), and philosophy (without any proviso) present utopian images because they confront men and women with *something that stands higher* than the particular men and women. Whether this 'higher-standing something' is fathomed as our own creation or, alternatively, as the source of our existence is irrelevant from this point of view. The sphere of objectivation-for-itself renders meaning to life precisely because it stands higher than empirical life. The sphere of objectivation-for-itself also *relativizes* our interests, goals and personal projects by virtue of being *absolute*.

After having relegated 'utopia' to the sphere of objectivation-for-itself, which embraces religion, art and philosophy, it seems as if we have lost track of the proposition, made prior to our last detour, that 'the decent person is the ultimate utopian reality'. What follows will make the detour justified.

Sometimes we perceive certain political events as if they were utopian in nature. I am pinpointing here real events, events of the past and the present, and not models which were concocted by philosophy and projected into a distant future. Those who have lived in periods of extreme political tension, who have witnessed the first few days of liberation or revolution, who have participated in the foundation of a new state or a new institution as the crowning gesture of previous human efforts, will retain the feeling of *once having been party to utopia*. The perception that utopias are fading, even if the institutions founded in the utopian moment have survived, normally belongs to this experience. But this perception provides us with the following puzzle: what has faded if the institutions have remained in place? In what sense was liberation a utopia if liberties were not curtailed afterwards? In short, what has changed? *Ethics have*. The perception of a lost utopia is only loosely linked to the changing character of social and political institutions; indeed, they may not have changed at all. But, at the time of their foundation, men and women lived and acted *on a heightened level of morality*, they all behaved as if they were all good, decent persons; or, at least, many of them did so. It is this massive increase in moral substance, the 'peak-experience' of self-abandon to the moral law within us or above us that makes certain moments look utopian, or indeed be utopian. One can get *foretaste of the best possible moral world* in such situations, the foretaste of a world of which we do not know whether it is possible at all.

A decent person is decent regardless of whether or not the political conditions lead to the general upsurge of morality amidst a non-utopian reality. But is it not relevant to suggest that the person who remains decent, who thus embodies the promise of the best possible moral world, whatever the circumstances, is the embodiment of *absolute utopia*? The painter can make a face more beautiful than in reality; the architect can invent a new structure. A metaphysical thinker can design as many spheres and emanations as she or he wishes. Speculation and creation know very few limits of imagination. But there is no imagination that could possibly invent a greater and more complete goodness than that of the good person. At this point, acting stands higher than speculation, for no virtuosity of the speculative mind can create something superior to the actor. *It is in morals that utopia becomes life*. The actor is utopian reality in two meanings of the term. First, the actor is a man or woman of absolute reality in so far as she or he exists as a living being for whom (in whom) existence and essence coalesce. And, second, the actor is utopian reality in so far as she or he is as absolute as the 'absolute spirit'. Like the images of the 'absolute spirit', the good person too relativizes interests, goals and projects by his or her very existence.

This is why non-decent, even positively wicked, persons recognize and respect decent persons. Or, if the decent are ridiculed and abused, this merely happens, as Goethe so well understood, because they are in their very existence a constant and tacit reproach to those who are not decent.

Decent persons relate intimately to the sphere of objectivation-for-itself (the 'absolute spirit'). There is not room here to discuss either the contents of this historically constantly changing relationship or the special relationship of the decent person to each particular constituent of the 'absolute spirit'. None the less, a few connections cannot be left unmentioned.

The sphere of objectivation-for-itself confronts men and women with something that stands higher than particular persons. Whatever the name of the supreme being or supreme beings, whatever the forms, the symbols, the media of artworks, religious creeds and philosophical systems, the recipient, the believer, the visionary all *ascend* to the Meaning that *emanates* therefrom. One does not dwell constantly on the heights of mystical experience, philosophical speculation, or self-abandon to an artwork. Moments of peak experience come and go, yet what is in between, everyday life and action, is not left untouched by them, because life has gained a meaning. Simultaneously, the experience of that 'higher-standing something' remains permanent as a background feeling, one which may return again to the centre of our conscience in a renewed contact with the absolute spirit.

Mutatis mutandis, the same can be said about the attitude of the decent person who has a 'feel' for that 'higher-standing something'. Any name can be given to it, but what matters is not the name but the attitude. Every time a decent person has to make a momentous decision, when she or he needs to concentrate on the moral content of an issue, the experience of something 'higher', 'sublime', enters the centre of his or her consciousness. The feeling of being carried by a supreme entity arises, as if someone else were acting inside the person. The person's conscience becomes enlarged, his or her emotions intensified, while the mind is at work with maximum speed and alertness. This is what happens in the moments of 'trial'. When those moments are gone, the experience of the 'higher-standing something' is relegated to the *background* of the consciousness of the decent person. She or he will continue to act decently, yet spontaneously, without giving it a thought. And, as soon as the next momentous decision approaches, the background feeling will move again to the centre of consciousness. The decent person is not an albatross. She or he can fly if this needs to be done, but is good at walking on solid ground too.

The existential choice is the foundation of the self: after all, the person chooses himself or herself. From this, however, the monocentricity of the self does not follow. Self-evident as this statement seems to be whenever the existential choice is attached to a vocation, a person or an idea, it is not obvious when we are discussing the existential choice of one's own goodness. Certain circumstances point, rather, in the opposite direction. It has been frequently stressed in hermeneutics that an artwork cannot be interpreted or understood as the expression of the artist's self. For example, Lukács distinguishes between two selves: the empirical self and the normative–aesthetic self. The creator of the work, guided by the homogeneous medium of a particular genre, leaves his empirical self behind. Although he remains the same person, he also becomes another person. The discrepancy between the empirical and the normative selves had already been noted by Aristotle, although he did not dramatize the issue. He just mentioned in passing that certain kinds of mental excellence and accomplishment are unrelated to morals. This is far more true today than it ever was, as a result of the increasing separation of cultural spheres in the modern world. The most subtle moral tale can be written or composed by the basest person, and Richard Wagner is a strong case in point.

A similar development can be observed in morals. Previously I have mentioned certain utopian conditions in political life under which men and women begin to act and behave on a heightened moral level *en masse*. Under the spell of the moment, egoists behave in an unselfish way, cowards act bravely, ambitious men manifest solidarity, misers give away their wealth. This is so because under utopian conditions men and women start to practise the utopia of the best possible moral world. But, as a rule, when the new institutions have been founded and stabilized, men and women return to their 'ancient' selves to a greater or lesser degree. These are the cases when one can distinguish between the empirical self and the normative moral self. Similar 'up and down' movements may characterize the private sphere as well. Dostoevsky, the keen observer of the 'up and down', dwelt at length on the portrayal of one of its forms, which he termed 'disorderly repentance'. Such 'ups and downs' may be found in the lives of decent persons too, with one difference. There is a discrepancy, sometimes even a contradiction, between the empirical and the normative selves of a non-decent person, but no such discrepancy may exist in the case of the decent person, because the distinction between the empirical self and the normative self is irrelevant in their case. For in the decent person the normative *moral self* and the *empirical* moral self coincide. This is what, in the final analysis, *authenticity* means. In a dense moral scenario, as opposed to 'morally normal' circumstances, something else is required from a decent person. 'Something else' is not tantamount to 'more', even if it can be. *Morally*, the self is indeed monocentric in so far as it is always the *same* (normative) moral personality that appears under both 'abnormal' and 'normal' conditions, in exceptional as well as in everyday situations. Yet each and every person is decent in his or her own way. The circumstance that the moral self is monocentric (normative, authentic) is not an indication of the monocentricity or polycentricity of the whole self. Our self is, after all, a composite unity of *all ties of meaning* (human beings are related to all bodies by the ties of meaning), and morality is just one tie of meaning, albeit a decisive one. Our character is far from being coextensive or cointensive with our moral character. Our psychological, mental, emotional or aesthetic character is also of tremendous significance.

Moral philosophy turns to men and women who seek an answer to such questions as 'What shall I do?', 'What is the right thing for me to do?' As Kant has keenly observed, the most decisive personal element in morals, that for which no other element can be an adequate substitute – that is, *love* – must be sidestepped so long as answers to such and similar questions are being sought. One can neither command 'Love!' nor insist that 'The right thing for you to do is to love.' Men of pre-modern times were not yet familiar with this quandary. So long as life remained traditional, so did emotions. One could then safely enjoin others to feel such and such on a particular occasion because this was the right thing to do. The increasing individuation and subjectivization of the human personality, two developments which, although different in kind, have reinforced one another, resulted in the new situation in which imperatives addressed to emotions have become problematic.[20] We still have *emotional preferences*, among them preferences from the moral point of view. But there is an increasing discrepancy between certain *universalistic* claims of our norms and our strongly culture-related (particularistic) emotional preferences. This is all the more so since emotional preferences also manifest themselves, in a very complex way, in preferences for certain emotional expressions. In our culture there is no agreement even on simple issues such as whether, on a certain occasion, emotions should be freely expressed or rather repressed. Certain feelings or emotions are of course generally disapproved for moral reasons. But certain others are regarded as merely culture-immanent or thoroughly individual–subjective manifestations, and, as such, adiaphoric.

Love is an emotion, or, rather, a general term which encompasses different emotions and emotional dispositions. There is love *qua* charity, love *qua* understanding, love *qua* attraction, love *qua* the manifestation of need or desire, love *qua* friendship, love *qua* respect, love *qua* adoration, love *qua* empathy, love *qua* sympathy, and so forth. As an emotion or emotional disposition, love shares the fate of all emotions in the modern world: we are ill at ease in making general evaluative statements about them. Yet love occupies a special place in morals because it is love that makes morals personal. Recognition is the recognition of personhood, but it is not personal. Modern men and women share the moral (and political) creed that each and every person should be recognized in his or her personhood precisely because recognition is due to each and every one. Recognition of personhood lacks all personal elements. Respect is due to everyone according to his or her moral merits. Yet since respect is *due*, and is due according to an ethical criterion, namely merit, there is nothing personal in the attitude of respect either. Love is different, for all kinds and types of love include a personal element. It is in love that the human bond is established and re-established, that it becomes concrete, a person-to-person affair, a thread which ties the living to the living.

Can one be a decent person without loving anyone? Can one live a decent life without love? The questions are rhetorical, as will be the answer: certainly not. The questions are rhetorical because they suggest the answer; the answer is rhetorical because it simplifies a highly complex matter. It is very unlikely that any person, decent or not, will never love anyone. But it is after all theoretically possible to be decent without ever having loved anyone, provided that the person in question recognizes all human beings, pays due respect to each and every one according to their merits, is just in judgement, develops certain basic virtues (none of which includes love), and, finally, observes norms as guidelines properly in situated actions. Such a decent person would deserve respect, yet would remain unlovable, alien from the rest of the human race. After all, our main joys and sufferings spring from love. She or he who knows nothing about these joys and sufferings can hardly be perceived as human.

The decent person is the morally normative person. She or he is the unity of the empirical and normative personality. In mentioning normativity, we also mean *authority*. As a decent person, the normative person is supposed to be the unity of external and internal authority. As a person of conscience, the decent person is the repository of internal authority. Yet, as the embodiment of the norm, she or he represents the external authority for non-decent persons. But can an unlovable person become an authority in matters of morals for people who are familiar with the joys and sufferings of love? Can such a person induce in all others the desire to imitate his or her goodness? Hardly. *A person who does not love, and is thus unlovable, cannot be the carrier or the embodiment of the norm of human goodness.*

Every decent person is decent in his or her own way. Every decent person also loves in his or her own way. The love of one is more passionate; the love of another is deeper. One expresses love; the other hides it. One person loves many; others love few. Yet all decent men and women manifest their goodness in their emotional attachment to other human beings. Although decent men and women are good for their own sake, they do the right things also for the sake of other persons. They do it not only out of duty but also *out of affection*.

The love of the modern person is not 'ideological'. It would be were it induced by general commandments or specified by concrete norms. But the commandments (to love our neighbours and hate our enemies) are misplaced when 'love' has acquired such a multiplicity of meanings. We understand that 'love' had a different sense in the biblical context: it was closer to 'the sense of justice' or 'recognition' in today's usage than to love as emotion. So far as concrete norms are concerned, we know that there can be immorality in love. But we are increasingly reluctant to associate, as our ancestors did, any concrete kind or version of love with immorality. We do not compartmentalize love; we do not systematize love. Nor do we establish a hierarchy between 'celestial' and 'terrestrial' love. It is precisely owing to the de-ideologization of love that love of a subjective and individualized kind can be so intimately connected with the goodness of the modern contingent person. Contingent persons do not have the inherited obligation to love this rather than that. They choose the objects (subjects) of their love as freely as they choose themselves.

At this crucial point we leave behind the normative discourse of moral philosophy to engage in a broader discourse concerning the possibility and the conditions of the good life. All moral philosophies hold in common that rectitude (decency) is the main component of the good life. This moral philosophy simply joins its predecessors by reconfirming this self-evident truth. Most moral philosophies add to this that a particular component of the good life is not yet the good life itself. Several other components should also be considered. I subscribe to this widely held opinion also. I would only add that the *prescriptive* (normative) aspect of morals (the subject matter of moral philosophy) does not exhaust the issue of ethics either. For there is more to the ethical attitude than can be the legitimate topic of a normative discourse. I shall address these problems in the third volume of *A Theory of Morals*, planned under the title *A Theory of Proper Conduct*.

Postscript

What has been accomplished in this volume can be summed up in a few words. I have engaged in writing a moral philosophy while being aware of the impossibility of inventing one. In order to answer the question addressed to all moral philosophies – 'What should I do?', 'What is the right thing for me to do?' – I decided to follow the path of modern contingent persons who have chosen themselves existentially under the category of the universal – that is, as good. We all know that good persons exist; we are also acquainted with good persons. The person who is good in the present world has chosen his or her goodness existentially, for no other (traditional) goodness is possible in a contingent world. If good persons exist, existential choice exists also.

Good persons are normative persons; they are the unity of the empirical self and the normative self. Thus, in following the path of good persons, I have been able to bring to the surface, as well as subject to theoretical scrutiny, moral norms which have been unearthed, invented, followed and observed by good persons. Moral philosophy, as philosophy, is a theoretical–speculative, not a practical, venture. But the attitude of good persons is practical, prescriptive. By bringing to the surface and scrutinizing the prescriptive, normative attitude, I have been able to elaborate a moral philosophy proper which appeals directly to men and women who seek morally good solutions in concrete life situations.

The normative (decent) person is the ultimate utopia. At the very moment when I decided to follow the path of such a person, I became engaged in establishing a utopian reality. At any rate, philosophy is a utopian reality by virtue of belonging to the sphere of 'objectivation-for-itself' (the 'absolute spirit'). In portraying the actions, decisions, and conflicts of the living utopian reality (the decent person), I have merely stuck to the rules of the philosophical genre.

Such a utopia addresses decent persons directly. Yet it also addresses non-decent persons, although only indirectly. What can non-decent persons do with the portrayal of normative persons, which they are not? Normative persons cannot be imitated in the sense of approximation – not, at least, in the modern world. One has to choose oneself as a decent person first, and then be decent in one's own way. This is how decency spreads, if it does at all, and not via imitation. One can also behave as if one were decent, but one does not learn this 'as if' from a moral philosophy. But, while decent persons cannot be imitated, they can be interpreted and reinterpreted. The interpretation and reinterpretation of the normative person can make the interpreter infinitely interested in the existential choice of goodness. Existential choice by definition cannot be determined, but the interpretation of the acts and the life of normative persons could trigger in those who are not decent an interest in being good. Moral philosophy addresses the non-decent person in precisely this manner. By bringing to the surface and scrutinizing the prescriptive, normative attitude of good persons, moral philosophy may awaken the interest and desire in some men and women who are not decent to choose themselves existentially under the category of the universal. And, even if such resolve does not occur, if the existential choice fails, goodness will still appear to them in an attractive light. Thus people may occasionally act the way decent people do, not because external factors so require, not because righteousness begins to pay its dividends, but simply because rectitude pleases. No philosophy can prove that it is better to suffer injustice than to commit injustice. Nor can any philosophy substantiate the notion that decent persons are in principle 'better off' than non-decent ones. Bertolt Brecht once remarked, 'formidable is the temptation to good.' What moral philosophy can do is to add its own arguments to this formidable temptation.

Notes

Chapter 1   The Contingent Person and the Existential Choice

1   I have borrowed this formulation from K. Baier's book *The Moral Point of View*, (Ithaca, NY: Cornell Univ. Press, 1958).

2   It was exactly because of this that Kant denied the existence and the possibility of moral conflicts.

3   I have pointed out in many of my writings that it is in the modern world that freedom and life have become the ultimate values, and that, whereas the value of freedom has been universalized, the value of life is still in the process of becoming universalized. An existential choice can occur before the person becomes consciously committed to the values of freedom and life; it may even happen that such a person will never 'distil' universal values out of their concrete manifestations. And, yet, whoever has chosen himself or herself existentially has already, by this very gesture, committed himself or herself to the universal values. Universal values inhere in the existential choice. One chooses onself as an autonomous being (one becomes autonomous through this choice), and by choosing oneself one also chooses one's own life as good life. The existential character of a choice (its being non-determined) should not be understood as a statement of ontological irrationality. Actually, the event we call 'existential' choice can easily be described in Aristotelian terms. It is a self-determining act; the cause is constitutive of the act itself and so constituted by the act: it is the final cause. Choosing myself as my destiny means, in Aristotelian terms, to actualize my *dunamis* (potentiality) as my *telos* (purpose or goal).

4   The expression 'hotel-dweller', and the meaning it covers, are borrowed from Michael Walzer.

5   I have discussed this problem in some detail in *General Ethics* (Oxford: Basil Blackwell, 1988), chs 1, 2 and 9.

6   The Other can know one better than one knows oneself, and one can know the Other better than one knows oneself. And still one has a privileged access to oneself and not to the Other, and *vice versa*. For this reason, as for a host of others, self-knowledge cannot be acquired in isolation. I discuss this problem in detail in *General Ethics*.

7 The idea that inauthentic beings are like puppets in a puppet theatre was elaborated by Kierkegaard. The anxious role-players in Irving Goffman's *Presentation of the Self in Everyday Life* (Harmondsworth: Penguin, 1953) lend themselves easily to such a Kierkegaardian reading.

8 Ibsen discovered this problem with great poetic sensitivity. Solness, the master builder, must follow his chosen path up to the very end. He cannot falter. He can die only after having proved to himself that he has remained himself; moreover, he meets his death willingly, just because of that. 'Remain true to yourself' was Ibsen's foremost maxim. Peer Gynt, who seeks adventure instead of choosing himself, and Hjalmar Ekdal, who remains unblessed, are both unautonomous and mediocre.

9 The structure of voluntary action is analysed in *General Ethics*. To choose ourselves ethically means, among other things, to take responsibility for our actions. Men and women who choose the ethical will never ask such questions as 'Am I my brother's keeper?'

10 The increasing complexity of modern morals is discussed at some length in *General Ethics*, where I identify two main changes in the structure of ethics (morals): the first has been accomplished; the second is still in the process of becoming. The inflation of reflexivity is a typical element of the second structural change. (See, in particular, *General Ethics*, ch. 9.)

11 In *General Ethics* I distinguish between two kinds of evil: the first I call the 'evil of the underworld', the second the 'evil of sophistication'. When the second kind of evil mobilizes the first, evil starts to spread like a plague and causes unspeakable harm. This interpretation of evil has nothing to do with the concept of the radicality of evil. (See *General Ethics*, ch. 10.) Actually, Kant too made this distinction, in the first section of *Religion within the Limits of Reason Alone*.

12 The first change in the structure of morals brings about the differentiation of *Sittlichkeit* (moral customs) and morality (personal, eventually subjective, relation to *Sittlichkeit*). The second structural change is responsible for carrying this differentiation to extremes.

13 I shall concretize this issue in chapters 2 and 3, in addressing the problem of the contemporaneity and uncontemporaneity of the Aristotelian image of the good man and the good citizen.

14 In sociological terms one should speak about the trivialization of norms and especially about the trivialization of institutional or institutionalized rules. Such norms or rules are not cultural, in the sense that they do not motivate actions. Where all norms and rules are trivialized, moral requirements for survival and recognition are kept to a minimum level. All the later works of Niklas Luhmann address this phenomenon from one or another angle.

15 All the heroes and heroines of Wagner's musical dramas are just contingent persons clad in a mythological garb.

234   *Notes to pp. 31–61*

Chapter 2   Everyday Virtues, Institutional Rules, Universal Maxims

1 The term 'utopian conditions' does not refer to imaginary conditions or to unrealizable ones. Rather, what I have in mind here are exceptional conditions. Utopian conditions are different in kind, but they all enhance the moral powers of quite average men and women. The first days of liberation are an example of the setting for such conditions, but not every utopian condition rests on the enthusiasm of the moment. In the first volume of Rousseau's novel, *La Nouvelle Héloïse*, it is a network of close friends that works in a morally elated, exceptional, i.e. 'utopian', way. In *Beyond Justice* (Oxford: Basil Blackwell, 1987), ch. 2, I discuss at some length how this network of friends operates.

2 How moral discourse was replaced with psychological discourse, how the concept of 'normality' took the place of that of 'morality', is a momentous and much-debated issue, best treated in Michael Foucault's *The History of Sexuality*, vol. I (New York: Vintage Books, 1980).

3 Of course, it is not only in the moral field that the two claims 'I do x for my own sake' and 'Doing x is its own reward' do not overlap. For example, I can safely say that I correct this manuscript for my own sake, but that correcting the manuscript is its own reward is a statement that, alas, I would hesitate to underwrite.

4 Men of the Enlightenment generally maintained that comparison enhances or at least reinforces harmful passions; sceptics could reconcile themselves with this fact, yet moralists could not. Rousseau dreamt about eliminating comparison from social life altogether; since quantification results in comparison, he banned quantification even from sports (see *Emile*). But, as a specimen of the kind of person who knows what is right but does what is wrong, Rousseau all too frequently compared morality with the alleged 'immorality' of others. Kant, so it seems, remained true to his maxim that persons should compare themselves with the moral law, but never with one another. Yet both agreed, and so did others, on one point: self-righteousness is a manifestation not of goodness, but of the lack of it.

5 This is not so within institutions, especially if they are hierarchically organized. But one does not choose such institutions; rather, one enters into them. See *Beyond Justice*, ch. 4.

6 This is the model of static justice. If it is the norms and rules themselves, rather than their application, that is contested, we talk about dynamic justice. The proceedings of dynamic justice allow people to denounce the rules of giving–receiving–reciprocating goods and services as unjust and wrong, and to make a case for alternative sets of norms that, to their mind, would be just, or more just.

7 Without this strong proviso one could underwrite *mafioso* ethics.

8 In *Beyond Subjective Morality* (New Haven, Conn.: Yale University Press, 1984) A. Fischkin demonstrates, in reporting conversations with his students, that people have a very acute sense for the appropriate

balance between giving and receiving, at least on the theoretical plane, when it comes to matters of liberality and generosity.

9   Most of our virtues can be termed 'beautiful' character traits, and most of our vices 'ugly' character traits. But 'beautiful' does not stand here simply for 'good', and 'ugly' for 'bad' or 'evil', for both aesthetic value categories emphasize one single aspect of a virtue or a vice. A character trait can be beautiful without being a virtue and certain bad character traits are not regarded as ugly at all. This question will be discussed thoroughly in the third volume of this trilogy, especially in the section on moral aesthetics.

10   This problem is discussed in detail in *General Ethics*, ch. 1.

11   It is obvious that not every standpoint, world-view, philosophy or learned opinion allows for decent practice, and that some of them have a greater affinity with decent practices than others. Still, many a standpoint opens the way for some decent practices (which ones depends on the standpoint), though none of them, not even the best, can serve as a substitute for practical decency.

12   The distinction between authentic and inauthentic existence became one of the central themes of twentieth-century existentialism. Seen from this perspective, Heidegger's *Being and Time* belongs to the existentialist trend. However, the distinction predates the first stirrings of existentialism and can be traced back to the Enlightenment, especially to Diderot and Rousseau.

13   To avoid a frequent misunderstanding: becoming oneself is not tantamount to becoming self-centred. Furthermore, the indestructibility of the kernel of one's personality does not make one mono-centred. If there are totally mono-centred persons (which I doubt), they must certainly be inauthentic.

14   By 'transparency' I do not mean psychological transparency. We make ourselves transparent if we present ourselves to another as we present ourselves to ourselves. Persons can psychoanalyse one another, but this possibility does not concern us here in the slightest. To offer one's own self to the Other for interpretation does not normally imply the use of any technique, even the practice of free association. It can be detrimental to sincere mutuality to use such techniques, or to talk about everything that just happens to enter our mind, especially where it can hurt the other person's feelings beyond repair.

15   Given that the vain person's good dreams result from an all-too-subjective constitution of reality, anxiety and insecurity can easily creep into those dreams. Particular character traits (such as vanity) combine with such a great variety of other patterns, moral and non-moral ones alike, that one can hardly make any generalized statement about them. Fiction does a better job in depicting the complexities of human characters. Yet I still plan to discuss the 'dream world' of subjectivity and its moral relevance in the final volume of this trilogy.

16   In totalitarian societies members of non-political institutions are usually forced also to be members of political ones. (e.g. in a typical Stalinist

state, a worker must be a trade-union member and a director must be a party member). Such obligatory combinations narrow down considerably the person's autonomy, and this circumstance should certainly be taken into account in moral judgements. No transfunctional institutions exist in totalitarian societies. Whenever a society commences the process of detotalization (that is, pluralism becomes accepted and not just tolerated in the social, if not also the political, domain), certain transfunctional institutions can emerge even if the state remains totalitarian (that is, political pluralism remains outlawed.)

17 For details consult *Beyond Justice*, ch. 3.
18 Sandel makes a similar proposition. Though I do not share the essence of his 'communitarian' criticism of Rawls's theory of justice, this idea strikes me as a good one.
19 Those who have read my book *Beyond Justice* will detect at this point an apparently serious inconsistency. Though I enumerate exactly the same maxims in my previous book, there I not only enumerate but also deduce them, while here I do not deduce them at all. It must be obvious to everyone who has undergone philosophical training that, if one has devised a language game, one can always deduce one's own principles. I deliberately forwent deducing these principles at the very moment when I embarked on this project – to accompany decent persons on their life ways and to explore the paths they tread in finding out what is the right thing for them to do. To deduce my maxims from the universal principle would have been a grave transgression of both the theoretical and the moral message of this book. Without trying to defend through references to philosophical authorities the viability of my attempt at a non-foundationalist approach, I remind the reader of Kant's *Groundwork of the Metaphysics of Morals*. Kant commences the discussion of morals from the standpoint of everyday reasoning, moves on to a metaphysics of morals, and then on again towards the critique of practical reason. There are three distinct theoretical approaches here, yet the practical result is completed already at the first stage.
20 I have discussed the ideas of justice in some detail in *Beyond Justice*, ch. 1.
21 The violation of the code of honour arouses the feeling of shame. Provided that the violator does not regard his *faux pas* as a moral matter, no pangs of conscience will follow. Though codes of honour do not play an eminent role in the moral universe of contingent persons, there are still institutions where such a code exists. Contingent persons can enter such institutions or stand in a close relation to persons who do so. If I am not mistaken, the officer corps still maintains a traditional code of honour, and so do a few other institutions.

Chapter 3   The Concerned Person, the Good Citizen, the Care of the World

1 I have addressed this problem in some detail in my essay 'The Good Person and the Good Citizen', in *The Power of Shame* (London: Routledge and Kegan Paul, 1985).

2 The accident of birth is an empirical universal for the simple reason that genetic patterns (the genetic code) do not determine the social destiny of the human infant. Nothing in the genetic code predetermines anyone to be born at a particular time, in a particular place and into a particular social class, stratum, estate or caste. How the two a priori of human existence (the social a priori and the genetic a priori) become dovetailed, what kinds of tensions result therefrom, and many related problems, are discussed in *General Ethics*.

3 Historical consciousness is the perception and the consciousness of social–political time, whereas historicity is the perception and the consciousness of the temporality of the person (life time). In *A Theory of History* (London: Routledge and Kegan Paul, 1982) I distinguish five main types of historical consciousness prior to our own. The contemporary confusion of historical consciousness and of historicity has resulted from their being discussed in concert, though far from identical. Hans Blumenberg, in his major book *Lebenszeit und Weltzeit* (Suhrkamp, 1986) addresses the same issue both phenomenologically and historically.

4 Justice is not a substance contained or not contained in an institution. It is the actors' perception and contestation that renders institutions just or unjust. I have elaborated a non-substantivist, perspectivist conception of justice, which relies heavily on my non-substantivist, perspectivist concept of rationality. See *Beyond Justice* and 'Everyday Life, Rationality of Reason, Rationality of Intellect', in *The Power of Shame*.

5 In the discussion of modern redemptive politics I rely heavily on the work of Ferenc Fehér. See his 'Redemptive and Democratic Paradigms in Political Philosophy', in Fehér and Heller, *Eastern Left, Western Left* (Oxford: Basil Blackwell, 1987).

6 Naturally decent persons never make common cause with evil. Indecent (non-decent) persons are not evil, though when an epidemic of evil strikes they are not immune to evil influence. Normally, however, indecent persons just do not consider actions or issues from the moral point of view, and/or give preference to what seems to be more useful, comfortable and agreeable in case of conflict, if they ever make a moral assessment.

7 There are two kinds of authorities in the judgement of moral character: the external and the internal one. The external authority is the community, the Others, the Eye of the Others, whereas the internal authority is practical reason, conscience, the internal voice. I first made this distinction in my essay 'The Power of Shame' (in *The Power of Shame*).

The chapter on moral authority in *General Ethics* places the issue in the general framework of a theory of morals.

8 Many decent persons have committed serious moral mistakes as a result of attraction to a totalitarian ethics. Both Bolshevism and (Italian) Fascism were greeted by many men and women (especially intellectuals) as the promise of the resurrection of communities, the long-awaited remedy for the sick egoistic 'merchant' ethics. The (false) promise of the revitalization of the heroic aspects of life was another point of attraction. How men and women can disentangle themselves from all the traps of evil political and social powers is discussed at some length in my essay 'The Power of Shame'.

9 See ch. 2, note 16.

10 World-historical responsibility is responsibility for the (future) world. The unique structural features of this kind of responsibility are discussed in *General Ethics*.

11 In both 'The Power of Shame' and *General Ethics*, I distinguish between conscience as the ultimate authority, and conscience as the sole authority, of moral judgement. Conscience as the ultimate authority manifests itself in independent thinking: we listen to the external authorities, but keep the last word to ourselves. Conscience as the sole authority is self-generating and as such totally subjectivist. Total subjectivism leads to total subjection (totalitarian personality).

12 The title of Robert Conquest's famous book *The Great Terror* encapsulates the identity of the subjective experience (terror as great fear) and objective functioning (terror as practice) in totalitarian societies. In an as yet unpublished study, Juan Corradi has dissected the working of terror (as great fear) in the context of the non-totalitarian dictatorship of generals in Argentina.

13 Fear, as an affect, is innate and manifests itself in well-known bodily and facial expressions (such as trembling, the active impulse to run away, a rapid heartbeat and going pale). However, pure fear occurs rarely, for, as in the case of all affects, cognitive aspects are integrated into the feeling itself, differentiate it and transform it into different emotions and orientative feelings. This process is discussed in detail in my book *A Theory of Feelings* (Assen: Van Gorcum, 1978).

14 By 'rationality of reason' I mean the ability to discriminate under the guidance of the main categories of value orientation (good/bad, good/ evil, sacred/profane, true/false, right/wrong, useful/ harmful, beautiful/ ugly, and the like) in accordance with the existing (valid) taken-for-granted norms and rules. By 'rationality of intellect' I mean the ability to test the rationality of one or more taken-for-granted norms or rules in justifying rejection or acceptance (of the standing norms or of alternative ones suggested to replace them). 'Rationality of reason' is an empirical human universal (ontological constituent of the human race), whereas 'rationality of intellect' became generalized in modern times as 'rationalism', after playing a marginal and intermittent role in earlier societies. I discuss the problem in all its broad ramifications in 'Everyday

Life, Rationality of Reason, Rationality of Intellectual', in *The Power of Shame*.

15 It is a mistake to identify intellectual virtues with rationality, and rationality with total rationalism. Not everything that is rational is good (or, for that matter, virtuous), and *vice versa*. The devil excels in rational argumentation. Hegel made this point in his lectures on the history of philosophy in discussing Zeno, the Sophists, the Sceptics and others.

16 It goes without saying that not only good citizens participate in the contestation of justice, but in certain cases they always participate. The 'referents' of the contestation, the victims of unjust practices, do not always participate in the process: they can be incapacitated for some reason or simply unable to participate (as in the case of mental patients or small children).

17 In *General Ethics* I discuss the difference between prospective and retrospective responsibility, on the one hand, and 'being responsible for', 'having a responsibility for', on the other. The latter means 'being in charge of' and as such is always a prospective kind of responsibility. But, if someone is in charge, his or her retrospective responsibility will be different, normally greater, than the responsibility of those who do not 'have' responsibility.

18 Habermas's conception of practical discourse can be accepted as the regulative practical idea of a fully democratic practice. In this interpretation the idea of practical discourse and that of just procedure coincide. In *Beyond Justice* I suggest subscribing to Habermas's theory as to a theory of justice while dismissing its claim to provide – as a discourse ethics – the model for a modern moral philosophy.

19 The argumentative–rationalist procedure of 'rationality of intellect' must always have recourse to at least one value or norm the validity of which is accepted by faith, by a gesture. Total rationalism is impossible, and the quest for it is self-defeating. 'Rationality of intellect' is normally surrounded by a non-rational aura (extending from rebelliousness to mystical experience and love). I discuss the related issues in 'Everyday Life, Rationality of Reason, Rationality of Intellect', in *The Power of Shame*.

20 Both the golden rule of justice and the golden rule of dynamic justice are discussed in detail in *Beyond Justice* (chs. 1, 3, 4).

21 I enumerate and discuss a few concepts of 'humankind' in chapter 1 of *Beyond Justice*. As for the analysis of the modern concept of humanism, see my essay 'The Moral Situation in Modernity', in Agnes Heller and Ferenc Feher, *The Post-Modern Political Condition* (Oxford: Basil Blackwell; New York: Columbia University Press, 1989).

Chapter 4 *How to Live an Honest Life*

1 The discussion of morals as a 'sphere' results from a gross misunderstanding of both Kant's and Weber's position. Hegel could not be interpreted in this manner, for what he terms *Sittlichkeit* encompasses

the whole social world (the family, the civil society and the state); if one terms the whole social world a moral 'sphere', one cannot refer to a moral sphere as a specific social sphere among many. The Kantian division between the theoretical and the practical use of reason is strict, but reason, as the upper faculty of desire, does not constitute a sphere, unless one describes transcendental freedom (the intelligible world) as a sphere, which would be a very strange thing to do. Even Weber, who relied upon the neo-Kantian distinction of value spheres, was always aware of the circumstance that morals as such cannot be described as a sphere in the same sense as science and politics can be. When he refers to morals in his theory of social-value spheres, he speaks about the legal–moral or religious–moral sphere, never a moral sphere as such. Both the religious and the legal sphere have a strong moral aspect, but they are different in kind. So is the political sphere and the morals inherent in it. Only within the framework of a conclusive discourse ethics is it reasonable to speak about a moral sphere. If morals can be equated with participation in a moral discourse, people 'do morals' whenever they get engaged in such a discourse, and so enter the 'sphere' of practical discourse. However, the equation of morals and practical discourse impoverishes the understanding of morals to a considerable extent. On this issue see also *Beyond Justice* and *General Ethics*.

2 The gesture of forgiveness is discussed in detail, with her usual eloquence, by Hannah Arendt, in *The Human Condition* (Garden City, NY: Doubleday, 1959).

3 In his genealogy of Greek and Roman ethics in *The History of Sexuality*, vols II and III (New York: Vintage Books, 1986 and 1988) Foucault makes a case for a proper balance between the aesthetic and ethic dimensions of human personality. As her lectures on Kant and a few of her latest writings indicate, Arendt sees judgement of taste as the juncture and the centrepoint of aesthetics and political ethics. Jean-François Lyotard, especially in his book *L'Enthousiasme* (Paris: Galilee, 1986) reintroduces the category of the aesthetic sublime into the discussion of political morality. Both Arendt and Lyotard (unlike Foucault) rely mainly upon Kant, and especially upon *The Critique of Judgement*. This issue deserves close scrutiny, given that both the identification of the aesthetic and the ethical dimensions, and their strict and complete division, arouse feeling of discomfort in everyday actors and philosophers alike.

4 Concrete norms are precise prescriptions for acting: they guide attitudes, behavioural patterns, judgemental patterns in their specific contexts. Abstract norms are transcontextual or supercontextual: their injunctions call for interpretation in every situated action and choice. Quite different concrete norms can become authentic interpretations of the same abstract norm. I discuss this problem in detail in *General Ethics*, ch. 2.

5 This particular duty (the duty towards ourselves) has recently fallen into disrepute, as being too strongly associated with the traditions of Prot-

estant ethics. But the core idea of the duty is not necessarily linked to this tradition. To develop one's own mental, emotional and physical abilities was morally credited in mainstream Greek thinking too. There is one kind of hedonism no moral philosophy or everyday ethics approves of, not even the hedonist brand, and this is the attitude of lingering in the world, of simply hanging around in life without any sense and purpose. In addition to being aesthetically displeasing, the gross neglect of one's human potentials makes one an easy prey to evil forces.

6 A moral norm is universal if it is regarded as valid in all human cultures (in principle, by all human beings). A moral norm can also be termed 'universal' if the actors who observe it observe it *as if* it were actually accepted as valid by every human being. I discuss the difference between abstract and universal norms in *General Ethics*.

7 I borrowed this model case from Gewirth, who exemplifies it with Jehovah's Witnesses and their strict refusal of blood transfusion, even if it may save the life of their sick children. See Alan Gewirth, *Reason and Morality* (Chicago: University of Chicago Press, 1978).

8 As far as I know, Lukács was the first to point out and to discuss this connection, in his book *The Young Hegel* (Cambridge, Mass.: MIT Press, 1976).

9 Neither Kant nor Hegel distinguished between abstract enthusiasm and concrete enthusiasm. From the position of the spectator (the position generally taken by Kant) the differentiation is of no relevance; from the position of the actors, however, it assumes great importance. I discuss this problem in some detail in the second part of *A Theory of Feelings*.

10 I mean here moral autonomy and not autonomy. One can remain morally autonomous (in doing the right thing) in a situation of very restricted personal autonomy (for doing what one wills). I analysed the difference in *General Ethics*.

11 One can be party to a value discussion if one shares a few values with the other parties prior to the discussion. There are different kinds of value discussion – from everyday discussion to a philosophical value discourse. Each of them can result in agreement and/or in disagreement. Value discourses concerning the matter of justice are normally conducted by (good) citizens. I present my ideas on the topic in *Radical Philosophy* (Oxford: Basil Blackwell, 1984), *The Power of Shame*, and *Beyond Justice*.

12 Followers of the school of discourse ethics dismiss phronesis as an antiquated ethical category. This is one reason why both Habermas and Apel reject all kinds of neo-Aristotelianism as just new attempts at fundamentalism. I want to prove that they are wrong.

13 Consistent consequentialism – that is, the attempt to construe the moral content of actions on the basis of their consequences – is one thing, and to consider, among other aspects, the foreseeable consequences of one's action before embarking on it is another. If the foreseeable consequences entail morally relevant issues, to consider them is not a pragmatic but a

practical exercise of our mental abilities. If the foreseeable consequences do not entail morally relevant issues, to consider them is a pragmatic exercise of our mental abilities and as such neither good nor evil, but still correct or incorrect, true or false, useful or harmful, and so forth. I discuss consequentialism in detail in *General Ethics*.

14 Whether there is such a thing as 'good death', and whether 'good death' follows from 'good life', or not, is an ancient philosophical problem. I shall return to this eminent topic in the final volume of this trilogy.

15 See *General Ethics*, ch. 10.

16 This is how Arthur Koestler reconstructs one of the fatal borderline situations of our century in his novel *Darkness at Noon*.

17 Specifically, *Radical Philosophy* and *Beyond Justice*.

18 The concepts 'best possible moral world' and 'best possible socio-political world' are used here in a quasi-transcendental sense. Since I do not subscribe to the hypothesis of transcendental freedom, my categories can be only quasi-transcendental. But quasi-transcendental they are, because they presuppose the presence of authentic a priori ideas. Such a priori ideas, however, need to be posited as historically emergent, yet without collapsing genesis and validity. For the ontological foundation of my moral theory see *General Ethics*, ch. 1, and the forthcoming final volume of this trilogy.

19 I discuss philosophy as rational utopia in *Radical Philosophy*.

20 The increase in subjectivity has made strong emotional injunctions obsolete in modern times. Traditions did strictly prescribe whom one should love, whom one should hate, whom one should fear, and how. Whoever did not feel the way she or he was supposed to feel, felt ashamed or guilty just because of this. Such generality of emotional dispositions has since withered. I discuss this matter in some detail in *A Theory of Feelings*.

Index